CW01655909

THE ILLUSTRATED ENCYCLOPEDIA OF THE

PYRAMIDS TEMPLES & TOMBS OF ANCIENT EGYPT

THE ILLUSTRATED ENCYCLOPEDIA OF THE PYRAMIDS TEMPLES & TOMBS OF ANCIENT EGYPT

Discover the fascinating and mysterious world of the pharaohs with insightful text and more than 400 stunning photographs

Lorna Oakes

southwater

For my husband John and all our many friends in Egypt

This edition is published by Southwater, an imprint of Anness Publishing Ltd, Hermes House, 88–89 Blackfriars Road, London SE1 8HA; tel. 020 7401 2077; fax 020 7633 9499

www.southwaterbooks.com; www.annesspublishing.com

UK agent: The Manning Partnership Ltd; tel. 01225 478444; fax 01225 478440; sales@manning-partnership.co.uk
UK distributor: Grantham Book Services Ltd; tel. 01476 541080; fax 01476 541061; orders@gbs.tbs-ltd.co.uk
North American agent/distributor: National Book Network; tel. 301 459 3366; fax 301 429 5746; www.nbnbooks.com
Australian agent/distributor: Pan Macmillan Australia; tel. 1300 135 113; fax 1300 135 103; customer.service@macmillan.com.au
New Zealand agent/distributor: David Bateman Ltd; tel. (09) 415 7664; fax (09) 415 8892

A CIP catalogue record for this book is available from the British Library.

Publisher: Joanna Lorenz
Managing Editor: Judith Simons
Project Editor: Claire Folkard
Designer: Jez MacBean
Illustrator: Chris Orr
Picture Researcher: Veneta Bullen
Production Controller: Stephen Lang
Editorial Reader: Jonathan Marshall

Previously published as *Sacred Sites of Ancient Egypt.*

ETHICAL TRADING POLICY

Page 1 *A detail from the so-called coronation chair of Tutankhamun.*
Page 2 *The majestic Sphinx before the pyramid of Khafre at Giza.*
Page 3 *Queen Tuya's jewel box from the tomb she shared with her husband, Yuya.*
Page 4 *The goddess Hathor welcomes Seti I into the Afterlife.*
Page 5 *Treasures from the tomb of King Psusennes of the 21st Dynasty.*

CONTENTS

Ancient Egypt in Context

The fourth millennium BC was a time of great importance to the ancient Egyptians. It was the main formative period, when the individual cultures of different areas were gradually replaced by that of Naqada, an important Predynastic centre in the south. The archaeological record has revealed the spread of the culture known as Naqada II, characterized by attractive buff-coloured pottery decorated with lively scenes of ships, animals and dancing women, throughout the Nile Valley and the Delta.

Political centralization seems to have followed in the wake of cultural unity and is encapsulated in the Narmer Palette, a famous ceremonial object now in the Cairo Museum, which was found at Hierakonpolis, another great, early southern centre. This depicts the early king Narmer (c.3100 BC), wearing the crown of Upper Egypt, subduing people of the Delta, and shows him a second time wearing the crown of Lower Egypt. The point at which unification took place is still a matter of discussion, although it is now thought that the Narmer Palette reflects an established situation, with a sole king already in control of the 'Two Lands', rather than recording the conquest of the north by a southern king, as was once proposed. Ongoing excavations at Abydos have brought to light the graves of kings of the Predynastic Period, who are now referred to as Dynasty Zero. Signs scratched on labels once attached to the grave goods of these rulers also attest to the development of writing at an earlier period than was previously thought.

From c.3100 BC, there is evidence for the existence of a capital city at Memphis. Finds from the related cemetery sites of Saqqara and Abydos show that at this time Egypt enjoyed a high level of artistic achievement, was engaged in far-flung trading relations and was administered by a highly organized and structured bureaucracy.

Although little is known of political events during the Old Kingdom (c.2686–c.2181 BC) which followed, the period is famous for its monumental architecture. The pyramids of Giza are testimony to the status of the kings and their control over resources of materials and labour, and not least the ability of the administration to organize such colossal enterprises.

This period of strength was followed by well over a century of insecurity, when the rule of Egypt was divided during the First Intermediate Period (c.2181–c.2055 BC). However, towards 2000 BC the kings who ruled from Thebes managed to establish control over the whole country. Mentuhotep II (c.2055–c.2004 BC), who reunited Egypt at the

▼ *During the 4th Dynasty, the kings of Egypt were buried in the famous pyramids at Giza in northern Egypt.*

▲ *In the New Kingdom, the royal tombs were situated in southern Egypt, in the remote area now known as the Valley of the Kings.*

beginning of the Middle Kingdom (c.2055–c.1650 BC), was always regarded with great reverence by later kings. In spite of the fact that Amenemhat I (c.1985–c.1955 BC) may have been a usurper and was probably assassinated, the Twelfth Dynasty kings were strong rulers who established control not only over the whole of Egypt but also over Nubia, where several fortresses near the Second Cataract were built to protect Egyptian trading interests.

The ensuing Second Intermediate Period (c.1650–c.1550 BC) was again a time of divided rule. The Hyksos kings, probably originating in the Syria–Palestine area, took over the Nile Delta, and the rule of the Egyptian kings was confined to the south. The texts known as The Story of Seqenenre and Apepi, as well as the Kamose Stela erected in the Temple of Amun at Karnak, tell of the attempts of the Egyptian kings to drive out the Hyksos, while the autobiography of Ahmose (a soldier in the army of King Ahmose) records their eventual success.

Many of the sites visited by tourists today belong to the New Kingdom (c.1550–c.1069 BC). The temples of Luxor and Karnak, the mortuary temples of the West Bank and the royal tombs of the Valley of the Kings are witness to the power and prosperity of Egypt at this time, as are the Tombs of the Nobles, the final resting places of the officials who served the kings of the Eighteenth, Nineteenth and Twentieth Dynasties. During this period, Egypt also controlled many of the petty states of Syria–Palestine and Nubia.

However, from the end of the Twentieth Dynasty, Egypt entered a period of comparative weakness, when the kings ruled the north and the high priests of Amun at Karnak ruled the south, although relations between the two seem to have been friendly. Egypt appears to have lost her former status in Syria–Palestine, while Nubia became independent, with a Kushite ruling family based in the city of Napata in the Sudan, to the south of the Fourth Cataract. These Kushite kings invaded Egypt in the mid-eighth century BC, and were later acknowledged as the Twenty-fifth Dynasty. In 701 BC, the Kushite king, Taharqo (690–664 BC), went to the aid of King Hezekiah of Jerusalem, who was threatened by Sennacherib of Assyria. Taharqo's temerity in supporting a rebellious vassal provoked Assyrian wrath: Egypt was subdued and became part of the Assyrian Empire for a time during the reign of Sennacherib's grandson, Ashurbanipal.

The governors of the Delta city of Sais at first ruled with Assyrian backing but were later to reign as the independent kings of the Twenty-sixth Dynasty. The Saite Period (664–525 BC) is regarded as an era of renaissance: culturally, there was a great deal of interest in the art and architecture of the past, which was consciously copied, but the period was also marked by a new realism in both sculpture and literature. Egypt was once again a united country under a firm central authority and became a power to be reckoned with on the world stage. Military campaigns were mounted to regain control of Nubia, and the Greek historian, Herodotus, describes an expedition sent by Nekau II (610–595 BC) to circumnavigate Africa.

Thereafter, the history of ancient Egypt is one of conquest by foreign powers: the Persians, Alexander the Great and finally Rome. ◆

Chronology and Geography

Predynastic Period	**before c.3100**
Early settlements of various cultures	
Development of farming	
Pottery and copper smelting	
Northward spread of Naqada II culture	
Evidence of kings at Abydos	
Earliest writing	

Early Dynastic Period	**c.3100–c.2686**
FIRST DYNASTY	c.3100–c.2890
Capital at Memphis	
Royal graves at Abydos	
Narmer Palette	
Bracelets from tomb of King Djer	*c.3000*
Labels of King Den	*c.2950*
SECOND DYNASTY	c.2890–c.2686
Peribsen	c.2700
Khasekhemwy	c.2686

Old Kingdom	**c.2686–c.2181**
THIRD DYNASTY	c.2686–c.2613
Step Pyramid of Djoser (Netjerikhet)	
FOURTH DYNASTY	c.2613–c.2494
Sneferu's pyramids at Meidum and Dahshur	
Great Pyramid of Khufu (Cheops)	
Pyramid of Khafre (Chephren)	
Pyramid of Menkaure (Mycerinus)	
FIFTH DYNASTY	c.2494–c.2345
Abusir pyramids of Sahure, Neferirkare and Niuserre	
Sun temples at Abu Gurab	
Saqqara Pyramid of Unas (Wenis): first Pyramid Texts	
Tomb of Ti	
SIXTH DYNASTY	c.2345–c.2181
Pyramid of Teti at Saqqara	
Pyramid of Pepi I (Meryre) at South Saqqara	
Pepi II (Neferkare)	c.2278–c.2184
Long reign of Pepi II	
Autobiography of Harkhuf from tomb at Aswan	
Tomb of Sabni and Mekhu	

First Intermediate Period	**c.2181–c.2055**
SEVENTH AND EIGHTH DYNASTIES	c.2181–c.2125
NINTH AND TENTH DYNASTIES	c.2160–c.2025
HERAKLEOPOLITAN RULERS:	
Khety (Meryibre)	
Khety (Wahkare)	
Merykare	
Ity	
ELEVENTH DYNASTY (pre-conquest)	c.2125–c.2055
THEBAN RULERS:	
Mentuhotep I	
Intef I, II and III	

Middle Kingdom	**c.2055–c.1650**
ELEVENTH DYNASTY (post-conquest)	c.2055–c.1985
Egypt reunited by Mentuhotep II	
TWELFTH DYNASTY	c.1985–c.1795
Amenemhat I (Sehetepibre)	c.1985–c.1955
King possibly a usurper, perhaps assassinated; capital at Itjtawy	
Senusret I (Kheperkare)	c.1965–c.1920
Period of joint rule (c.1965–c.1955) with his father	
White chapel at Karnak	
Amenemhat II (Nubkaure)	c.1922–c.1878
Tomb of Sarenput II at Aswan	
Senusret III (Khakaure)	c.1874–c.1855
Egyptian control of Nubia strengthened	
Amenemhat III (Nimaatre)	c.1855–c.1808
Interest in land reclamation in the Faiyum	
Queen Sobekneferu (Sobekkare)	c.1799–c.1795
THIRTEENTH AND FOURTEENTH DYNASTIES	c.1795–c.1650

Second Intermediate Period	**c.1650–c.1550**
FIFTEENTH DYNASTY	c.1650–c.1550
Delta ruled by Hyksos kings	
SIXTEENTH DYNASTY	c.1650–c.1550
Numerous 'kings', perhaps tribal chiefs and vassals of the Hyksos	
SEVENTEENTH DYNASTY	c.1650–c.1550
Egyptian kings ruling in south	
The Story of Seqenenre and Apepi	
Kamose Stela; Kamose's attempt to drive out Hyksos	

New Kingdom	**c.1550–c.1069**
EIGHTEENTH DYNASTY	c.1550–c.1295
Ahmose (Nebpehtyre)	c.1550–c.1525
Hyksos expelled	
Autobiography of Ahmose son of Ebana at el-Kab	
Amenhotep I (Djeserkare)	c.1525–c.1504
Alabaster shrine at Karnak	
Tuthmosis I (Aakheperkare)	c.1504–c.1492
First royal tomb in Valley of the Kings	
Foundation of tomb builders' village at Deir el-Medina	
Queen Hatshepsut (Maatkare)	c.1473–c.1458
Joint rule with Tuthmosis III	
Funerary temple at Deir el-Bahri	
Expedition to Punt	
Obelisks at Karnak	
Sole reign of Tuthmosis III (Menkheperre)	c.1458–c.1425
Consolidation of Egyptian empire	
Hall of Records and Festival Hall at Karnak	
Tomb of Rekhmire at Thebes	
Amenhotep II (Aakheperure)	c.1427–c.1400
Tomb of Sennefer	
Tuthmosis IV (Menkheperure)	c.1400–c.1390
Tombs of Menna and Nakht at Thebes	
Amenhotep III (Nebmaatre)	c.1390–c.1352
Prosperous period marked by temple building	
Luxor temple	
Colossi of Memnon	
Tomb of Ramose	
Amenhotep IV/Akhenaten (Neferkheperurawaenre)	c.1352–c.1336
Capital moved to Akhetaten (Tell el-Amarna)	
Worship of the Aten	
Distinctive artistic style	
Tutankhamun (Nebkheperure)	c.1336–c.1327
Capital moved back to Thebes	
Restoration of traditional religion, funerary practices and beliefs	
Ay (Kheperkheperure)	c.1327–c.1323
Tomb in Western Valley	
Horemheb (Djeserkheperure)	c.1323–c.1295
Building at Karnak and Luxor	
Tombs at Saqqara and Valley of the Kings	
NINETEENTH DYNASTY	c.1295–c.1186
Ramesses I (Menpehtyre)	c.1295–c.1294
Throne inherited from Horemheb by army commander	
Seti I (Menmaatre)	c.1294–c.1279
Temple of Osiris at Abydos	
Hypostyle Hall at Karnak	
Ramesses II (Usermaatre Setepenre)	c.1279–c.1213
Battle of Qadesh against Hittites; peace treaty and marriage to Hittite princess	
Capital moved to Per-Ramesses in Delta	
Ramesseum and Abydos temple	
Building and embellishment at Luxor and Karnak	
Temples at Beit el-Wali, Derr, Wadi es-Sebua and Abu Simbel in Nubia	
TWENTIETH DYNASTY	c.1186–c.1069
Ramesses III (Usermaatre Meryamun)	c.1184–c.1153
Medinet Habu	

Third Intermediate Period	**c.1069–c.747**
TWENTY-FIRST TO TWENTY-FOURTH DYNASTIES	c.1069–c.747
North ruled by kings from Delta; South governed by High Priests from Thebes and local rulers	

Late Period	**c.747–332**
TWENTY-FIFTH DYNASTY	c.747–656
Kushite Dynasty	
Assyrian Conquest	*671*
Assyrian destruction of Thebes	*664*
TWENTY-SIXTH DYNASTY	664–525
Saite Dynasty	
TWENTY-SEVENTH TO THIRTIETH DYNASTIES	525–332
Persian Conquest	*525*
LAST EGYPTIAN DYNASTY	380–343
Conquest of Alexander	*332*

Ptolemaic Period	**332–30**
Ptolemy I	*305–282*
Defeat of Antony and Cleopatra	*30*

[All dates are BC]

MEDITERRANEAN SEA
N
Rosetta
Buto
Alexandria
Port Said
Tanis
Wadi Natrun
Sais
Bubastis
Per-Ramesses
Suez Canal
Ismalia
Leontopolis
Heliopolis
LOWER EGYPT
Giza
CAIRO
Abusir and Abu Gurab
Saqqara
Memphis
Dahshur
Suez
Faiyum
Lisht
Siwa Oasis
Hawara
el-Lahun
Meidum
Herakleopolis
Beni Suef
GULF OF SUEZ
Bahr Yussef
Serabit el-Khadim
Monastery of St Anthony
Bahariya Oasis
el-Minya
Sinai Peninsula
Beni Hasan
el-Ashmunein
Antinoopolis
Tuna el-Gebel
Tell el-Amarna
Assiut
MIDDLE EGYPT
RED SEA
Farafra Oasis
River Nile
Sohag
Abydos
Dendera
Naqada
Valley of the Kings
Thebes (Luxor)
West Bank
Dakhla Oasis
Hierakonopolis
Edfu
Gebel Silsila
Kom Ombo
Kharga Oasis
Elephantine
Aswan
UPPER EGYPT
New Kalabsha
First Cataract
Beit el-Wali
Philae
NUBIA
Lake Nasser
Gerf Hussein
Wadi es-Sebua
Amada
Qasr Ibrim
Abu Simbel

Part One: Burial Places

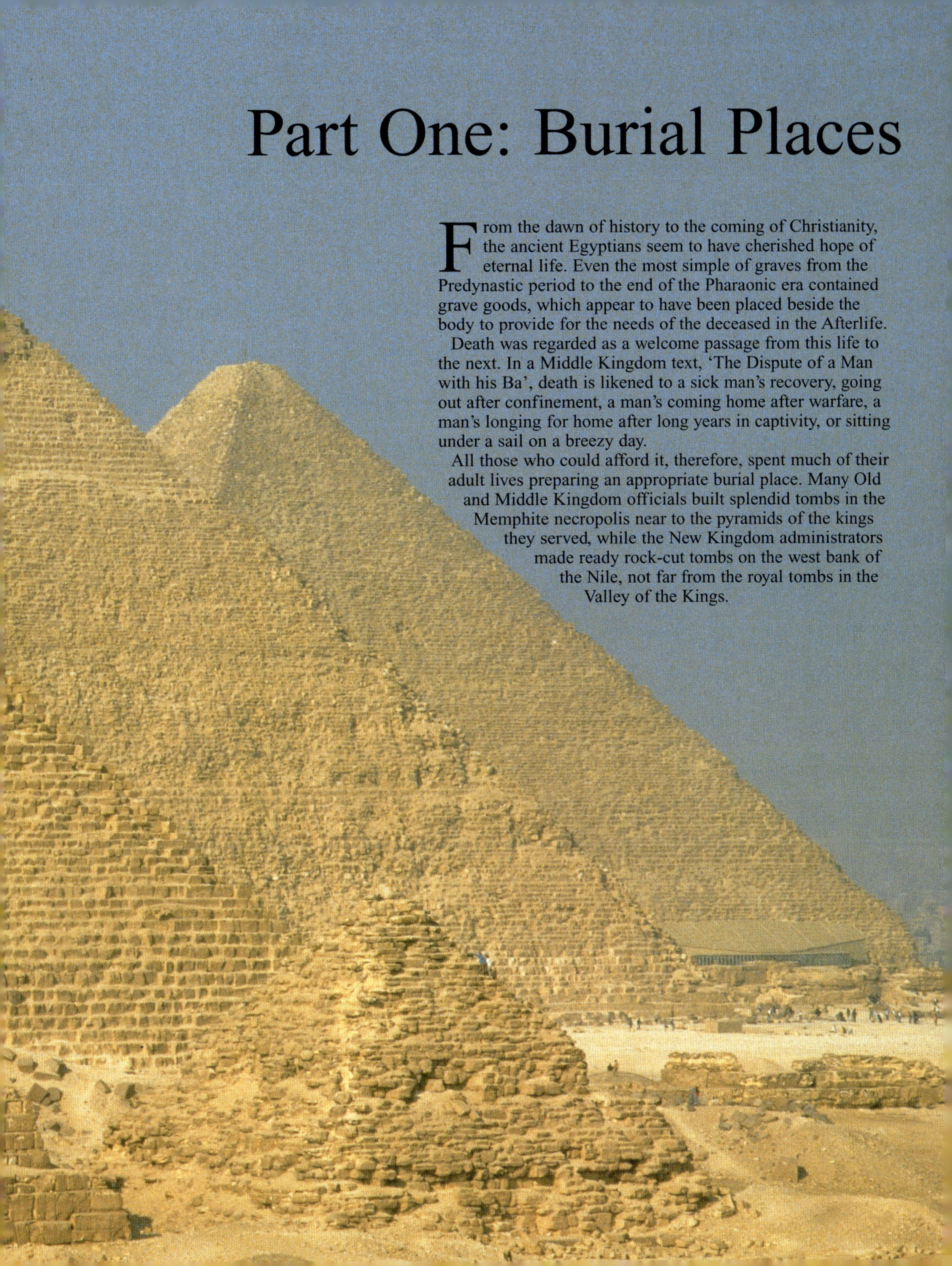

From the dawn of history to the coming of Christianity, the ancient Egyptians seem to have cherished hope of eternal life. Even the most simple of graves from the Predynastic period to the end of the Pharaonic era contained grave goods, which appear to have been placed beside the body to provide for the needs of the deceased in the Afterlife.

Death was regarded as a welcome passage from this life to the next. In a Middle Kingdom text, 'The Dispute of a Man with his Ba', death is likened to a sick man's recovery, going out after confinement, a man's coming home after warfare, a man's longing for home after long years in captivity, or sitting under a sail on a breezy day.

All those who could afford it, therefore, spent much of their adult lives preparing an appropriate burial place. Many Old and Middle Kingdom officials built splendid tombs in the Memphite necropolis near to the pyramids of the kings they served, while the New Kingdom administrators made ready rock-cut tombs on the west bank of the Nile, not far from the royal tombs in the Valley of the Kings.

The Rediscovery of Ancient Egypt

Egypt has always been a source of fascination for the traveller. The romantic landscape of the River Nile, with its magnificent antiquities set among the palms of the fertile valley, and the allure of the barren desert stretching away to the horizon never fail to capture the hearts and minds of visitors. But one visit is never enough. The first acquaintance makes such an impact that we are left totally speechless with wonder. With the second and third visits we start to believe our eyes, and the great antiquity and achievements of this ancient civilization begin to sink in. Add to this the charm of the people, their friendliness and unfailing good humour, courtesy and hospitality, and we are permanently hooked.

From the time of Herodotus onwards, Greek and Roman visitors to Egypt were fascinated by the pyramids and the Valley of the Kings. European interest was awakened in the seventeenth century, when the first attempts were made to record the monuments. This eventually led to rivalry between European nations and the race began to build up the Egyptian collections in the great museums of the world.

◀ *A watercolour painted in 1923 by Douglas Macpherson shows a statue of Tutankhamun guarding the entrance to his burial chamber, which was entirely filled by a nest of four gilded wooden shrines placed over the sarcophagus.*

Early Travellers to Egypt

The earliest traveller known to have fallen under the spell of Egypt was the Greek historian Herodotus (c.490–c.420 BC). He visited Egypt in the mid-fifth century BC, and later recorded his travels in Book Two of his great work *The Histories*. This work is primarily about the war between Greece and Persia in the earlier part of that century, but it is much more than a blow-by-blow account of events. Herodotus is often called the 'Father of History' because of his breadth of vision and the far-ranging scope of his work. He was interested in the deep-rooted causes of the war, the previous history of the powers involved, and the achievements and customs of their peoples. Because Egypt was part of the Persian Empire at the time of the war, he included a section on Egypt. Nobody had ever written anything like it before.

The travels of Herodotus

Concerning his trip to Egypt, Herodotus wrote: 'I went and saw for myself as far as Elephantine, but further information is from hearsay'. The truth of his account is sometimes doubted. Writing about the building of the Giza pyramids, for instance, he was referring to a period 2,000 years before his own time, and he had to rely on what he was told by the Egyptian priests. He often provided two or more versions of an event, leaving his readers to make up their own minds. However, on the history of the Twenty-sixth Dynasty (664–525 BC), he is the best ancient source. Modern archaeology continues to prove that much of what he said about this period was true.

Strabo

The Greek historian and geographer Strabo (c.63 BC–c.AD 21) spent several years in Alexandria, the capital planned by Alexander the Great, though he did not live to see it built, on the Mediterranean coast. It was extended and embellished with additional buildings by the Ptolemies, who ruled Egypt after him. Strabo's description is one of the main sources of information about it:

> *The city has magnificent public precincts and royal palaces, which cover a fourth or even a third of the entire area. For just as each of the kings would from a love of splendour add some ornament to the public monuments, so he would provide himself at his own expense with a residence in addition to those already standing.*

Alexandria's public buildings included the great Museum, with its covered walk and dining hall for the convenience of scholars studying at the nearby Library. The two harbours and the lighthouse are also mentioned by Strabo, as well as the Theatre, the Gymnasium and the Temple of Serapis.

The whole city was criss-crossed with streets at right angles to each other, wide enough to take large numbers of horses and carriages. Strabo's description is particularly useful because much of the ancient city has disappeared under later building or now lies below the sea. It is exceptionally valuable to the teams of modern archaeologists who are now bringing parts of the old city to light.

Strabo also visited Upper Egypt, and described the tourist attractions of the day, such as the Colossi of Memnon and the royal tombs in the Valley of the Kings. About the latter he wrote: 'Above the Memnonium [the Ramesseum], are the tombs of the kings, which are hewn in stone, are about 40 in number, are marvellously constructed, and a spectacle worth seeing'.

▼ *At his Tivoli residence, Hadrian encapsulated the places and works of art he had seen on his travels in Greece and Egypt.*

▲ *Although recent excavation has revealed more of the site, the two gigantic statues of Amenhotep III are all the tourist usually gets to see of this once enormous mortuary temple, which served the cult of the deceased king.*

The Colossi of Memnon

Strabo was rather scathing on the subject of these two massive statues, which represent Amenhotep III (c.1390–c.1352 BC) and mark the site of his once great funerary temple. In Strabo's day, however, they were identified with the mythical King Memnon of Ethiopia, said to be the son of the Dawn, a hero who had gone to the aid of the Trojans against the Greeks.

The statues had been damaged by an earthquake in 27 BC, and one of them was reputed to give out weird noises. Most tourists were greatly impressed and gathered daily to hear the statue speak. Strabo cynically put the mystery down to the machinations of the local priests.

Hadrian saw the same statue in AD 130, but it did not 'speak' until the second day of his visit. A poetess in the imperial retinue, Julia Balbilla, carved on the statue a verse in praise of Memnon and Hadrian. The inscription can still be read today.

Hadrian

When the Roman emperor Hadrian (AD 117–138) arrived in Egypt in AD 130, he went first to Alexandria. There he spent some time in learned discussions with the scholars in the Museum. He then sailed up the Nile accompanied by his favourite, Antinous, who was accidentally drowned during the trip. In memory of his friend, Hadrian founded a new city, Antinoopolis, which was laid out on a grid along Greek lines, with two colonnaded main streets crossing at right angles and embellished with baths, temples and a theatre.

Graffiti inscribed by the tourists of antiquity bear witness to the interest aroused by Egypt's buildings and monuments during the Roman Period. Paramount among these were the obelisks inscribed with hieroglyphs, which the Romans could not decipher. Several emperors had obelisks taken to Rome, where they still stand today. The Roman naturalist Pliny the Elder wrote that the Emperor Augustus (27 BC–AD 14) used the obelisk set up in the Campus Martius in Rome as a sort of calendar, based on measurements of its shadow at various times throughout the year. Apparently it did not work. Emperor Constantine (AD 312–337) removed an obelisk of Tuthmosis III from its original site at Thebes and took it to Alexandria to await shipment to his new capital of Constantinople. Constantine died before the obelisk reached its destination, but Theodosius I finally set it up in the Hippodrome in AD 390.

Hadrian took an even more personal interest in the antiquities, and had some of them taken home to Italy to enhance his villa at Tivoli. It does not seem to be true, however, as scholars once thought, that he tried to recreate complete buildings. The building known today as the Serapaeum at Tivoli was once widely considered to be a 'replica' of the Temple of Serapis at Canopus near Alexandria, but is now identified as a triclinium (dining room). ◆

► *Portrait bust of the Emperor Hadrian who spent much of his reign travelling around the Empire, visiting Greece in AD 125 and 128 and Egypt in AD 130.*

The Reawakening of European Interest

After the fall of the Roman Empire, Europe forgot about Egypt for a time. Egypt became a Muslim country, and it was in any case difficult for Europeans to travel beyond Cairo and the Nile Delta. During the Middle Ages, most interest was focused on Egypt's links – real or otherwise – with the Bible. The pyramids at Giza, for instance, were fancifully identified as 'Joseph's granaries'. For the most part, Egypt was merely a staging post on the well-worn pilgrim route to Jerusalem during this time. Any European interest in Egypt lay in its associations with early Christianity rather than in the land of the pharaohs.

Religious missions

It was only in the seventeenth century that European expeditions to Egypt began again, and these were undertaken mainly for religious reasons. Monks went to Cairo to preach the gospel, but some of them took the opportunity to travel further afield. In 1672, the Dominican priest Father Vansleb was instructed by Jean Baptiste Colbert, chief minister of Louis XIV of France, to collect coins and ancient manuscripts while in the country. He visited the Red and White Monasteries at Sohag and the Monastery of St Anthony on the Red Sea. He also took an interest in the antiquities, particularly the mummies. On opening a pit at Saqqara, he came upon a room full of mummified birds and took some examples back to Europe. Travelling further south, he was the first European to describe Antinoopolis.

Slightly later, between 1714 and 26, another French priest, Claude Sicard, went on to explore the rest of the country. Father Sicard was the leader of the first Jesuit mission to Cairo and eventually he drew up the first scientific map of Egypt. This showed the precise locations of Memphis and Thebes, and

▼ *An early 19th-century watercolour engraving by Louis François Cassas shows the Sphinx and the pyramid of Khafre at Giza.*

all the main temple sites. He also pinpointed ten open tombs in the Valley of the Kings.

Early descriptions

The best account to survive from this early period, however, was written by Richard Pococke, Bishop of Ossory in Ireland, who visited Egypt in the late 1730s. His description of the Valley of the Kings, where he found 18 tombs (although only nine were open), was published in 1743 under the title *Observations on Egypt*. He also produced a map of the Giza pyramids, but this is schematic in the extreme and his description of the site does not agree with what is found on the ground.

Pococke's contemporary, the Danish traveller Friderik Norden, also visited the pyramids. He was a naval marine architect, and in 1755 he published a much more accurate account than Pococke's in his *Travels in Egypt and Nubia.* He had been commissioned by King Christian VI of Denmark to collect information of antiquarian interest; he travelled the length of Egypt and eventually penetrated Nubia. Frustrated in his attempt to reach the Second Cataract, he got as far as Derr, where he wrote an account of the temple of Tuthmosis III (c.1479–1425 BC).

During his travels, Norden recorded a huge amount of information on the monuments of ancient Egypt. His book was widely read by scholars and laymen alike, and its importance in providing accurate plans and drawings cannot be exaggerated. He was also interested in contemporary life. He warned that the local people were suspicious of foreign travellers, being convinced that they were all treasure seekers and practitioners of black magic, and crowds gathered to see them. In order to allay any such suspicions, Norden advised prospective travellers not to try to touch the antiquities, but to adopt Turkish dress, 'a pair of mustachios' and 'a grave and solemn air'. The first picture of a scene in a tomb in the Valley of the Kings was published in 1790 by the Scottish traveller, James Bruce. During his visit to the tomb of Ramesses III (c.1184–1153 BC) he was fascinated by a scene in a small side chamber, depicting harpists playing before some of the gods. Bruce's drawing is now lost but seems to have been elaborated by the plate-engraver who took many liberties with the original. Having never seen any ancient Egyptian art, he interpreted it according to contemporary taste in the neo-classical style. Although his illustration of the harpists affords some amusement today, the tomb of Ramesses III has ever since been known as 'Bruce's tomb'. ◆

▲ *Richard Pococke's 'map' of the Valley of the Kings. Although not accurate in the modern sense, archaeologists have been able to identify the tombs Pococke visited from the accompanying plans.*

Napoleon's Expedition to Egypt

In 1798, Napoleon Bonaparte of France mounted a great expedition to Egypt with the dual purpose of reducing the power of his chief adversary, England, and exploring a lost civilization. His military expedition was a failure, but his survey of Egypt brought the wonders of the ancient land to the attention of the whole of Europe.

Before leaving for Egypt, Napoleon ordered leading French scholars to assemble teams of professional surveyors, engineers, mathematicians, astronomers, chemists and botanists, as well as artists, architects and archaeologists. These experts were to survey and record all aspects of Egyptian life, past and present. The French soon made themselves masters of Cairo, after defeating the Mameluke rulers, but were beaten at sea by Nelson's English fleet at the Battle of Abukir Bay. Finding themselves stranded in Egypt, the French Commission on Arts and Sciences spent the next three years mapping the whole country, recording archaeological sites and monuments, and studying the flora and fauna and contemporary life of the Egyptian people.

Description de l'Egypte

The result was a massive work, the *Description de l'Egypte,* published in 20 volumes between 1809 and 1828. This monumental, lavishly illustrated work caused a tremendous sensation among the scholars and cognoscenti of Europe, depicting as it did the splendours of ancient Egypt as they had never been seen before. The Commission's artists had drawn precise views of many of the pyramids. Khufu's Great Pyramid and the Sphinx had been carefully measured and studied.

Further south, the Commission explored the Valley of the Kings, where 16 tombs were located. The map of the valley, drawn for the expedition by Jollois and de Villiers, two young engineers, was the first accurate map of the area ever to be made. They also discovered a secondary valley, the Western Valley, and in it the tomb of Amenhotep III (c.1390–1352), whose existence had not previously been known.

▲ *Napoleon Bonaparte who, in 1798, mounted an expedition aimed at the conquest of Egypt. This was accompanied by a special commission that recorded the flora, fauna and contemporary culture of Egypt and surveyed the antiquities.*

▲ *The Commissioners engaged in their survey. The results were published in* Description de l'Egypte, *which reawakened interest in the area.*

▲ *Members of Napoleon's expedition measure the Sphinx, as depicted in a drawing by Vivant Denon from* Voyages dans le Basse et la Haute Egypte.

In addition, the Commission recorded several of the temples of Upper Egypt, with their unimaginable images still bright with colour. Apparently the sight of the Luxor and Karnak temples as they rounded a bend in the Nile so overwhelmed the troops with the expedition that they spontaneously 'formed ranks and presented arms to the accompaniment of the drums and the bands'. Metaphorically speaking, this must also have been the reaction of the intelligentsia of Europe as the volumes were published.

A popular version of the *Description,* the work of Vivant Denon, was published in 1802. This book, the *Voyages dans la Basse et la Haute Egypte,* became an enormous bestseller. It ran to 40 editions and was also translated into English and German. The book brought the discoveries made in Egypt to a much wider readership and, together with the *Description de l'Egypte,* led to a wave of Egyptomania that swept across Europe. However, this renewed interest also sadly led to the unscrupulous looting of antiquities by private collectors and museums alike.

Vivant Denon

Egyptology owes a great deal to Baron Dominique Vivant Denon (1747–1825). He had served at court under Louis XV and also as ambassador of France at St Petersburg and Naples under Louis XVI and, despite his distinguished career, he managed to survive the French Revolution unscathed. The Empress Josephine, who found him a place on Napoleon's expedition to Egypt, later befriended him.

Denon proved himself to be a talented artist and undertook much of the Commission's illustrative work, albeit sometimes in very difficult conditions, surrounded by Mamelukes and Arabs taking potshots at him. He also complained at the little time he had at his disposal in the Valley of the Kings. Allowed only three hours to record six tombs, he exclaimed:

> *How was it possible to leave such precious curiosities, without taking a drawing of them? How to return without having at least a sketch to show? I earnestly demanded a quarter of an hour's grace: I was allowed twenty minutes; one person lighted me, while another held a taper to every object I pointed out to him, and I completed my task in the time prescribed with spirit and correctness.*

On his return from Egypt, Denon was appointed Director General of Museums, and he went on later to found the Musée Napoléon, now the Louvre, in Paris. ◆

▼ *Vivant Denon, whose discourse and publications made a great contribution to the rise of Egyptology.*

European Rivalry: Champollion and Young

One of the most important antiquities to be studied as a result of Napoleon's expedition was the Rosetta Stone. This slab of black basalt was discovered in 1799, incorporated into an old wall, by a French officer inspecting the building of Fort Julien, near Rosetta in the Delta. After the French defeat, the British seized the stone and today it is in the British Museum, London.

The stone was inscribed in three different kinds of writing. One section was in Greek, which could be read, one was in Egyptian hieroglyphs and the other was in a cursive script. The race was soon on to decipher it. The main contestants were the French linguist Jean-François Champollion (1790–1832), his compatriot Sylvestre de Sacy (1758–1832), the English scientist Dr Thomas Young (1773–1829) and the Swedish diplomat Johan David Akerblad (1763–1819). Both Champollion and Young had been child prodigies and were conversant with Greek, Latin, Hebrew, Arabic and Aramaic, as well as several European languages.

Deciphering the hieroglyphs

All four scholars recognized the importance of the Rosetta Stone as the key to a modern understanding of the history and culture of ancient Egypt. Each had a copy of the three texts, but it was 20 years before any real progress was made. The Greek text proved to be a decree celebrating the anniversary of the coronation of Ptolemy V (205–180 BC). It was guessed that the other two sections of the inscription were versions of the same text. The first clue came in the name of Ptolemy. This could be read in Greek and was found in the hieroglyphic version inside a cartouche, the oval outline that, it was also guessed, enclosed the names of a king. Young compared this cartouche with two others inscribed on an obelisk that had been brought to England from Philae and is now in Kingston Lacy, Dorset. On this he was able to recognize the names of both Ptolemy and Cleopatra, since they have several letters in common. However, he failed to crack the code because he refused to believe that, apart from use in foreign names (the Ptolemies were Macedonian), the hieroglyphs could have an alphabetic or phonetic value. He firmly believed that the hieroglyphs were symbols that conveyed the sense of a whole word. The breakthrough came when Champollion, aided by his knowledge of Coptic (the last written form of the ancient Egyptian

▲ *Jean-François Champollion did most to decipher Egyptian hieroglyphs by realizing that a sign could represent both an idea and a sound.*

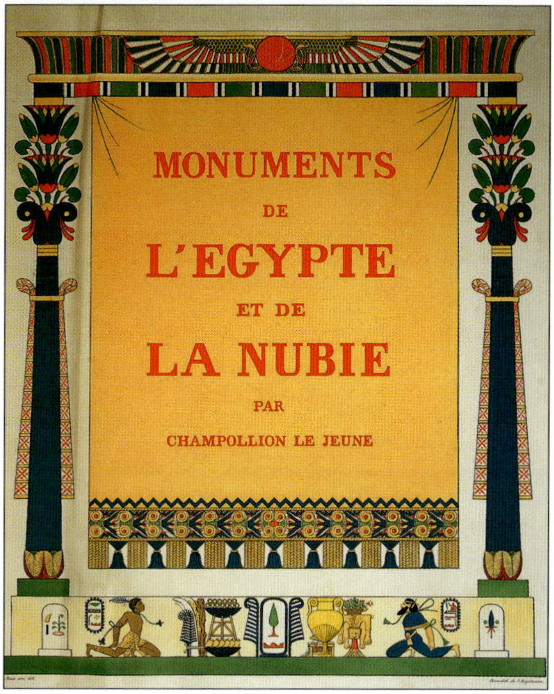

language, which employed mostly Greek characters), realized that hieroglyphs could convey both an idea and a sound value. In 1822, he was able to study some copies of texts from the temples of Tuthmosis III (c.1479–c.1425 BC) and Ramesses II (c.1279–1213 BC) in Nubia. Again, the royal names were identifiable because they were written in cartouches. These kings were also known from the classical authors, and Champollion was able to refer to Coptic to confirm his intuition about their identities and the way in which the language worked. He knew that *ra* means 'sun' in Coptic, and in the cartouche he saw a sun disc that

▶ *In 1828, Champollion travelled through Egypt and Nubia reading inscriptions. In this book he proved the accuracy of his decipherment.*

not only expressed the idea of 'sun' but the sound *ra* in Egyptian. He already knew the letter 's' from the Greek form of the name of Ptolemy (Ptolemaios). Guessing that the middle symbol was *mes,* he arrived at the name 'Ramesses'. Champollion made his discoveries known in September 1822 in a lecture to the Paris Académie des Inscriptions et Belles Lettres, now famous as the *Lettre à M. Dacier.* He then went on to study as many texts as he could lay his hands on in Turin, Aix and Livorno, and at last fulfilled his ambition to visit Egypt. During his 15-month trip, he travelled from Alexandria to Abu Simbel and beyond, reading the ancient texts along the way. Each one confirmed the views he had expressed in his lecture. Writing to Dacier, he said:

> *Now that I have followed the course of the Nile from its mouth to the Second Cataract, I am in a position to tell you we need change nothing in our Alphabet of the Hieroglyphs, our alphabet is correct: it applies equally well to the Egyptian monuments built during the time of the Romans and the Ptolemies and – what is of much greater interest – to the inscriptions in all the temples, palaces and tombs dating from the time of the pharaohs.*

Champollion was, however, scathing about the efforts of his rivals. Akerblad, he reckoned, could not read 'three words of an Egyptian inscription'. Although Young had made a valuable contribution to the decipherment of the Rosetta Stone, had correctly asserted that the second of the scripts was a cursive form of hieroglyphs and had published an article in the Encyclopaedia Britannica on the subject, Champollion dismissed his efforts as 'mere bragging'. For his part, Young refused to believe that Champollion had accurately cracked the code. ◆

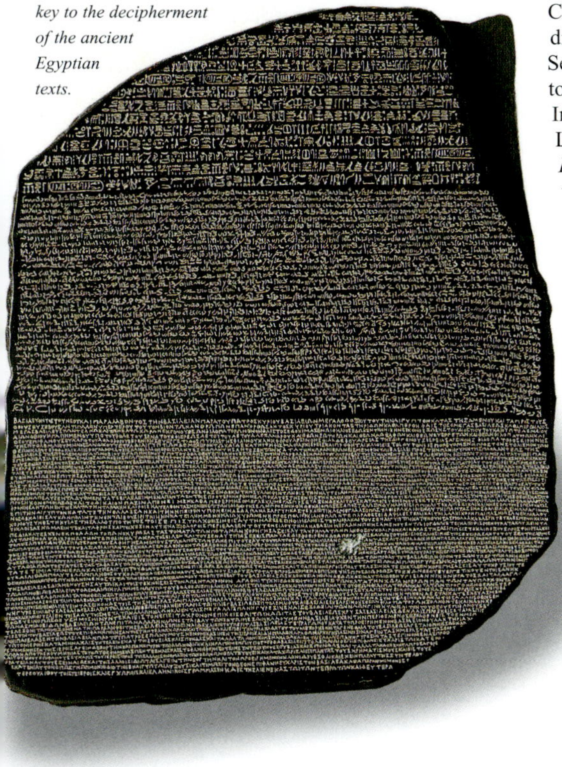

▼ *Written in Greek and ancient Egyptian, using three scripts (Greek, Egyptian hieroglyphs and demotic), the Rosetta Stone held the key to the decipherment of the ancient Egyptian texts.*

The Race for the Antiquities

The discoveries that were made during Napoleon's expedition gave rise to a passion for all things Egyptian throughout Europe, and led to a lucrative trade in ancient artefacts, eagerly sought by both private collectors and public institutions. There were large fortunes to be made by the major collectors of the antiquities, and such was the competition between them that fights often broke out between the rival gangs of workers at the excavation sites.

Bernadino Drovetti

Drovetti had served as a colonel during Napoleon's expedition to Egypt. He became Consul General of Egypt in 1810, and for the next 19 years used his position to carve out a career as an antiques dealer. He often directed excavations himself and took an active part in the looting of antiquities, ably assisted by his agent Jean-Jaques Rifaud, a sculptor from Marseilles. When he had amassed a significant collection he offered the finds to Louis XVIII, hoping that they would be bought for the Louvre in Paris. But the king thought the price too high, so Drovetti sold the collection to the King of Sardinia, who presented it to the Turin Museum in 1824. Some of the best pieces of royal sculpture, including the famous seated statue of Ramesses II (c.1279–c.1213 BC), are in this collection today and the Turin Museum was the first to own such an important group.

Drovetti then embarked on another collection, which he again offered to France. This time it was bought by Charles X, on the recommendation of Champollion, on behalf of the Louvre, where it became the nucleus of the Egyptian Antiquities section. Friedrich Wilhelm III of Prussia bought a third collection in 1836 for the Berlin Museum.

Henry Salt

Not to be outdone, the British Consul General, Henry Salt, also collected antiquities on the instructions of Sir Thomas Banks, one of the Trustees of the British Museum. However, he was bitterly disappointed when he was offered a mere £2,000 for what he had assembled. This did not even cover the cost of excavation and transport. Furthermore, the museum refused to buy the best item in the collection, the beautiful alabaster sarcophagus of Seti I (c.1294–c.1279 BC). This was later bought by Sir John Soane, who paid as much for it as Salt had received for the rest of the collection, and it is the centrepiece of Sir John Soane's Museum in Lincoln's Inn Fields, London.

A second collection made by Salt was offered to the British Museum, but was finally sold to the French king Charles X and presented to the Louvre. Among its many important pieces was the Karnak kinglist, which made the Louvre collection as important as that of Turin.

▼ Belzoni's drawing of the Temple of Karnak. Only the tops of the pillars and pylons stood out from the mounds of accumulated sand and rubble.

◀ *Bernardino Drovetti, standing centre left, whose collection formed the nucleus of the Turin Museum.*

'The Patagonian Samson'

Belzoni had enjoyed a varied career before entering Salt's service. At one time he had entertained ideas of becoming a monk, but he later appeared as 'The Patagonian Samson' in a music-hall act at Sadler's Wells Theatre in London. He was extremely tall and immensely strong, and the climax of his act was to appear on stage strapped into an iron harness carrying a dozen or so people who formed a 'human pyramid'.

Giovanni Belzoni

Salt's right-hand man in the difficult process of transporting the antiquities to Europe was the adventurer Giovanni Belzoni. He first visited Egypt in 1814 with the idea of interesting the Turkish viceroy, Mohammed Ali Pasha, in a water-raising device he had invented. Unfortunately for Belzoni his machine was rejected, and he was left penniless as he had sunk all his funds into the project. In despair, he left Cairo in 1816. But as luck would have it, he was approached by the scholar and explorer Jean-Louis Burckhardt, who introduced him to Salt. Burckhardt suggested that they should try to remove the colossal fallen bust of Ramesses II from the Ramesseum and transport it to England.

▲ *Giovanni Belzoni, seen here in Turkish dress, was given money by the British Consul General to collect antiquities for the British Museum.*

By means of four great levers the bust was raised sufficiently for a huge raft on rollers to be placed underneath it, and Ramesses began the first stage of his long, slow journey to London. It took ten days to cover less than 2km (1 mile). The local rulers put many difficulties in the way, but eventually the statue reached the River Nile.

While waiting for a ship big enough to carry the bust to Cairo, Belzoni used the time to visit the Valley of the Kings, where he explored the magnificent tomb of Seti I. Belzoni was also a talented artist and faithfully copied all the painted reliefs and texts he found in Seti's tomb. His drawings were later exhibited to great public acclaim in London and Paris. Even Champollion went to have a look at Belzoni's work and copied a number of the texts in support of his theories on decipherment.

During the wait for a ship, Belzoni also excavated at Karnak, where he discovered 18 statues of the lioness-headed goddess Sekhmet, a kneeling statue of Seti II (c.1200–c.1194 BC) and several sphinxes, all of which are today in the British Museum collections. Belzoni also took part in the excavation of Abu Simbel and made accurate records of the temple. ◆

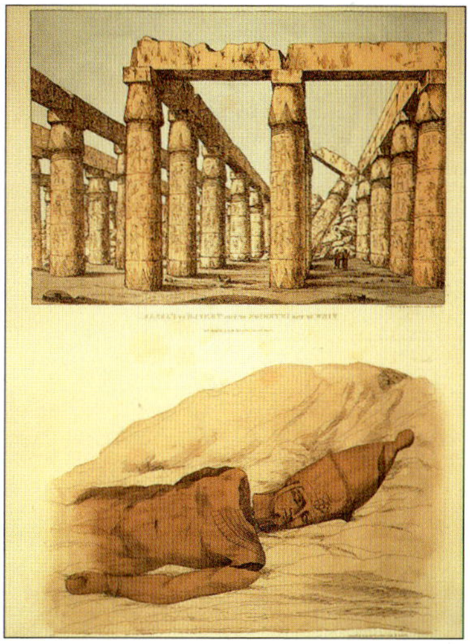

▲ *Illustrations from a book by Belzoni of Karnak and a colossal statue, thought to be of Ramesses II, that he found there.*

The Founders of Egyptology

The nineteenth century saw the development of an ever-increasing body of serious travellers to Egypt. By this time, these travellers' main interest lay in making careful records of the antiquities, rather than in removing them from their original settings to the museums of Europe.

John Gardner Wilkinson

The work of Sir John Gardner Wilkinson (1797–1875) laid the foundations of Egyptology in Britain. Arriving in Egypt in 1821, he spent the next 12 years systematically studying the main archaeological sites of Egypt and Nubia, including Karnak, the tombs of the Valley of the Kings and Gebel Barkal, the sacred mountain near the Fourth Cataract. He made precise copies of the tombs at Beni Hasan, identified the 'Labyrinth' described by the classical authors as the mortuary temple of Amenemhat III (c.1855–c.1808 BC) at Hawara and was the first to draw up a detailed plan of Tell el-Amarna, the city of Akhenaten (c.1352–c.1336 BC). Some of his most valuable work was in the field of epigraphy, which is the study of ancient inscriptions. He made exact copies of the texts he came across during his excavations, and identified the names of many of the ancient Egyptian kings for the first time. The detailed precision of his work far outclassed that of his contemporaries, and it remains a veritable mine of information for modern Egyptologists.

Wilkinson was interested in more than the monuments, however, and on his return to England wrote a massive work entitled *The Manners and Customs of the Ancient Egyptians*. Using his copies of scenes from the tombs, papyri and other inscriptional material, he produced a vivid portrayal of the daily life of the ancient Egyptians. Later, he made a detailed study of the famous kinglist known as the Turin Canon, and helped to establish the correct order of the rulers of ancient Egypt.

▼ *A watercolour painting by Lepsius depicts the city of Thebes, showing the ruins of the temples of Luxor and Karnak.*

▶ *John Gardner Wilkinson was the first British scholar to make a science of Egyptology. He was particularly famous for his copies of tombs and their inscriptions.*

Carl Richard Lepsius

In 1842, Carl Lepsius (1810–84) was commissioned by Friedrich Wilhelm IV of Prussia to lead an expedition to Egypt. Before this he had spent years studying Champollion's grammar in order to learn hieroglyphs, and had visited the major European collections of Egyptian antiquities. As with the earlier expeditions, Lepsius' main task was to record the monuments and to take home antiquities. His team included the artist Joseph Bonomi and the English architect James Wild. On his return he published his findings in a monumental work, *Denkmäler aus Aegypten und Aethiopien* (1849–58), a book comparable in scale to Napoleon's *Description de l'Egypte.*

Lepsius' work is particularly important because it describes many sites where there was considerably more to see at the time of his visit than there is today. Many of them have suffered at the hands of looters as well as from the ravages of time. In fact, some of the most important finds of recent times came about through his work. Professor Geoffrey Martin's rediscovery of the tombs of Maya, Tutankhamun's treasurer, and the king's general, Horemheb, were made possible by surveys and descriptions made by Lepsius of the tombs at Saqqara dating from the New Kingdom (c.1550–c.1069 BC). They lay buried beneath the sand as the joint expedition of the Egypt Exploration Society and the National Museum of Antiquities in Leiden set to work in 1975.

In 1865, Lepsius was rewarded with the post of Keeper of the Egyptian Antiquities Department in the Berlin Museum, and some months later he led another expedition to Egypt, this time to the little-explored area of the Delta. At Tanis, he discovered the Canopus Decree: this document, written in Greek and Demotic, proved useful to scholars engaged in decipherment because it could be compared with the Rosetta Stone. Until his death in 1884, Lepsius produced many more publications, and was also the editor of the leading German Egyptological journal, the *Zeitschrift für ägyptische Sprache und Altertumskunde.* Lepsius did more than anyone else to put Germany, particularly the Berlin Museum, on the map in the field of Egyptology. ◆

▼ *The antiquities and 15,000 casts Lepsius brought home from Egypt formed the nucleus of the Berlin Museum's Egyptian collection.*

Mariette and French Egyptology

Auguste Mariette (1821–81) first became interested in Egyptology in 1842 while he was sorting through some papers left to his family by his cousin Nestor L'Hôte. L'Hôte had accompanied Napoleon's expedition to Egypt and had produced several drawings for Champollion, some as yet unpublished. Mariette spent the next seven years learning hieroglyphs and studying Coptic before finding employment in the Louvre, where he made an inventory of all the museum's ancient Egyptian texts.

◀ *Auguste Mariette, the founder of the Egyptian Antiquities Service and the Bulaq (now Cairo) Museum. He discovered the Serapaeum, the burial place of the Apis bulls, and the valley temple of the Old Kingdom king Khafre, at Giza.*

The Serapaeum

In 1850, Mariette was sent to Egypt to collect papyri, but because he was given a rather lukewarm reception in the monasteries of the Wadi Natrun he decided to try his luck elsewhere. He eventually arrived at Saqqara, the cemetery site for the ancient capital Memphis. On seeing a sphinx half-buried in the sand he was immediately reminded of the words of Strabo:

There is also a Serapaeum at Memphis, in a place so sandy that dunes of sand are heaped up by the winds: and by these, some of the sphinxes which I saw were buried even to the head and others were half visible; from which one might guess the danger if a sandstorm should fall upon a man travelling on foot towards the temple.

Mariette felt irresistibly led by these words towards the Serapaeum, which was the burial place of the mummified remains of the Apis bulls. Each of these sacred animals was regarded during its lifetime as the representation on earth of the deity Apis (a manifestation of Ptah, the creator god of Memphis) and was kept in a special stall near his temple. After death the bulls were associated with the Underworld gods Sokar and Osiris, and were laid to rest at Saqqara.

The avenue leading to the temple took two years to clear and it was only in the face of much official opposition that Mariette was allowed to complete his work in the Serapaeum itself. However, he was eventually able to restore some kind of order to the chaos found in the subterranean passages and burial chambers, where the sarcophagus lids had been prised off and many had been smashed. The Serapaeum subsequently became a major tourist attraction and its discovery brought Mariette much acclaim. He often conducted important visitors to the Serapaeum in person and on such occasions the galleries were lit by hundreds of children carrying candles, giving an effect described as dreamlike and magical. Inside the last burial chamber, the guests found a table set with silver goblets and a bottle of champagne, with folding chairs ready to receive them.

▲ *Mariette's discovery in the Serapaeum of an undisturbed Apis burial, with the bull's mummy, jewellery and gold, brought him worldwide fame.*

▲ *Mariette's excavation methods are criticized today. He often requisitioned the male population of villages to further the work and used dynamite.*

▲ *Found by Mariette in the valley temple, this diorite statue of King Khafre protected by the hawk god Horus is a masterpiece of Egyptian art.*

Khafre's valley temple

Mariette's second most important discovery was the valley temple of the pyramid of the Fourth Dynasty king Khafre (c.2558–c.2532 BC) at Giza. At the time of its discovery, it had been virtually reduced to a heap of enormous stones. He began work on it in 1853, when he partly excavated the interior, and completed it in 1858. In the course of the excavation he blew apart some of the collapsed monoliths in order to remove them from the temple. He is often criticized for the fact that here, as elsewhere, he failed to publish his finds adequately. But in this case he did discover one of the masterpieces of the Old Kingdom (c.2686–c.2181 BC), the great diorite statue of Khafre himself (now in the Cairo Museum).

In 1858, Mariette was appointed Director of the Egyptian Antiquities Service, and the viceroy gave him the authority and means to excavate wherever he wished. He set up the Bulaq Museum near Cairo to exhibit his finds. ◆

Amelia Edwards

It was entirely by chance that Amelia Edwards (1831–92) first became interested in Egypt. She and a friend had gone to France on a sketching holiday and had been plagued by weeks of rain. After discussing whether to return to England or 'push on further still in search of sunshine', they decided to go to Egypt. She later wrote:

For in simple truth we had drifted hither by accident with no excuse of health or business or any serious object whatsoever and had just taken refuge in Egypt as one might turn aside into the Burlington Arcade... to get out of the rain.

In spite of this rather prosaic start to her relationship with Egypt, once she was there it was clearly a case of love at first sight. On looking out of her window on the first morning of her stay she was immediately captivated by the scene:

It was dark last night, and I had no idea that my room overlooked an enchanted garden, far-reaching and solitary, peopled with stately giants beneath whose tufted crowns hung rich clusters of maroon and amber dates... Yonder, between the pillared stems, rose the minaret of a very distant mosque; and here where the garden was bounded by a wall and a windowless house, I saw a veiled lady walking on the terraced roof in the midst of a cloud of pigeons. Nothing could be more simple than the scene and its accessories; nothing at the same time more Eastern, strange, and unreal.

Before going to Egypt, Amelia Edwards had already achieved some success as a writer and journalist. She was to become one of the most prominent writers of her age, and her work included several travel books, the most famous of which is the record of her six-month journey up the River Nile, *A Thousand Miles up the Nile*.

▲ *Amelia Edwards wrote the best-selling book* A Thousand Miles Up the Nile *(1877) and founded what is now the Egypt Exploration Society.*

A Thousand Miles up the Nile

It is typical of Edwards' enterprise and courage that she and her friend decided to make the most of their trip to Egypt by chartering a *dahabeeyah* (a flat-bottomed, wooden boat) and engaging a crew with a view to sailing up the Nile to Aswan and then beyond the borders of Egypt into Nubia. This was in 1873, the year David Livingstone died and before General Gordon had made his first journey to Khartoum, a remarkable feat for two women at that time.

By far the greater part of *A Thousand Miles up the Nile* is devoted to the monuments she visited. The modern tourist sees them in their reconstructed state, but when Miss Edwards went to Egypt over a century ago, many of the tombs and temples were filled with the rubble and driven sand of past centuries. Describing the ruins of Luxor Temple she wrote:

These half-buried pylons, this solitary obelisk, those giant heads rising in ghastly resurrection before the gates of the temple were magnificent still. But it was as the magnificence of the

◀ *A 19th-century painting of the Cairo Bazaar that so fascinated Amelia Edwards on her arrival.*

Preparing for the voyage

The hiring of Miss Edwards' *dahabeeyah* was much more difficult than house-hunting. Added to the problems of weighing up the merits of the available boats was the fact that they frequently changed their position on the river. The prices varied from day to day and the 'certificates of recommendation' by former travellers had 'a mysterious way of turning up again and again on board different boats and in the hands of different claimants'.

Eventually Amelia and her friend found a craft to their liking. After scurrying to the nearest stores to make a few last-minute purchases, they went on board and set about transforming the sparsely furnished saloon of the *dahabeeyah* into a cosy Victorian parlour. As Miss Edwards remarked, 'It is wonderful what a few books and roses, an open piano and a sketch or two will do'.

▲ *Nile cruises became very popular after the publication of Amelia Edwards' book.*

prologue to a poem of which only garbled fragments remain. Beyond that entrance lay a smoky, filthy, intricate labyrinth of lanes and passages. Mud hovels, mud pigeon houses, mud yards, and a mud mosque, clustered like wasps' nests in and about the ruins. Architraves sculptured with royal titles supported the roofs of squalid cabins. Stately capitals peeped out from the midst of sheds in which buffaloes, camels, donkeys, dogs and human beings were huddled together in unsavoury fellowship.

Amelia began work on the book on her return to England in 1874. She read extensively and consulted respected Egyptologists on matters of historical and archaeological detail. She also took up the study of hieroglyphs. By 1878, she was writing reviews and articles on Egyptology for weekly journals such as The Academy, and quickly became an authority in her own right.

The Egypt Exploration Fund

Amelia Edwards' greatest work was the founding of the Egypt Exploration Fund (now Society). She was very concerned about the state of the ancient monuments; many were suffering from neglect; others were being vandalized. The Egyptian government had neither the interest nor the resources necessary to protect them. In 1879, Miss Edwards wrote to Auguste Mariette, the founder of the Cairo (Bulaq) Museum, to ask whether it might be possible to finance excavation in the Delta by public subscription in England. She also enlisted the support of several English Egyptologists and Biblical scholars.

Amelia's most enthusiastic supporter was Sir Erasmus Wilson, an eminent surgeon who was already engaged in writing a popular history of Egypt. He was also very wealthy and had just spent £10,000 transporting the obelisk now known as Cleopatra's Needle to England. When *A Thousand Miles up the Nile* was published, Wilson was so impressed with it that he wrote to Amelia, and thus began a long friendship. She advised him on his book and he was always willing to give financial support to any scientific survey or excavation by the British in Egypt. Others were less easy to persuade. The Oriental Department of the British Museum was totally opposed to Miss Edwards' efforts, although help came from elsewhere in the Museum, notably from the Department of Coins and Medals. The Egypt Exploration Fund was eventually set up in March 1882, with R. S. Poole and Amelia Edwards as Honorary Secretaries and Sir Erasmus Wilson as Treasurer.

The Fund found many supporters in the United States, where Miss Edwards embarked on an extensive and exhausting lecture tour in 1889. During the five months she was there, she lectured 115 times and travelled to 16 different states. Her labours were well rewarded and the subscriptions flowed in.

First chair in Egyptology

The strenuous tour of North America had left Amelia's health seriously impaired, but her devotion to the Fund impelled her to go to Millwall Docks in London in October 1891 to supervise the arrival of antiquities from Egypt and their dispersal to various museums. A lung infection resulted, from which she never recovered. She died the following spring, bequeathing a sum of money to found the first chair in Egyptology at University Collge, London, with the proviso that Flinders Petrie should be the first professor. ◆

The Father of Modern Egyptology

Sir William Matthew Flinders Petrie (1853–1942) was the pioneer of modern archaeological methods in Egypt. In great contrast to his contemporaries, his main anxiety was to halt the destruction of the ancient remains.

Petrie had received little formal education but his father had taught him the principles of surveying and geometry. After practising on Stonehenge, father and son planned to visit Egypt to survey the Great Pyramid. In the end, his father did not go, and Petrie undertook the task alone. Nobody had ever done anything like it before. He spent several weeks setting up the survey points and making accurate plans, which he published in 1883. He also spent much time weighing up the possible methods by which the pyramids might have been constructed.

He was horrified by what he saw going on in the valley temple of Khafre:

Mariette most rascally blasted to pieces all the fallen parts of the granite temple by a large gang of soldiers, to clear it out instead of lifting the stones and replacing them by means of tackle... Nothing seems to be done with any uniform and regular plan, work is begun and left unfinished; no regard is paid to future requirements of exploration, and no civilized or labour-saving devices are used. It is sickening to see the rate at which everything is being destroyed, and the little regard paid to preservation.

In his time, Petrie excavated at most of the important archaeological sites. He worked principally at the Predynastic cemeteries at Naqada, the Delta sites of Tanis and Naucratis, the city of Akhenaten at Tell el-Amarna, the Faiyum pyramids of Senusret II (c.1880–c.1874 BC) and Amenemhat III (c.1855–c.1808 BC), and the remains of the cemetery and ancient city of Abydos.

▲ *Flinders Petrie, the pioneer of modern archaeological methods in Egypt and the first Professor of Egyptology at University College, London.*

Excavations at Abydos

Although frustrated in his ambition for many years, in 1899 Petrie was eventually granted the concession to dig at Abydos. There he found that the site had been dug over many times, both by dealers and by local farmers looking for mudbrick to grind up for use as fertilizer on their land. Mariette had removed statues from the site for the Bulaq Museum. Worst of all, the Frenchman Emile Clément Amélineau had worked over the royal tombs of the Early Dynastic Period (c.3100–c.2686 BC) and had done untold damage in the process. It had been rumoured that he was interested only in large, intact, saleable objects and that he broke those he was not able to carry away: Petrie found that this appeared to be true. Moreover, because Amélineau had treated his workmen badly and offered them no reward for objects they found, there seemed to have been much pilfering from the site.

When Petrie began to rework the site, he found much that Amélineau had missed, including some of the grave stelae that marked the royal tombs and small tablets indicating the graves of officials. Most important of all were the little ivory and ebony labels originally attached to grave goods, which gave the

▼ *The members of Petrie's teams led a spartan life. At the age of 83, Petrie and his wife Hilda (in the helmet) used this old green bus in Palestine.*

▲ *Ivory comb of King Djet from the Early Dynastic cemetery at Abydos.*

names of some of the kings, each one recording an important event in a particular year of the king's reign. From these, Petrie was able to collect the names of all the kings of the First Dynasty (c.3100–c.2890 BC) and to suggest the order in which they had reigned.

During his excavation of the tomb of King Djer (c.3000 BC), Petrie found part of an arm wrapped in bandages, later found to be wearing a set of four exquisite bracelets made of gold, lapis lazuli, amethyst and turquoise. After carefully examining the jewellery, he entrusted the precious burden to James Quibell, the Chief Inspector of Antiquities for Lower Egypt, to deliver to the Cairo Museum. However, the museum's assistant conservator was interested only in the jewellery, and threw away the arm and the linen, thus destroying the earliest evidence for mummification. As Petrie remarked, 'a museum is a dangerous place'.

This discovery also demonstrates the superior way in which Petrie treated his workers. He always believed in paying his men properly for anything that they found so that he could be sure they would bring their finds to him rather than take them to the dealers. In this instance, the workmen could see the jewellery inside the wrappings, but left the arm undisturbed while they went to find one of Petrie's assistants. In the evening, the arm was unwrapped in the presence of the workmen and the gold of the bracelets weighed against sovereigns. The men were paid handsomely 'to ensure their goodwill and honesty for the future'.

Petrie's interest in objects of everyday life also marks him as remarkably astute. In his day, these would usually have been passed over in favour of the more spectacular. From the small finds made at Kahun, the settlement of the workers on Senusret II's pyramid at el-Lahun, it is possible to build up a complete picture of life within the community.

Honeymoon on a coal barge

Petrie was aided in his work by his wife, Hilda Urlin, one of his former students. Their wedding breakfast, a glass of milk and a bun at a café opposite Victoria Station in London, before catching the boat-train to Calais on the first stage of their journey to Egypt, anticipated the austerity of their married life. After nearly two weeks in Cairo they set off for Dendera. The train went no farther than Nag' Hamadi, so they hired a boat for the rest of the journey. Unfortunately, the wind dropped and they were forced to spend the night in cramped conditions under the half deck. They breakfasted on the remains of the previous night's supper of bread, 'little fritters', beans and jam. A colleague, Norman de Garis Davies, was with them, and all three had to share a single knife and tin mug provided by the boatmen. When they were still 16km (10 miles) from their destination at two in the afternoon, they decided to walk the rest of the way. Hilda claimed to have enjoyed this 'most delightful adventure' of her 'honeymoon on a coal barge'. ◆

▲ *This carved ivory label was once attached to a pair of sandals from the royal cemetery at Abydos. King Den is shown smiting his enemies.*

Sequence dating

Petrie devised an ingenious method, called sequence dating, of putting into chronological order the finds from his excavations at Naqada, Hu and Abadlya. He cut 900 strips of cardboard, each 17cm (7in) long, to represent 900 of the 4,000 tombs he had excavated. On each he recorded the number of pots of various types he had found in the grave, as well as other objects such as palettes and beads. By comparing the contents of each grave, he was able to work out a probable chronological order. Assuming that designs would become more complex over time, Petrie assigned the earliest sequence dates to the simplest artefacts, using a numerical sequence from 30–80 (the numbers 1–29 were kept free in case earlier objects were found). He was able to divide the pottery and associated grave goods into two main phases, now usually called Naqada I (c.4000–c.3500 BC; red pottery with white decoration) and Naqada II (c.3500–c.3100 BC; buff-coloured pottery decorated with red motifs such as ships, ostriches and dancing women). Although adjustments have been made in the light of more recent discoveries, the system is still used by archaeologists today.

The Development of the Pyramid Complex

The Predynastic Period in Egypt lasted from around the mid-sixth millennium BC to c.3100 BC. During this long, formative period, the many individual cultures of different parts of Egypt were gradually replaced by those now called Naqada II (c.3500–c.3100 BC) and III (c.3100–c.3000 BC). Naqada was a site in the south of Egypt excavated by Sir Flinders Petrie in 1895, and it gave its name to a particular type of burial that had distinctive grave goods. At the same time, the various settlement centres gradually developed into a politically unified state ruled by a king.

Some of the most impressive archaeological remains of the Early Dynastic Period (c.3100–c.2686 BC) are the mudbrick mastabas, or burial places, of the kings and their officials at Saqqara, Abydos and Naqada. Mastaba, from an Arabic word meaning 'bench', is the name given to a type of tomb that looks rather like the mudbrick benches seen outside Egyptian houses. The burial chamber was below ground, surrounded by storerooms filled with goods for the use of the deceased in the Afterlife. Above ground, a mudbrick superstructure was built with an offering chapel attached. In later examples, the offering chapel was incorporated into the superstructure. It was from these mastaba tombs that the later royal pyramid complexes developed, while the mastaba form continued to be used by high-ranking officials whose burial places were usually clustered around those of the kings they had served.

◀ *Amenemhat III's pyramid at Hawara was the last large pyramid to be built in Egypt.*

Early Dynastic Period Mastabas

The earliest type of mastaba had a pit cut into the desert plateau. This was divided by mudbrick walls into the burial chamber and storerooms. There was no way into the burial chamber from outside, so the tomb was finished only after the burial had taken place. Later in the Early Dynastic Period, access to the burial place was provided by a staircase leading into the tomb, so it could be constructed before the body was buried. Precautions against robbers were apparently necessary, because in several tombs portcullises blocked the stairway.

During the Old Kingdom (c.2686–c.2181 BC) the storerooms were incorporated into the superstructure, from which a shaft led down to the burial chamber below ground. Stones often blocked the shaft. The main offering niche also became part of the internal plan, and eventually developed into a funerary chapel, decorated with scenes depicting the life of the tomb owner.

▲ *These two small dolomite vases with gold lids fastened with gold wire came from the tomb of the 2nd Dynasty king Khasekhemwy at Abydos.*

Abydos

As recently as about a century ago, the history of the earliest dynasties was still unknown. Flinders Petrie described the period before King Sneferu (c.2613–c.2589 BC), first king of the Fourth Dynasty, as 'a blank', but he did more than any other Egyptologist to fill the gap, with his discoveries in the First and Second Dynasty mastaba tombs of Abydos. Emile Amélineau had excavated these between 1894–8, but much had been missed. Petrie re-dug the site much more meticulously and was able to chart the development of the architecture of the tombs, which he was convinced were the burial places of the earliest kings. He also found objects inscribed with the names of previously unknown kings and was able to suggest a tentative chronology. This has recently been confirmed by the find at Abydos, by a team from the German Archaeological Institute led by Gunther Dreyer, of a clay seal, giving the names of the first five kings of the dynasty in order. The members of the team have continued the work on architectural

▼ *Remains of 1st and 2nd Dynasty tombs discovered by Walter B. Emery at Saqqara; thought to be royal tombs when first excavated, they are now known to have belonged to officials.*

development, and have found evidence for several stages of building in some tombs. They have also studied the links between the Early Dynastic Period tombs and those of the Predynastic Period nearby. They are now postulating a Dynasty Zero preceding the First Dynasty, thus pushing back the boundaries of the known history of Egypt.

Graves of a typical Predynastic type have been found in Cemetery U at Abydos. Here, graves of the Naqada I and II and later periods have been found. Some Predynastic tombs of the latest stage have several chambers, and it is thought that these belonged to the Dynasty Zero kings. One originally had nine rooms, but was later extended to 12. The storerooms were filled with large numbers of pottery vases, some of local origin and others imported from Canaan. In the burial chamber were traces of a wooden shrine and an ivory sceptre very similar to those that later formed part of the royal insignia.

The first tombs of the Early Dynastic Period (c.3100–c.2686 BC) were found in Cemetery B. The most elaborate belonged to King Aha, probably the second king of the First Dynasty. This tomb too, seems to have been extended at various times. Surrounding the tomb were a large number of subsidiary graves for retainers. From a study of the skeletal remains it seems that the bodies were all of young men aged about 25, and that they were killed in order to accompany their royal master to the Afterlife.

The tomb of Djer

According to ancient Egyptian tradition, Abydos was the burial place of Osiris and, in the late Middle Kingdom (c.2055–c.1650 BC), the tomb of the First Dynasty king Djer (c.3000 BC) was remodelled as the god's tomb. Emile Amélineau found a stone statue representing Osiris lying on his side (a reference to the myth in which the god was killed by his jealous brother Seth). However, much of the original burial remained and Petrie, during his re-excavation of the site, found the now famous set of four bracelets still attached to part of a mummified arm.

The remaining First Dynasty tombs lie a little to the west. They, too, were brick-lined pits but some also had a further lining of wood panelling. They were also surrounded by the graves of servants. The superstructures have long since disappeared, but the grave markers remain, carved with the names of their royal owners.

Lying some distance away from the tombs themselves are the associated funerary enclosures, which were probably used for the funerary cults of the dead kings. Of those belonging to the First Dynasty kings little remains, but some that belonged to the kings of the Second Dynasty are still impressive. The best preserved belonged to King Khasekhemwy (c.2686 BC), and its double walls still stand to a considerable height. The outer surface of the inner wall is built in the 'palace façade' style, with a series of elaborate niches and false doors. Just inside the entrance to the enclosure were some small buildings. The funerary complexes, together with the tombs themselves, may well be the prototype of the Step Pyramid. A further clue may lie in the fact that the entrance to each of the Abydos enclosures is on the south-eastern corner, just like the entrance to the Step Pyramid complex.

▲ *The grave marker of King Djet from his tomb at Abydos. The* serekh *bearing his name is surmounted by Horus, thus associating the king with the god.*

Saqqara

Between 1936–56, Walter B. Emery found further mastaba tombs at Saqqara, the chief necropolis of Memphis. These had many rooms containing high-quality grave goods arranged around a central burial chamber. The fact that the tombs were much bigger than those at Abydos (excluding the funerary enclosures) led Emery to think that he had found the true royal tombs at Saqqara, and that the tombs at Abydos were cenotaphs only. This theory has now been discounted, and the Saqqara tombs seem to have belonged to high officials. First, the number of tombs at Saqqara was much larger than the number of known kings, and second, seal impressions bearing the names of the same rulers turned up in several tombs. These seals were also inscribed with the names of senior officials. In the case of Mereruka, an official of the First Dynasty king Qa'a (c.2890 BC), a stela bearing his name was found near the main offering niche, making ownership of the tomb clear. This stela was the forerunner of the decoration of the false door of later funerary chapels and of the tomb autobiography, which was intended to justify the life of the deceased and provide his passport to immortality. ◆

The First Architecture in Stone

Until the beginning of the Third Dynasty (c.2686 BC), the main building materials were wood, reeds and mudbrick. The first building in the world to be constructed completely in stone was the Step Pyramid of King Djoser (c.2667–c.2648 BC) at Saqqara. Before this time, only a few details, such as doorways or the paving of a tomb chamber, had been made of stone. According to Manetho (an Egyptian priest who wrote a history of Egypt in the third century BC to impress Ptolemy II with the great splendour and antiquity of the civilization he had inherited), the inventor of the art of building in stone was Imhotep. That he was at any rate in charge of building operations at the Step Pyramid is clear from the discovery there of the pedestal of a statue of King Djoser bearing the words: 'The Chancellor of the King of Lower Egypt, the first after the King of Upper Egypt, Administrator of the Great Palace, Hereditary Lord, the High Priest of Heliopolis, Imhotep, the builder, the sculptor'.

▲ *The Step Pyramid of King Djoser (c.2667–c.2648 BC), the world's first stone-built building. Previously, wood, reeds and mudbrick were used.*

Djoser's Step Pyramid

The Step Pyramid itself developed from the mudbrick royal mastabas of the Early Dynastic Period (c.3100–c.2686 BC) at Abydos. There, a mound of sand covered the burial chamber, perhaps representing the first land that appeared from the primordial ocean and on which creation took place, thus linking the themes of creation and re-creation. The mudbrick mastaba developed into a stone-built tower, and the mound became a ladder, which the king would climb to join the 'imperishable stars', a claim made in the Pyramid Texts, the funerary texts that accompanied royal burials during the Late Old Kingdom and First Intermediate Period (c.2350–c.2055 BC).

In the Step Pyramid complex, architecture that had previously been carried out in mudbrick, wood and reeds has been translated into stone. The wall surrounding the whole complex is built of small blocks of dressed limestone in imitation of the mudbrick 'palace façade' style of Early Dynastic tombs and enclosure walls.

The entrance to the complex is at its south-eastern corner. Roofing in ancient Egypt was usually in the form of palm logs, and the entrance passage was roofed with such 'logs' copied in stone. There are no real doors at the actual entrance, but the vestibule has carvings in stone of huge wooden doors, forever open. Even the hinges have been reproduced, and the right-hand door has a slit to show which panel should be 'closed' first.

Inside the entrance stands a colonnade of 20 pairs of half-engaged columns. These imitate huge bound bundles of reeds. Although no buildings in this medium have survived in Egypt, until very recently the Marsh Arabs of southern Iraq used reeds to build their homes and strengthened the corners with reed bundles. Similar buildings are also known from Sumerian seals of the third millennium BC. It is sometimes

◀ *Papyrus plants made of stone, with triangular stems and open umbels, form half-engaged columns and capitals in the Northern Court.*

▲ *Bundles of reeds are used by the Marsh Arabs of southern Iraq to strengthen buildings. Stone versions were used in the Step Pyramid buildings.*

said that the Step Pyramid columns are half-engaged (joined to the wall) because the architect, uncertain of the new technique, was not sure that they would be strong enough to support the roof if they were free-standing. It is much more likely that they were direct copies of the way reed columns were used in house construction.

Dummy shrines

Plant forms are much in evidence elsewhere in the complex. The dummy buildings of the *heb sed* court and North and South Houses are translations into stone of different types of shrines to local gods, which until this time had been made of wood and reeds. The most common type represents a rectangular wooden-framed tent with an arched roof. The shrine stands on a pedestal. The curved roofs of the larger ones are supported with poles carved in imitation of the trunks of conifers. The poles suggest that the actual shrines were open at the front to reveal the image of the god. They would have been temporary rather than permanent structures in real life, providing a shelter for the god's image at festivals.

The second type of shrine, seen in the North and South Houses of the complex, was larger and stood directly on the ground. These shrines, too, were open-fronted but the image of the god was shielded by a reed screen between the poles over the lower part of the building. The fact that reeds were actually used in this way in the construction of real reed shrines is suggested by the carving of their knotted ends. This stylized knotting became a standard architectural motif known as the *kheker* frieze.

In the third version of the temporary shrine, of which Temple T is an example, all four walls are plain and are strengthened at the corners by bound reed bundles. Another roll lies across the top of the wall, but here the loose ends of the reeds form a plain frieze. Inside, however, is another building, imitating one made of mudbrick.

▲ *Palm-log ceilings are still features of Egyptian village houses. Stone imitations were used in the entrance lobby of the Step Pyramid complex.*

All these designs, including the double shrine, became features of later ancient Egyptian temple architecture, as did the papyrus column and open papyrus capital first seen in engaged form decorating the walls of the Northern Court. ◆

► *Stone shrines to house statues of the gods surround the* heb sed *court where the king would be able to celebrate his jubilee in the Afterlife.*

From Step Pyramid to True Pyramid

Two of Djoser's successors, Sekhemkhet (c.2648–c.2640 BC) and Khaba (c.2640–c.2637 BC), attempted to build step pyramid complexes but failed to complete them. There are also some provincial step pyramids, including one at Seila on the fringe of the Faiyum Oasis. It has been suggested that this may have belonged to the first king of the Fourth Dynasty, Sneferu (c.2613–c.2589 BC), which would bring the number of pyramids associated with him to four. Five of the step pyramids are tentatively associated with Huni (c.2637–c.2613 BC), Sneferu's predecessor. However, later kings did not copy this type of royal burial, although some features were incorporated into pyramid complexes belonging to later periods.

The Meidum Pyramid

Sneferu's three main pyramids were built at Meidum and Dahshur. Today, the Meidum Pyramid appears across the cultivation as a ghostly three-staged tower surrounded by a great heap of debris. It is often suggested either that the pyramid collapsed in antiquity, leaving the first stages of the building revealed, or that later builders used the pyramid as a quarry. Even the ownership of the pyramid is sometimes disputed. In the past, some scholars preferred to believe it was the work of Huni (largely because, at the time, no other pyramid had been attributed to him). However, all the texts found at the site, albeit from later periods, mention Sneferu rather than his predecessor, and as the ancient name of Meidum is Djed Sneferu ('Sneferu endures'), it seems likely that the pyramid belonged to him. The fact that the two stelae found in the mortuary chapel were uninscribed is rather a puzzle. Not only would a name have definitely established ownership but it was also considered extremely important in ancient Egyptian funerary belief to perpetuate the name of the deceased, otherwise he might cease to exist in the Afterlife.

▲ *It is possible that the Meidum Pyramid was never finished, explaining its present appearance. This may be why the stelae are uninscribed.*

Sneferu began work on the Meidum Pyramid early in his reign. It was originally conceived as a seven-stepped tower, but a further step was added later. This seems to have been completed by Sneferu's 14th year but then, probably during the latter part of his reign, Sneferu had the steps filled in to form a true pyramid.

The Meidum Pyramid complex set the pattern for the rest of the Old Kingdom (c.2686–c.2181 BC). It consisted of the main pyramid and at least one subsidiary pyramid within an enclosure, together with a mortuary temple, to ensure the king's immortality. This was connected by a causeway to the valley, or lower, temple, situated at the edge of the flood plain. The valley temple was linked to the River Nile by a canal, so that the funeral procession of the king could land here and the body be taken up the covered causeway for burial within the pyramid in relative privacy. The Meidum Pyramid is also remarkable for the first use of corbelling to roof the burial chamber.

The pyramids of Dahshur

For some unknown reason, in mid-reign Sneferu temporarily abandoned Meidum and began to build two further pyramids, the Bent and the Red Pyramids, further north, at the new necropolis of Dahshur.

▲ *The Bent Pyramid is so-called because of the change of angle about halfway up. Much of the high-quality Tura limestone casing remains.*

The Bent Pyramid seems to have been something of an experiment as the angles had not yet been satisfactorily worked out. There is evidence to suggest that the Bent Pyramid began as a small pyramid with a slope of 60 degrees, but that subsidence threatened to cause it to collapse. Thereupon further layers were added round the inner core so that the angle was more gentle. The problems continued, however, and it was eventually decided to proceed at an even less severe angle. Consequently the profile of the pyramid has a distinct bend towards the top.

The Bent Pyramid is noteworthy for the large amount of outer casing of fine Tura limestone that remains in situ. Further, both the burial chamber and the antechamber of the Bent Pyramid are roofed in magnificent corbelling. The mortuary chapel, on the other hand, is a very simple affair. Inside were an offering table and two stelae, both inscribed with the name of Sneferu. However, it was in the valley temple that Sneferu's funerary cult was carried out by later kings.

The Red Pyramid is perfectly constructed. There is no sign of experimentation whatsoever, and it is generally recognized as the first true pyramid. It was built of local limestone containing iron oxide, which gives it the reddish colour from which it gets its name. The outer casing of white Tura limestone has almost entirely disappeared, but the pyramid is otherwise intact. Noteworthy features are the low angle of inclination (43 degrees) and the horizontal line of the core blocks. In earlier pyramids, the blocks were laid at an angle in the belief that this method gave greater stability to the building. As in the Bent Pyramid, the antechamber and burial chamber are roofed with very fine corbelled blocks.

Excavations by Dr Rainer Stadelmann of the German Archaeological Institute have revealed a large number of graffiti scribbled on pieces of limestone casing by the builders of the Red Pyramid. The most interesting thing about these inscriptions is that they are dated. One, from a corner of the pyramid, implies that Sneferu began to build it in the 30th year of his reign. Another, which had originally been placed about 30 courses of stone higher up, was dated four years later. From these marks, it has been possible to deduce the length of time it took to build a pyramid, in this case about twenty years.

The mortuary temple was on the east side of the Red Pyramid and the ground plan has been reconstructed. Enough remained to make possible a reconstruction on paper of the temple's original appearance. It seems to have been much larger than the mortuary temples of the Meidum and Bent Pyramids, and was a worthy forerunner of the even larger Great Pyramid of Khufu at Giza. Lying in the mortuary temple is the reconstructed pyramidion, or solid limestone capstone, that once topped the pyramid. ◆

▼ *The Red Pyramid is second only in base size to the Great Pyramid of Khufu but is about 15m (49ft) lower because of its more gentle angle.*

How the Pyramids were Built

The first step in building a pyramid was to choose a suitable site. This had to be on the west side of the Nile because the west was where the sun set and where the dead were thought to enter the Underworld. The pyramid also needed to be situated on high ground, away from the danger of flooding at the time of the Nile's inundation. However, it could not be too far away from the bank because the river would be used to transport blocks of fine-quality limestone for the outer casing from Tura, on the other side of the Nile. The site chosen would be at a point on the desert plateau that would provide a firm rock base capable of supporting the great weight of the pyramid without any risk of cracking. It would also need to be within easy reach of the capital, so that the king could go to inspect the building work whenever he wished.

Site preparation

No plans for a pyramid exist, although there are extant plans of tombs in the Valley of the Kings. However, the building of a pyramid was not a haphazard affair and the measurements were accurate to a high degree. The workers had first to prepare a firm foundation by removing the loose sand from the rock. Then the rock base had to be made absolutely flat. The workers may have done this by building low mud walls all round the base and cutting channels in a grid pattern over the surface. Then they would have filled the channels with water and marked the level it reached. After the water had drained away, protruding rock would have been cut back to the level indicated, and any depressions filled with stones to make a perfectly level surface.

Each side of the pyramid had to face one of the cardinal points. The builders probably established true north first and worked out the other directions from that. They may have found true north by taking a sighting on a particular star in the northern sky. They would then observe the rising and setting of the star and mark its appearance and disappearance on an artificial horizon. By bisecting the angle thus made, they would obtain a north-south line. They had instruments for drawing right angles, so they would then have been able to find east and west. Next, they had to make the base perfectly square, with all four sides exactly the same length and the corners perfect right angles.

The workforce

Herodotus claimed that the Great Pyramid was built using slave labour, with 100,000 men at a time working in three-monthly shifts, for a period of 20 years. The idea of slave labour is now discounted, and it is thought more likely that the work did not carry on throughout the year, but only during the three months or so of the inundation period, when the workforce could not be employed on the land.

▼ *An artist's impression of the construction of the Giza pyramids, based on a drawing of Heinrich Leutemann. Groups of workers haul the massive blocks into position.*

Raising the blocks

Sometimes a rocky outcrop was used as the core of the pyramid to save work. The inner chambers and passages would have been constructed independently and the actual pyramid built around them. Some of the royal pyramid builders seem to have changed their minds about their preferred location of the burial chamber. The inner pyramid would then be built of limestone cut from the desert plateau. When the main structure was finished, the pyramid was completed by encasing it in blocks of finely cut and dressed limestone from Tura. Sometimes granite was used for the lower courses.

The precise method of raising the pyramid is not known. Pulleys were apparently not invented until Roman times. However, the Greek historian Herodotus tells of levers being used to raise the blocks from one level to the next. It has also been suggested that workers operating in teams used ramps to haul the blocks into position. As the pyramid grew in size so the ramp would have been raised to enable the workers to reach the next level. The main problem with this is that the ramp would eventually have been as huge as the pyramid itself and would have reached an immense distance into the desert. No trace of such a structure has definitely been identified at any of the various pyramid sites. Another idea is that the ramp wound around the pyramid and was dismantled when the pyramid was completed. Construction methods are still hotly debated. ◆

▲ *Scene from a stela of Ahmose I commemorating the reopening of the quarries at Maasara in his 22nd year, showing oxen hauling a stone block.*

▼ *The production of mudbricks, as depicted in the tomb of Rekhmire at Thebes. Mudbrick remains an important building material in Egypt today.*

The Pyramid Texts

The Pyramid Texts are a collection of spells that were meant to ensure the resurrection of the king and his union with the gods in the sky. The texts appear for the first time covering the walls of the burial chamber and adjoining rooms in the pyramid of the last king of the Fifth Dynasty, Unas (c.2375–c.2345 BC), which was erected near the Step Pyramid of Djoser at Saqqara. Similar collections are found in the burial suites of the Sixth Dynasty kings Teti (c.2345–c.2323 BC), Pepi I (c.2321–c.2287 BC), Merenre (c.2287–c.2278 BC) and Pepi II (c.2278–c.2184 BC).

These texts are our best source of information about religious belief in the Old Kingdom. Not only do they shed light on beliefs concerning the king's Afterlife, but they also make many references to ancient Egyptian mythology. One text from the passageway leading to Unas' burial chamber reads:

This Unas comes to you, O Nut,
This Unas comes to you, O Nut,
He has consigned his father to
the earth,
He has left Horus behind him.
Grown are his falcon wings,
Plumes of the holy hawk;
His ba has brought him
His magic has equipped him.

Nut, the sky goddess, welcomes Unas to the Afterlife with the words:

Make your seat in heaven,
Among the stars in heaven.

Another spell, this time from the ante-chamber, calls on the gods for assistance. Shu, the god of air, is asked to lift the king up, while Nut bends down to take his hand. The king is also thought to climb up to the sky on a ladder:

Hail, daughter of Anubis, above the
hatches of heaven,
Comrade of Thoth, above the
ladder's rails,
Open Unas' path, let Unas pass!

Sometimes the king calls on a celestial ferryman, in fact the ferryman of the gods, to take him across the water that was thought to separate earth and sky:

▲ *The first Pyramid Texts were found in the burial chamber of Unas. In these, he climbs a ladder to be united with his father Re-Atum.*

Awake in peace...
Sky's ferryman, in peace,
Nut's ferryman, in peace,
Ferryman of gods, in peace!
Unas has come to you
That you may ferry him in this boat
in which you ferry the gods.

Should the ferryman refuse, a solution to the problem could be found in the form of Thoth, the god of wisdom, who is often represented as an ibis:

If you fail to ferry Unas,
He will leap and sit on the wing
of Thoth,
Then he will ferry Unas to that side!

Most of all, the king desires to spend eternity united with his father, Re, the sun god:

Re-Atum, your son comes to you,
Unas comes to you,
Raise him to you, hold him in
your arms,
He is your son, of your body,
forever!

Although the texts are found in pyramids only towards the end of the Old Kingdom, the material embodied in them may be much older. An indication of this can be seen in a text of King Teti, which seems to make reference to a time when burials were much simpler:

Oho! Oho! Rise up, O Teti!
Take your head,
Collect your bones,
Gather your limbs,
Shake the earth from your flesh!

The same text implies that commoners are excluded from heaven, which is the prerogative of kings:

Stand at the gates which bar
the common people!
The gatekeeper comes out to you,
He grasps your hand, takes you into
heaven, to your father Geb.
He rejoices at your coming,
Gives you his hands,
Kisses you, caresses you,
Sets you before the spirits, the
imperishable stars.

Teti is also seen sailing with the sun god, a theme that first occurs in the Pyramid of Unas:

Teti will take his pure seat in the
bow of Re's barque:
The sailors who row Re, they shall
row Teti!
The sailors who convey Re about
lightland,
They shall convey Teti about
lightland!

In the burial chamber of Pepi I there are several references to the myth of Osiris, with whom Pepi is united in the Afterlife. Pepi is said to be:

...the Great One...fallen on his side,
He who...in Nedyt was cast down.

This is an allusion to the murder of Osiris by his jealous brother, Seth. Pepi, like Osiris, hopes to be raised from the dead and to become Orion.

▲ *Texts from the tomb of Teti describe how he takes his seat in the sun god's boat and sails with him across the sky. Another text tells how his father Geb welcomes him into heaven.*

Your hand is grasped by Re,
Your head is raised (by all
the gods)
Lo, he has come as Orion,
Lo, Osiris has come as Orion...

You shall live!
You shall rise with Orion in the
eastern sky,
You shall set with Orion in the
western sky. ◆

► *The ceilings of royal burial chambers were decorated with stars as the king, on death, hoped to take his place in heaven among the 'imperishable stars'.*

The Abusir Necropolis

Several of the kings of the Fifth Dynasty (c.2494–c.2345 BC) built their pyramids at Abusir, a name that is ultimately derived from Per Wsir, which means 'Place of Osiris'. The pyramids here are not as large as those of the Fourth Dynasty kings, and it has been suggested that this smaller size reflects a corresponding decline in royal power. That this might not be so is perhaps borne out by the fact that the quality of the materials used and the standard of much of the workmanship remains high. When in 1902–8 the German Egyptologist Ludwig Borschardt excavated the pyramid complex of Sahure (c.2487–c.2475 BC), the second king of the Fifth Dynasty, he found a great number of painted, delicately carved reliefs.

▲ *Remains of the pyramid of the 5th Dynasty king Sahure, at Abusir, where the pyramids are much smaller than those at Giza.*

Pyramid complex of Sahure

Although Sahure's complex is the best preserved of those at Abusir, the pyramid itself is in a dilapidated condition. Once the outer casing had been removed, the inner core deteriorated into a heap of rubble. The core had been formed of five or six steps built with rough blocks of local limestone, held together with mud mortar. Borschardt found evidence for a wide 'construction gap' on the northern side of the pyramid, which gave the builders room to work on the inner chambers while the construction of the pyramid itself went on around them. Granite had been used to line parts of the passageway leading to the burial chamber and for the portcullis that blocked the first section. The burial chamber itself was built entirely of Tura limestone and was roofed with three layers of huge limestone blocks placed at an angle.

Sahure's valley temple was on the edge of the Abusir Lake, from where a ramp led to a portico. The roof of this building was decorated with gold stars on a blue ground and supported by eight granite columns with palmiform capitals. Granite had also been used for the lower part of the walls and black basalt for the floor. The upper walls were of limestone carved with reliefs showing the king as a sphinx trampling his enemies.

The causeway was also decorated in relief and included scenes showing the gods leading prisoners representing Egypt's enemies – Asiatics and Libyans. These set a trend that was followed until the end of the Pharaonic Period.

The mortuary temple is the most interesting part of Sahure's complex, and became a model for those of later kings. It consists of five parts: entrance hall, open court, five niches for statues, storerooms and a sanctuary. The open court was paved with basalt and surrounded by a cloister decorated with scenes of the king receiving booty and smiting his enemies. Granite columns and palm-frond capitals again supported the starry roof. Running around the outside of the court was a wide corridor decorated with an entirely different type of relief. On the northern side the king was shown fishing and fowling in the

◀ *Travertine/calcite altar from Niuserre's sun temple at Abu Gurab. The shape has been interpreted as a huge hieroglyph meaning 'May Re be satisfied'.*

▶ *Following earlier tradition, the great officials of the 5th Dynasty were buried near their royal masters. The tomb of Ptahshepses, shown here, is one of the most splendid.*

marshes, and on the southern side he was depicted hunting with his courtiers and his successor, Neferirkare (c.2475–c.2455 BC). These reliefs are today in the Berlin Museum.

Neferirkare planned a pyramid complex at Abusir. His pyramid was to have been bigger than that of his predecessor, but it was never finished. Although the mortuary temple seems to have been hurriedly completed in mudbrick, only the foundations of the causeway and valley temple had been finished. When his son, Niuserre (c.2445–c.2421 BC), became king, he removed these elements from his father's complex and incorporated them into his own.

Tomb of Ptahshepses

Close to the pyramid of Sahure is the magnificent tomb of his vizier, Ptahshepses. The complex includes a portico, with the earliest-known example of columns with lotus-bud capitals, an offering room with statue niches, a huge courtyard surrounded with square pillars and a burial chamber with the fine granite sarcophagus still in situ.

◀ *Calcite bowls from the court of Niuserre's sun temple, used in the purification of offerings.*

Sun temples

Near to their pyramids, the kings of the Fifth Dynasty built sun temples to honour Re, the Heliopolitan sun god, at Abu Gurab. The Abusir Papyri and other documents mention six, although only two have been found so far, those of Userkaf (c.2494–c.2487 BC) and Niuserre. Userkaf's was the first royal building in this part of the necropolis, his pyramid being at Saqqara, close to the Step Pyramid of King Djoser. The remains, such as they are, were excavated between 1954–7 by a team from the Swiss Institute in Cairo. Niuserre, who also built his own sun temple at the nearby site of Abu Gurab, added extensively to Userkaf's temple.

Niuserre's sun temple is in a much better state of preservation. Although not much remains on the site today, the German expedition of 1898–1902 found enough clues to make possible a reconstruction on paper. It seems that the sun temple was part of a larger complex with the same component parts as a pyramid complex, including a valley temple and connecting causeway. Like the pyramid complex, it may have had a funerary function. The sun god was one of the chief gods of the Afterlife, and was also the main creator god. If the sun temple is considered to be part of the pyramid complex, there is no need to see the monuments of the kings of the Fifth Dynasty as being in any way inferior to those of the Fourth. ◆

The Abusir Papyri

Details of the cult of the dead king can be found in an archive called the Abusir Papyri. They date from the reign of King Djedkare (c.2414–c.2375 BC) and are mostly concerned with the administration of the mortuary cult of King Neferirkare (c.2475–c.2455 BC). They provide an insight into the duties of the priests involved in the daily ritual, as well as important festivals. They laid down which offerings were to be brought on given dates, supplied rotas for guard duty, and indicated the organization of the workforce. There are also inventories of temple furniture and ritual vessels, and sets of accounts of the temple's income and expenditure.

Mudbrick Pyramids

Some of the kings of the Middle Kingdom (c.2055–c.1650 BC) built mudbrick pyramids in the Faiyum Oasis. They do not exactly follow the Old Kingdom model, and display a number of unusual features.

The pyramid of Senusret II

Senusret II (c.1880–c.1874 BC) built his pyramid at el-Lahun, an important agricultural centre near the Middle Kingdom capital, close to where the Bahr Yusef leaves the Nile and enters the Faiyum. The pyramid was built around a core of limestone, over which a limestone framework was erected and filled with mudbrick. The upper part of the pyramid was entirely of mudbrick. The exterior was then cased in limestone, with the blocks of the bottom course set into a trench cut into the rock.

Senusret departed from usual practice by placing the entrance on the southern side of his pyramid instead of on the northern side. This may have been intended to outwit potential robbers but, if so, it failed. All that was left of Senusret's burial was a gold *uraeus*, the royal headdress in the protective form of a rearing cobra, and a few leg bones, presumably of the king.

Very little remains of the mortuary and valley temples or the causeway. Surrounding the pyramid were two walls, one of stone and one of mudbrick. Beyond the outer wall, trees had been planted in pits sunk into the rock and filled with earth. Inside the enclosure wall on the northern side of the pyramid was a row of eight mastaba tombs, at the eastern end of which was a small pyramid. It is not clear whether this was a subsidiary tomb connected with the king's own burial or whether it was intended for a queen. Between the enclosure walls on the southern side of the pyramid were four shaft tombs. One

▲ *A statue of Amenemhet III from his pyramid complex at Hawara. His burial chamber was cut from a single block of quartzite.*

▼ *The first of the mudbrick pyramids belonged to Senusret II who built his final resting place at el-Lahun in the Faiyum.*

► *Amenemhet III planned to be buried at Dahshur but seems to have abandoned the idea when the pyramid began to show signs of structural stress. He built a second pyramid at Hawara.*

of these was the burial place of Princess Sithathoriunet, and contained a collection of jewellery, which was part of her funerary equipment.

The Labyrinth

Amenemhat III (c.1855–c.1808 BC), famous for his land reclamation schemes, sited one of his pyramids at Hawara in the Faiyum. Like that of Senusret II, it was built of mudbrick and cased in limestone. It was almost 60m (197ft) tall and was the last large pyramid to be built in Egypt. On the southern side of the pyramid was a vast structure known to Herodotus and other classical authors as the Labyrinth. It covered an area of 6 hectares (15 acres) and had 12 covered courts, six in a row facing north and six facing south, with the gates of the one range exactly fronting the gates of the other, with a continuous wall around the outside of the whole. Inside, the building was of two storeys and contained 3,000 rooms, of which half were underground with the other half directly above them.

Herodotus wrote that he was not allowed to see the underground rooms because they contained the tombs of the kings who built the Labyrinth and also the tombs of crocodiles, which were worshipped in the Faiyum. However, he was allowed to see the rest and could hardly believe his eyes as he wandered through this maze of rooms, galleries and courtyards. None of this remains today, and even when Flinders Petrie excavated the site in 1888–9 he could recognize very few details of this most unusual of mortuary temples. ◆

▼ *Carved limestone crocodiles representing the god Sobek once adorned the 'Labyrinth', in fact the mortuary temple of the Hawara pyramid.*

The workers' town of Kahun

Not far from Senusret's valley temple was the town of Kahun, where the workers on the pyramid lived. This site was exhaustively excavated by Flinders Petrie, who discovered a vast number of domestic objects in the form of pottery, loom weights, mirrors, combs, stone and faience vases for perfumed oils and ointments, pots of kohl used as eye-liner, rush baskets of various shapes and sizes, rush sandals, carpenters' tools, fish hooks, agricultural implements and toys. There was even a rat trap. Different types of houses and their interior decoration also came to light. A large number of documents were found, including wills and some extremely interesting gynaecological and veterinary papyri. From these, it has been possible to build up a full picture of life in this town, which was the first of the pyramid workers' towns to be discovered and excavated.

Royal Jewellery of the Twelfth Dynasty

Several of the daughters of the kings of the Middle Kingdom (c.2055–c.1650 BC) were buried in shaft graves near to their father's pyramid. Some of the shafts contained sumptuous collections of diadems, bracelets, pectorals and collars. Middle Kingdom jewellery is considered to be some of the most exquisite ever made, either in ancient Egypt or elsewhere. Both in terms of inspiration and craftsmanship it is unparalleled.

▲ *The stunning gold diadem of Sithathoriunet was found in her tomb in the funerary complex of Senusret II.*

Jewellery of Princess Sithathoriunet

When Flinders Petrie and Guy Brunton explored the shaft tomb of Princess Sithathoriunet in 1914, they found little apart from her red granite sarcophagus and a set of canopic jars, the vessels which accompanied each burial to house the internal organs. Then they discovered a niche in the wall that had been plastered over. Inside were five boxes containing Sithathoriunet's jewellery, a mirror, razors and pots for cosmetics.

▶ *The silver mirror of Sithathoriunet is a jewellery masterpiece. It is supported by a head of Hathor mounted on an obisidian handle.*

The prize piece in this collection is a diadem in the form of a broad band of gold decorated with the *uraeus* (the royal cobra) and rosettes. It also has two gold plumes and three sets of detachable gold streamers. It would have been worn on top of a wig made up of dozens of long braids held in little gold clasps. The cobra's head is made of lapis lazuli and the eyes of garnets set in gold rims. The rosettes are inlaid with lapis, carnelian and green faience in imitation of feldspar and turquoise. The diadem is now on display in the Cairo Museum.

There are also two pectorals (chest ornaments) in the collection. One has the name of the princess's father, Senusret II (c.1880–c.1874 BC), worked into the design and the other the name of her nephew, Amenemhat III (c.1855–c.1808 BC), during whose reign she died.

The toilet articles are as beautiful as the jewellery. Among them are some elegant black vases for perfumed oils and ointments, but the masterpiece is the mirror. This consists of a thick silver disc surmounting a handle of obsidian in the form of an open papyrus plant. Below the umbel, which is covered in electrum (an alloy of silver and gold) is the head of Hathor, goddess of sexual love, worked in gold with eyes of lapis lazuli. The head has Hathor's charac-teristic cow's ears, symbolizing her nurturing role: she was worshipped as a universal mother goddess, but was particularly associated with kings. The mirror is double-faced, both sides being identical. Around the neck are four rings inlaid with carnelian, stone and faience, as is the pointed corolla of the base. The triangular shape of the papyrus stem is outlined in granulation work. This mirror would have ensured that the princess, whose name included that of Hathor, putting her under the protection of the goddess, enjoyed her gifts of eternal youth and beauty in the Afterlife.

Jewellery of Princess Neferuptah

A further collection of jewellery and toilet articles was discovered in 1956 at Hawara in the tomb of Princess Neferuptah, possibly a daughter of Amenemhat III. One of the most impressive pieces is a broad collar composed of six bands of tubular beads made of feldspar and carnelian, with little gold beads between them. Below this is a border of golden droplets inlaid with feldspar heads in repoussé work. The collar is balanced by a counterpoise consisting of a miniature falcon head above a series of narrow bands of beads, which match the main part of the collar. Matching pairs of bracelets and anklets complete the set.

▲ A beautiful pectoral found in Princess Meret's tomb at Dahshur shows her father Senusret III as a griffin trampling his foes.

Jewellery of Princess Meret

Some of the Middle Kingdom kings built mudbrick tombs at Dahshur. Princess Meret, daughter of Senusret III (c.1874–c.1855 BC), was buried close to his pyramid there. Two finely wrought pectorals were among the funerary equipment found in her tomb. They are made in the form of shrines. Inside at the top, Nekhbet the vulture goddess, protector of kings, hovers with outspread wings above the image of the king trampling his enemies. One pectoral includes the name of her father and the other that of Amenemhat III, her brother.

▲ Princess Neferuptah's collection included matching sets of bracelets and anklets. They were made of gold, carnelian and feldspar.

◀ The intact tomb of Princess Neferuptah, found under a ruined mudbrick pyramid at Hawara, revealed another rich collection of jewellery. The princess was found wearing this collar.

Jewellery of Princess Sathathor

Princess Sathathor was also buried at Dahshur, close to the pyramid of Senusret III whose sister, and possibly wife, she was. Her jewellery includes a pectoral in the form of a shrine, with the name of her father, Senusret II, inscribed inside it. This is protected on each side by two striped falcons wearing the Double Crown of Upper and Lower Egypt.

Another delightful piece is a belt of gold cowrie shells and tiny beads. The clasp is formed of two half cowrie shells, which slide together along grooves to make a whole as they fasten the belt. ◆

The Pyramids of the Kushite Kings

From the beginning of the New Kingdom (c.1550–c.1069 BC), kings abandoned the practice of burial within a pyramid and opted instead for a tomb in the Valley of the Kings in Western Thebes. The tradition of pyramid burial was, however, revived by the Kushite kings of the Twenty-fifth Dynasty, whose capital was at Napata in Upper Nubia. Egyptian control of Nubia had been lost after the end of the New Kingdom, and Nubia had developed as a separate kingdom. During the same period, several independent rulers, each powerful in his own district, had governed Egypt. The Kushite king, Piy (c.747–c.716 BC), marched north around 728 BC and brought the whole of Egypt under his control. His success was recorded on a great stela originally set up in the temple at Gebel Barkal and now in the Cairo Museum.

▲ *From the time of Taharqo, the Kushite kings were buried at Nuri in large elaborate tombs, which reflected Egyptian royal burial places.*

Burials at el-Kurru

The Kushite rulers regarded themselves as the true successors of the great Egyptian kings and emulated their activities in many ways, including that of building pyramids. Piy, his father, and several of his successors were buried in pyramids at el-Kurru. The style of these was rather different from the traditional structures, however. They were much more modest in size and had steeply sloping walls. Like the early Egyptian tombs, they seem to have evolved from mastabas. However, they appear to have been modelled on small 'private' pyramids, known from the craftsmen's village at Deir el-Medina, rather than on the vast royal structures from the height of the Pyramid Age. Apart from the kings' tombs, 14 queens were also buried in pyramids at el-Kurru.

Piy and his immediate successors, Shabaqo (c.716–c.702 BC) and Shabitqo (c.702–690 BC) were buried on beds within the tomb chamber. But from the time of Taharqo (690–664 BC), the kings adopted the Egyptian practice of using coffins and sarcophagi. Mummification was practised and the grave goods included traditional *shabti* figures, small statuettes of servants who would do whatever work was necessary in the

◀ *Pyramids of the kings and queens of Meroe in the North Cemetery. They were built on a ridge in imitation of Egyptian pyramids.*

▲ *One of Taharqo's* shabtis. *Kushite kings were buried in Egyptian-style coffins and sarcophagi. Bodies were mummified and provided with* shabtis.

► Shabtis *of Taharqo from his pyramid at Nuri. They were exceptionally large and made of serpentine, calcite and black granite. The features of the king indicate that he was Nubian, and the texts reflect the interest of the Kushite kings in earlier periods.*

Afterlife. One distinguishing feature was the continuation of the Kushite practice of horse burials. The royal chariot horses were apparently sacrificed, decapitated and buried standing in pits in a special cemetery near the pyramids of el-Kurru.

Nuri

From the time of Taharqo, members of the Kushite royal family were buried at Nuri. Here the pyramids were much larger than those at el-Kurru and the chapels were decorated with reliefs. A stela built into the pyramid showed the king, in Egyptian fashion, before the gods. Taharqo's pyramid was the largest of all and was built in two stages, the inner pyramid having been encased with limestone. The subterranean rooms were also more elaborate than in any other of the Nuri tombs. The entrance was on the eastern side and led eventually to a doorway with a moulded frame and cavetto (concave) cornice. From there a tunnel led to an antechamber with a barrel-vaulted ceiling. In the burial chamber, there were six great pillars cut from the rock. These divided the room into three, each part having a barrel-vaulted ceiling. A shallow pit had been cut into the floor to take the sarcophagus, and four niches were incorporated into the walls. Surrounding the burial chamber was a 'moat' reached by a flight of steps.

The last royal burial at Nuri took place at the end of the fourth century BC. From this time, the city of Meroe in the Sudan became important, and the kings built their pyramids there. Meroe remained the royal cemetery for much of the next 600 years, until the disintegration of the kingdom in around AD 350. ◆

◄ *Taharqo, the most famous of the Kushite kings, dressed as a pharaoh. He kneels before the falcon god, Hemen, who holds a cobra in his talons. The deity is a Nubian version of the Egyptian god Horus.*

The Pyramids of Giza

Giza was the most important royal necropolis of the Fourth Dynasty (c.2613–c.2494 BC), and it is where the most famous of all the pyramids were built. Although today the three main pyramids have been almost engulfed by the sprawling suburb of Giza, they still retain their awe-inspiring majesty. These colossal monuments are not the only sights worth seeing at Giza. They are surrounded by the smaller pyramids of queens and princesses, and the mastaba tombs of high officials, several of which can now be visited. Recent excavation has also revealed a cemetery where dwarfs were buried. In life, these men were highly respected and held important posts, and in death they were considered to be worthy of a tomb close to their royal master.

A further exciting find in recent years has been the discovery of the town inhabited by the workers who built the pyramids. It came to light during work on the construction of a sewage system for the villages near to the Great Pyramid. An extensive settlement site dating from the Old Kingdom (c.2686–c.2181 BC) was discovered near the valley temple of Khufu. Hundreds of objects relating to the daily life of the workers and their families have been found here, and the associated cemetery has also been discovered.

◀ *Visited by Herodotus in the mid-5th century BC, and one of the Wonders of the Ancient World, the Giza pyramids are now closed in rotation as a means of conservation.*

The Great Pyramids

The most famous of all the landmarks of present-day Egypt, and one of the Wonders of the Ancient World, the Giza pyramids were the burial places of the Fourth Dynasty kings, Khufu, Khafre and Menkaure. Each pyramid was part of a larger complex consisting of a mortuary temple, a causeway, a valley temple and subsidiary pyramids, while the pyramid of Khufu is surrounded by five boat pits.The pyramids were robbed in antiquity, but the contents of the concealed tomb of Queen Hetepheres, the mother of Khufu, give some idea of the richness of the burials of the kings. The pyramid complexes are surrounded by 'streets' of mastaba tombs belonging to the officials who served as administrators or were in charge of the funerary cults of the deceased kings. Current excavation is beginning to shed light on the lives and deaths of the workers who toiled to build the memorials to the ancient kings. ◆

▲ *The Great Pyramid of Khufu was the largest of the three pyramids at Giza. It appears smaller than that of Khafre, which was built on higher ground.*

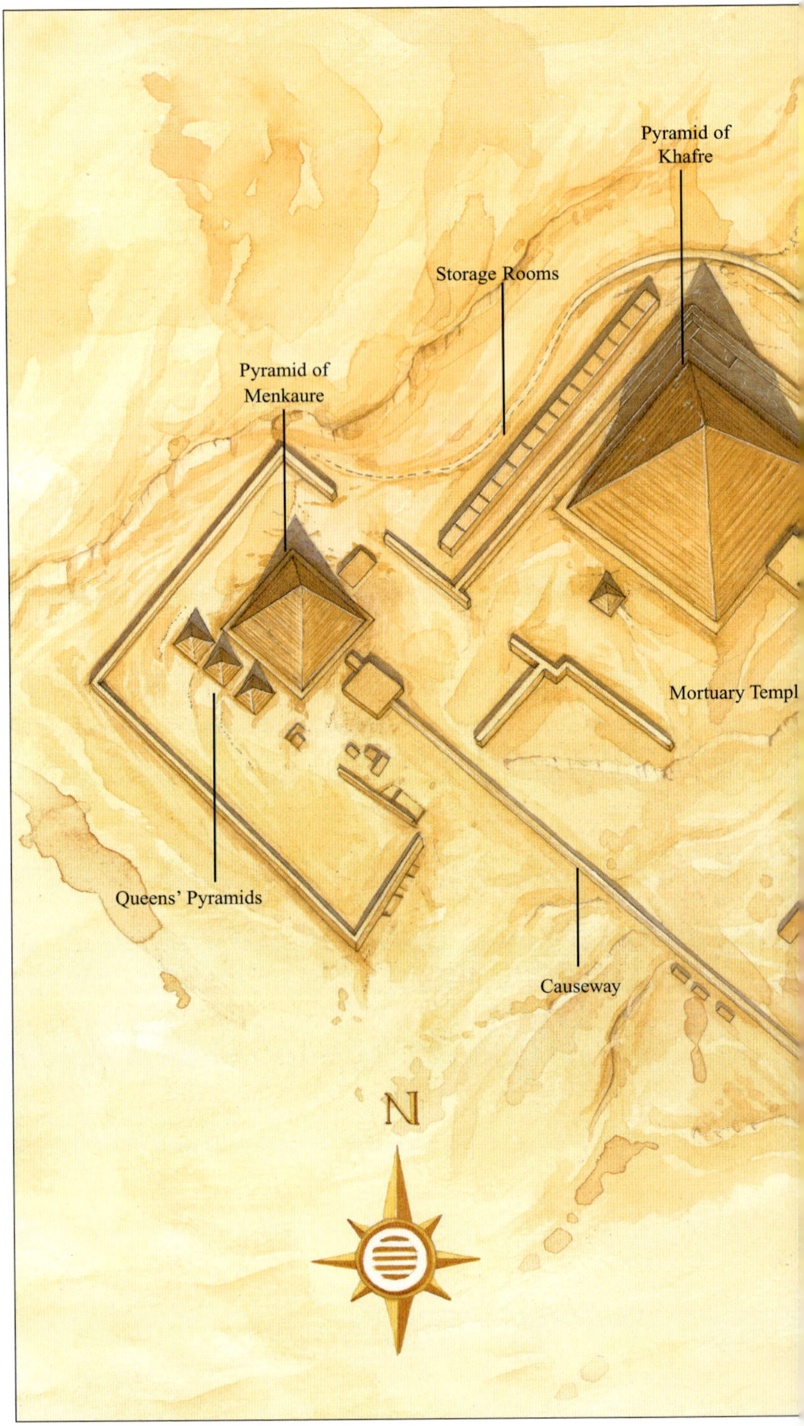

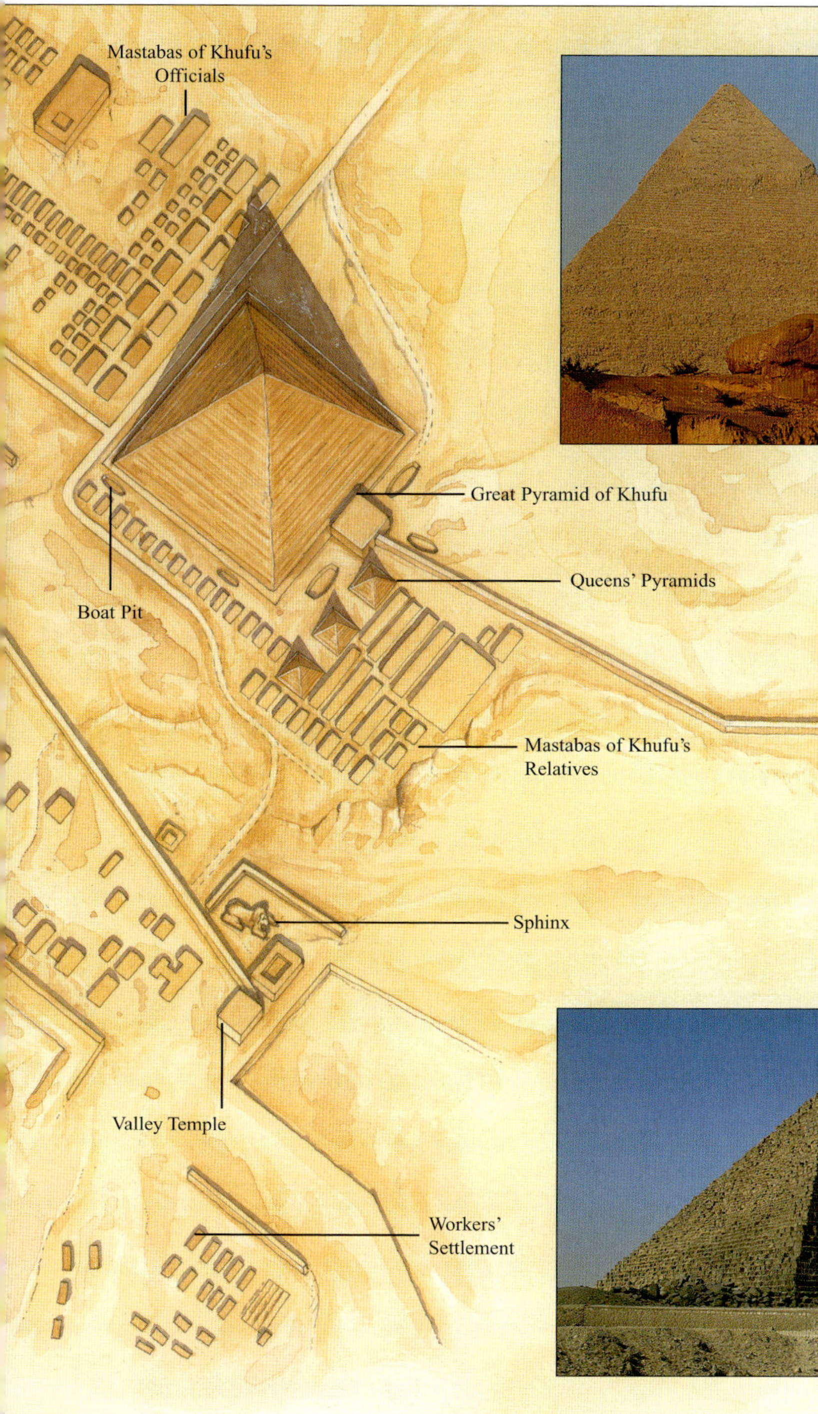

▲ *Khafre's pyramid retains its outer casing at the top. In the foreground is the Sphinx, thought to be a portrait of this 4th-Dynasty king.*

▼ *Menkaure's is the smallest of the three main pyramids at Giza. The great gash in the north face was made by Caliph Othman in* AD *1196.*

The Great Pyramid of Khufu

The Great Pyramid of the Fourth Dynasty king Khufu (c.2589–c.2566 BC) is the largest of all the pyramids. It was originally 140m (460ft) tall but is now 3m (10ft) less. At the base, the sides each measured 140m (460ft), but are now only 127m (417ft) because the pyramid has been stripped of its limestone casing. Some of this was removed in antiquity, but much was also taken in the ninth century AD when the caliphs built the city of Cairo. Amelia Edwards thought this gave the pyramid an unfinished look, as if the workmen 'were coming back tomorrow morning'. It is estimated that about 2,300,000 blocks, each weighing an average of 2.3 tons (although some weigh much more) went into the building of the pyramid.

The original entrance is on the north face and is 15m (49ft) above ground level, surmounted by a double vault. The lower entrance, used by tourists today, was made in the ninth century AD when an entry was forced on the orders of Caliph Mamun.

▲ *The Great Pyramid at Giza, largest of all the pyramids, was stripped of its casing of white limestone in antiquity and during the 9th century.*

Inside the Great Pyramid

There are at least three chambers inside the pyramid. From the entrance, a corridor leads downwards for 18m (60ft) and then divides. One branch leads on down to an underground chamber, which was left unfinished. The other climbs up towards the Grand Gallery, where it again divides. A horizontal tunnel leads to a second chamber, misleadingly known as the Queen's Chamber, while another tunnel winds precipitously to connect with the descending corridor.

The Grand Gallery is corbelled in the manner of Sneferu's pyramids and is a wonderful example of craftsmanship and precision. An antechamber once blocked by three granite slabs leads from it into the King's Chamber, the walls of which are lined with granite. The sarcophagus is plain and uninscribed. It has been suggested that the two chambers lower down the pyramid were intended as burial chambers, but first one and then the other was found to be too small to house the large granite sarcophagus, so it became necessary to alter the plans. This would have been possible, as the internal chambers were constructed while the main work of building the pyramid went on around them. The King's Chamber is roofed with nine granite slabs weighing about 400 tons. Above are five weight-relieving chambers, one above the other, designed to carry the enormous weight of the rest of the pyramid.

Two small shafts, once thought to be for ventilation, lead north and south from the burial chamber to the outside. Recent research by the German Archaeological Institute has shown that they are nothing to do with the circulation of air, but had a purely ritual use. They were to provide a direct route to heaven for the soul of the king. According to the same

▲ *The Grand Gallery leads from the ascending corridor to the burial chamber of Khufu. The walls are 8.5m (28ft) high and 47m (154ft) long and are corbelled, each layer of limestone blocks projecting about 6cm (2½in) beyond the one on which it rests.*

◀ *The only surviving image of Khufu, builder of the Great Pyramid, this tiny limestone statuette is in the Egyptian Museum, Cairo. Although the figure is tiny, just 7.5cm (3in) tall, the face is full of character.*

study, the three internal chambers also had a ritual purpose and the team would dispute the suggestion that they represent changes in plan.

The Queen's Chamber also has a similar pair of shafts, which were partly explored when the pyramid was closed for conservation in 1992. A tiny robot penetrated 65m (213ft) into the pyramid before it was stopped by a 'door' with two copper handles. It is hoped that exploration will continue in the near future. A new gilded limestone capstone was made to celebrate the turning of the millennium.

The pyramid complex

Although little remains today, the pyramid once possessed a valley temple, causeway and mortuary temple. The mortuary temple was much bigger than those of the Meidum and Dahshur pyramids. It had a colonnade surrounding a large court paved with basalt. The limestone walls had carved reliefs. According to Herodotus, the causeway was also decorated with reliefs, and some pieces have now come to light to support his statement. The valley temple has almost completely disappeared, although some basalt paving blocks found in 1990 by Dr Zahi Hawass, Director-General of the Giza Pyramids and Saqqara, may once have belonged to it.

On the south side of the pyramid, there were three small pyramids belonging to the queens Henutsen, Meritetis and Hetepheres, Khufu's mother. Khufu's own (tiny) secondary pyramid was found in 1991 by Zahi Hawass. The complex is completed by five boat pits, which either represented or contained boats to enable the deceased king, in his identification with the sun god, to make his celestial voyages. To the east of the complex lie the mastabas of his relatives, while those of his officials are to the west. ◆

Images of Khufu

If there were ever any statues of Khufu in the temple complex they have vanished without trace. The only surviving image of this king is a tiny statuette found by Flinders Petrie at Abydos and now in the Cairo Museum. In fact Khufu's only firm link with the pyramid is his cartouche in the topmost of the relieving chambers above the burial chamber.

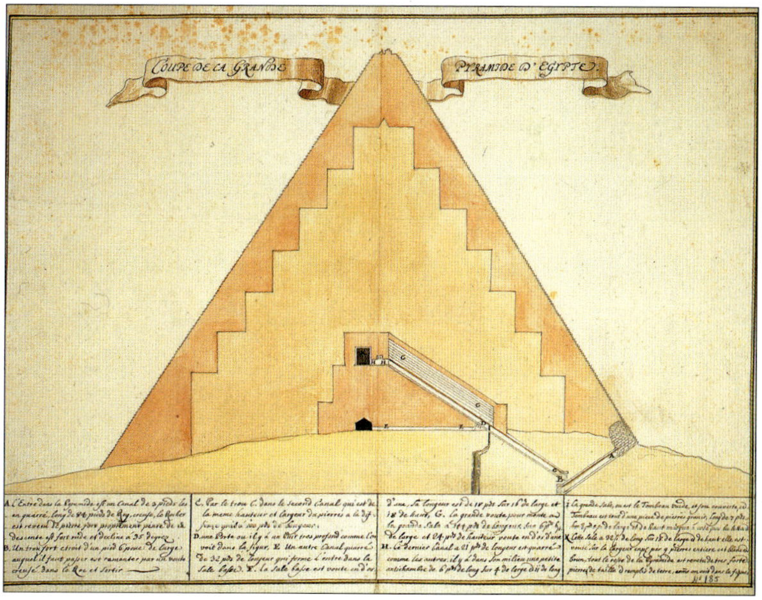

▶ *This plan of the interior of the Great Pyramid by Benoit de Maillet was published in 1735 before the descending corridor had been fully explored.*

The Pyramid of Khafre

The pyramid complex of Khafre is the most complete of all the Giza pyramids. Because it was built on slightly higher ground and rises at a sharper angle, the pyramid itself appears to be larger than Khufu's, although it is actually second in size. Near the top it still retains some of its original casing stones. The other component parts of the complex, especially the valley temple, are also much more in evidence here.

There are two entrances to the pyramid on the north side, of which the lower one is used by tourists today. This leads to a passage that first descends and then rises, before running horizontally to the burial chamber, which is just below ground level. The Italian adventurer Giovanni Belzoni entered the burial chamber on 2 March 1818, as his inscription proclaims. Inside was an empty plain red granite sarcophagus, with no inscriptions.

In its heyday, the pyramid was served by a magnificent mortuary temple, 110m (360ft) long, with two pylons, a transverse vestibule and a rectangular hall, both embellished with columns. Then came a large court surrounded by a columned portico where there would have been statues of the king. Behind this were five small chapels, storehouses and an inner sanctuary. Sadly, the temple has been used as a quarry over the centuries, and little of its ancient splendour can be seen today.

▲ *The pyramid of Khafre, which still retains part of its original high-quality Tura limestone casing. Khafre's funerary complex is the best preserved of the three at Giza.*

Khafre's valley temple

Although it has lost its roof, much remains of the causeway along which the king's body would have been brought from the valley temple. Khafre's magnificent valley temple is the best preserved of any that have come to light so far. It was discovered by Auguste Mariette in 1858, and is sometimes known as the Granite Temple because of

◀ *Khafre spared no expense on the construction of his valley temple. It is lined with huge blocks of polished Aswan granite and the floors are paved with alabaster from Hatnub.*

the huge blocks of polished red Aswan granite from which it was constructed. These enormous blocks were cut with astounding precision. Some have even been cut so that they turn corners. The floors are of polished alabaster.

In the T-shaped hall are emplacements for 23 statues of Khafre. These would have been illuminated by light entering through slits high up on the walls. Only the bases of most of these statues remain, but Mariette found one splendid complete version lying in a well in the vestibule. It is a little larger than life-size and is made of polished diorite from the quarries at Toshka in Nubia. Khafre is seated on the throne of the Two Lands. Behind him sits Horus, in the form of a falcon, with his wings folded protectively around the king's head.

The king's body would have been transported from the capital, Memphis, by boat. A quay has been discovered in front of the Sphinx temple, and it may have continued in front of the valley temple.

The site of the secondary pyramid has now been located to the east of the pyramid. Only the foundations of the superstructure remain, but when the underground section was explored one of the two passages was found to end in a niche that once contained the remains of a wooden shrine. This may have held a statue of the king; in some tomb scenes such a shrine housing a statue of the deceased is shown being dragged towards the tomb.

The Sphinx

Egypt's earliest colossal royal statue, the Sphinx, is also an integral part of Khafre's complex. In spite of some of the more bizarre theories recently put forward, most Egyptologists regard the Sphinx as a portrait statue of the king carved from an outcrop of rock that remained after the quarrying of limestone for the interior of the Great Pyramid. Rather than leaving it as something of a blot on the landscape, it was transformed into this symbol of royal power, a lion's body with the head of the king.

◄ *Twenty-three diorite statues of Khafre once graced his valley temple, although only this one, now in the Cairo Museum, survives intact. The king is protected by Horus, the falcon god.*

▲ *The famous Sphinx is carved from an outcrop of rock on the Giza Plateau. The lion's body symbolizes royal power, while the head is a portrait of Khafre. The features strongly resemble the diorite statue of the king.*

During the New Kingdom (c.1550–c.1069 BC), the Sphinx was regarded as a manifestation of the sun god. Between its paws is the famous Dream Stela, an inscribed tablet that records the promise to the prince Tuthmosis, later Tuthmosis IV (c.1400–c.1390 BC), that the sun god would ensure that he became king of Egypt, though he was not the heir, should he clear away the sand that had drifted around the Sphinx and do any necessary repairs. Much conservation work has been done on the Sphinx in recent years, and the Sphinx Temple has also been restored. ◆

The Pyramid of Menkaure

The pyramid built by the Fourth Dynasty king Menkaure (c.2532– c.2503 BC) at Giza is only about half the size of those of his predecessors, Khufu and Khafre. The reason for this is unclear. Perhaps their building projects had put too great a strain on Egypt's resources. The builders may have been running out of suitable sites on the Giza Plateau. Or perhaps the kings now felt they needed to show more deference to the sun god, as witnessed by the small size of the royal burial places and the contemporary building of sun temples at Abusir during the Fifth Dynasty (c.2494–c.2345 BC).

Architectural innovations

Whatever the reason for its diminished size, the construction still used costly materials and the pyramid was designed with several original features. For instance, although it was partly cased in Tura limestone, 16 courses of red granite blocks were used for the lower section. Further, the entrance on the north side of the pyramid leads down to a horizontal chamber decorated with a false door motif. The lintel above the entrance to the horizontal corridor is carved in imitation of a rolled reed curtain. These are the first signs of decoration inside a pyramid since the time of Djoser (c.2667–c.2648 BC). Another new feature was the complexity of the burial suite. A horizontal passage with three portcullises leads to an antechamber. From here, a second passage leads down to the burial chamber, lined with granite. When the English explorer Howard Vyse entered the pyramid in 1837 he found a sarcophagus carved with the 'palace façade' motif. It was removed for shipment to England, but was unfortunately lost in a storm at sea. A wooden coffin found in an upper

▼ *Despite being only about half the size of those of his predecessors, the pyramid of Menkaure was nonetheless built of costly materials, with granite being used for the casing of the lower part.*

► *Remains of the mortuary temple are still visible on the east side of the pyramid. Offerings to the king would have been brought here daily.*

chamber and containing the remains of a mummy was dispatched on a different ship and is now in the British Museum in London. The style of the coffin, however, dates it to the Twenty-sixth Dynasty, or Saite Period (664–525 BC), while the bones are from the Christian era. Attached to the burial chamber was a room divided into six small niches and probably intended as a store for the king's funerary goods.

Mortuary and valley temples

The remains of an unfinished complex mortuary temple can be seen against the eastern face of the pyramid. It consists of a vestibule leading from the causeway, a large open court, a pillared portico leading to the sanctuary and various ancillary rooms, presumably for cultic equipment. Building was started in limestone, although the intention appears to have been to case it in granite. Menkaure seems to have died before it was completed because the temple has been hurriedly finished off in mudbrick. The unfinished nature of the complex made its excavation by George Reisner in 1899 especially interesting, because it provided information about how the work had been done. When Reisner stripped away the mudbrick he could see that the limestone walls were being prepared to take the granite facing when the construction was interrupted. On the core blocks he found levelling lines, measurements and even the names of workers marked in red paint.

Not much remains of the limestone causeway. Like the valley temple, this is often said to have been completed by Menkaure's son, Shepseskaf (c.2503–c.2494 BC), but there is little evidence for this. The valley temple itself, even in Reisner's time, lay beneath the sand. He found it by projecting the axis of the causeway from the entrance of the mortuary temple, and was fortunate enough to make some wonderful discoveries. First he found the pair-statue of Menkaure and his queen, Khamererenebty. He went on to find four more masterpieces of ancient Egyptian art, the famous triads showing Menkaure with the goddess Hathor and a local deity, which are now in the Cairo Museum.

Three small pyramids lie to the south of Menkaure's, one of which might have been intended as the king's subsidiary pyramid, later adapted to accommodate a queen. The body of a young woman was found in the central pyramid. ◆

◄ *The mudbrick valley temple was embellished with beautiful schist triads showing Menkaure protected by Hathor and various local deities.*

Hathor

The king was thought to be the child of the gods. As the living king was regarded as Horus, his mother was often held to be Isis. However, in the triads that decorated Menkaure's valley temple, Hathor, whose name means 'House of Horus', plays that role. As a cow goddess she nurtures the king with her milk. In the Pyramid Texts the king is asked on his arrival in paradise, 'Are you Horus, the son of Osiris? Are you the god, the eldest one, the son of Hathor?'

Stories from Herodotus

In Book Two of *The Histories*, Herodotus related the stories of Cheops (Khufu c.2589–c.2566 BC) and Chephren (Khafre c.2558–c.2532 BC) as told to him by Egyptian priests during his visit to the pyramids in the mid-fifth century BC. He clearly regarded them as tyrants. In contrast, Mycerinus (Menkaure c.2532–c.2503 BC) was seen as a good king.

Oppressive rule

'Cheops…brought the country into all sorts of misery. He closed all the temples, then not content with excluding his subjects from the practice of their religion, compelled them without exception to labour as slaves for his own advantage. Some were forced to bring blocks of stone from the quarries in the Arabian hills to the Nile, where they were ferried across by others who hauled them to the Libyan hills. The work went on in three-monthly shifts, 100,000 men in a shift. It took ten years of this oppressive slave-labour to build the track along which the blocks were hauled, a work, in my opinion, of hardly less magnitude than the pyramid itself, for it is 5 furlongs [1km] in length, 60ft [18m] wide, 48ft [15m] high at its highest point, and constructed of polished stone blocks decorated with carvings of animals. To build it took, as I have said, ten years, including the underground sepulchral chambers on the hill where the pyramids stood: a cut was made from the Nile, so that the water from it turned the site of these into an island. To build the pyramid itself took 20 years: it is square at the base, its height equal to the length of each side; it is of polished stone blocks, beautifully fitted, none of the blocks being less than 30ft [9m] long. The method employed was to build it in steps, or as some say, tiers or terraces. When the base was complete, the blocks for the first tier above it were lifted from the ground by contrivances made of short timbers; on this first tier there was another, which raised the blocks a stage higher, then yet another which raised them higher still. Each tier or storey had its set of levers, or it may be that they used the same one, which being easy to carry, they shifted up from stage to stage as soon as its load was dropped into place. Both methods are mentioned, so I give them both here. The finishing-off of the pyramid was begun at the top and continued downwards, ending with the lowest parts nearest the ground. An inscription is cut upon it in Egyptian characters recording the amount spent on radishes, onions and leeks for the labourers. And I remember distinctly that the interpreter who read me the inscription said that the sum was 1,600 talents of silver...

But no crime was too great for Cheops: when he was short of money, he sent his daughter to a bawdy house with instructions to charge a certain sum, they did not tell me how much. This she actually did, adding to it a further transaction of her own; for with the intention of leaving something to be remembered by after her death, she asked each of her customers to give her a block of stone, and of these stones (the story goes) was built the middle pyramid of the three which stand in front of the great pyramid. It is a 150ft [45m] square.

Cheops reigned for 50 years according to the Egyptian's account, and was succeeded after his death by his brother Chephren. Chephren was no better than his predecessor: his rule was equally oppressive, and, like Cheops, he built a pyramid, but of a smaller size (I measured both of them myself)... The pyramid of Chephren lies close to that of Cheops; it is 40ft [12m] lower than the latter, but otherwise of the same dimensions; its lower course is of the coloured stone of Ethiopia.

Chephren reigned for 56 years, so the Egyptians reckon a period of 106 years, all told, when the temples were never opened for worship and the country reduced to the greatest possible misery...'

◀ *A bust said to be of the Greek historian Herodotus, who was one of the first travellers to Egypt to write of his experiences there.*

▲ *Herodotus visited the pyramids in the mid-5th century BC and was given his information by the priests who looked after the site.*

The reign of Menkaure

'The next king of Egypt to rule after Chephren was Mycerinus, the son of Cheops. Mycerinus, reversing his father's policy of which he did not approve, reopened all the temples and allowed his subjects, who had been brought into such abject slavery, to resume the practice of their religion and their normal work. Of all the kings who ruled in Egypt he had the greatest reputation for justice in the decision of legal causes, and for this the Egyptians give him higher praise than any other… He used to compensate out of his own property any man who was dissatisfied with the results of his suit, and so leave him nothing to complain of… Such were the generosity and mild rule of Mycerinus, when the first of his troubles fell upon him: his daughter, who was his only child, died. Wishing, in the excess of his grief at this calamity, to give his daughter a tomb which should be different from any other, he had a wooden cow made, hollow inside and plated on the outside with gold, to receive her body. The cow was not buried, but was still to be seen in my day at Sais, standing in a richly decorated chamber of the royal palace; incense of all kinds is burnt before it every day, and at night a lamp is always kept lighted in the room. Close by in another chamber, the priests told me, are some statues, which represent the concubines of Mycerinus: there are, indeed, 20 or so naked wooden figures of great size in this chamber, but as to whom they represent I can only pass on such information as was given to me.

There is another, and quite different, story told about the cow and the statues; according to this, Mycerinus conceived a passion for his daughter and violated her, and distress at the outrage drove her to hang herself: she was entombed in the cow, and her mother cut off the hands of the servants who had allowed the king access to her. The statues represent the servants, and like their living originals, have no hands. Personally I think this story is nonsense, especially in its explanation of the servants' missing hands; I could see for myself that they had simply dropped off through age. They are still there, plainly visible, lying on the ground at the statues' feet...

After the death of his daughter, a second calamity fell upon Mycerinus: he received an oracle from Buto to the effect he was destined to live for only six more years and to die within the seventh. He sent back an angry message to the shrine, and reproached the god with the injustice of allowing a man so pious as himself to die so soon, when his father and uncle, who had closed the temples, forgotten the gods, and afflicted their fellow men, had lived to a good old age. In answer to this there was another message from the oracle, which declared that his life was being shortened precisely because he had not done what he ought to have done...Mycerinus, convinced by this that his doom was sealed, had innumerable lamps made, by the light of which he set himself every evening to drink and be merry, and never ceased by day or night from the pursuit of pleasure, travelling about from place to place amongst the pools and woodlands...His object in this was by turning night into day to extend the six remaining years of his life into twelve, and so convict the oracle of falsehood.' ◆

The Tomb of Hetepheres

Queen Hetepheres was the wife of Sneferu (c.2613–c.2589 BC) and the mother of Khufu (c.2589–c.2566 BC). It seems likely that she was originally buried at Dahshur, near her husband, but that her tomb was violated soon after she was laid to rest. Perhaps because of this, her reburial was ordered and a shaft grave assigned to her on the east side of Khufu's Great Pyramid, near the three small pyramids, the northernmost of which is also thought to be hers. The shaft tomb was discovered in 1925 by the staff photographer of the Harvard-Boston expedition led by George Reisner. It was found to contain some beautiful gilded wooden furniture, which is now displayed in a new gallery in the Cairo Museum.

Hetepheres' furniture

The furniture includes a large portable canopy and a box for the curtains that went with it. Both are inscribed with the name of Hetepheres' husband, and the rest of the furniture dates to his reign. One of the best pieces is a beautifully crafted, gilded wooden sedan chair, a mode of transport commonly seen in the tombs of high-ranking officials of the Old Kingdom (c.2686–c.2181 BC). Unfortunately, the wood could not withstand the ravages of time, but the gold work is spectacular. The finials of the carrying poles take the form of elegant palmiform capitals, and the chair is decorated with strips of gold chased in imitation of reed matting. The ebony panels of the backrest are decorated inside and out with exquisite hieroglyphs worked in gold, each one a little masterpiece. The inscription reads:

> *Mother of the King of Upper and Lower Egypt, follower of Horus, controller of the butchers of the acacia house, one for whom everything she says, is done, the god's bodily daughter, Hetepheres.*

There are also two gilded wooden chairs decorated with papyrus clusters and delicate inlay work, as well as a bed and headrest, also of gilded wood. Other objects found in the tomb include a tubular leather case for walking sticks, a large gilded jewellery box containing silver bracelets inlaid with precious stones and a small box containing razors and three elegant golden vessels.

▼ *This narrow side panel from one of the boxes found in Hetepheres' tomb shows the name of her husband, Sneferu.*

▲ *This gilded wooden chair was placed in Hetepheres' tomb for her use in the Afterlife, but was likely to have seen service in her lifetime.*

The body of the queen has not been found. A beautifully carved alabaster sarcophagus was found in the shaft but it was empty. However, an alabaster canopic chest discovered in the tomb was found to contain the queen's internal organs, and it is some of the earliest evidence for the practice of including the organs in the burial in this manner.

However, the American archaeologist Mark Lehner has recently suggested that her original burial place was, in fact, the shaft-grave and it was this that was robbed in antiquity. He thinks her body, but not the canopic chest, was then removed to the satellite pyramid, which was also later violated. This would explain the damage to the funerary equipment found in the shaft grave and the presence there of the canopic chest and the empty sarcophagus. ◆

▲ *Furniture found in the tomb of Hetepheres would have been used by her on royal progresses through Egypt, which took place at regular intervals. It included a portable canopy, a chair, a bed and a headrest.*

Khufu's Boats

Boat pits as part of a funerary complex are known from the First Dynasty (c.3100–c.2890 BC). Boats have always played a significant role in the lives of the Egyptians, and were also important in a funerary context. In the Pyramid Texts, there are many references to the boat of the sun god Re, and to the fact that the king in his Afterlife expected to accompany Re in his daily journeys across the sky.

Five boat pits are associated with Khufu's burial within the Great Pyramid complex. Two lie to the south of the pyramid, and three others were found to the east. Both of the southern pits were sealed by huge blocks of limestone. One of these was opened and was found to contain a large wooden boat that had been taken apart for storage. This was restored over a period of ten years by Ahmed Yussef Mustafa, and was finally reassembled in 1968. It is now housed in a specially constructed museum nearby. The function of the craft is unknown. It may have been a solar boat, in which the deceased king, identified with the sun god Re, would cross the sky each day. It may have been used as a state barge in real life, or it may have been the boat that brought the king's body from the capital at Memphis to his pyramid for burial. That it might have had a practical use before burial is suggested by the fact that it shows signs of having been in water. Nevertheless, it could also have been part of the funerary equipment intended to provide the king with everything he needed in the next world.

The other pit on the southern side has not yet been opened, although there are plans to do so in the future. However, using modern technology it has been

▶ *One of Khufu's boats reconstructed from timbers found in one of five boat pits surrounding his pyramid is now on display in the Boat Museum at Giza.*

▲ *In this scene from the Valley of the Kings, the sun god Re sails through the Underworld and accompanies the king on his journey to the Afterlife.*

▼ *An aerial view of some of the empty boat pits lying close to the Great Pyramid.*

possible to see inside the pit without opening it. An endoscopic image has been obtained, which proves that there is indeed a boat inside. The other three pits are empty, and it is not known whether they ever contained boats or whether the pits themselves were intended to represent boats.

Khufu's boat was made of cedarwood from Lebanon. Shipments of wood from Byblos are known from the reign of Sneferu (c.2613–c.2589 BC). They are also mentioned on the Fifth Dynasty stela known as the Palermo Stone, which records important events from the beginning of the First Dynasty to the end of the Fifth Dynasty (c.2345). No nails were used in the construction of the boat: the planks were fastened together with ropes and pegs.

The boat is 43m (141ft) long and 6m (20ft) wide. It has a very shallow draught, making it suitable only for use on the River Nile. There are two cabins, a long central one, presumably for the use of the king, and a smaller one at the prow, probably for the captain. Two large steering oars are located in the stern and the boat was rowed by ten pairs of oars. There is no mast and so no provision for a sail. ◆

The Eastern and Western Cemeteries

The Great Pyramid is the central monument in a large necropolis. Behind the three queens' pyramids to the east of Khufu's pyramid, several members of the royal family were buried, some in mastabas and some in rock-cut tombs. The mastabas of the Sixth Dynasty official Qar and his relative Idu are also situated in the Eastern Cemetery. Officials of Khufu's reign lie in mastaba tombs in a cemetery to the west.

The tomb of Meresankh III

One of the most beautiful and best-preserved tombs in the Eastern Cemetery is that of Queen Meresankh III. She was the granddaughter of Khufu and the daughter of two of his children, Kawab and Hetepheres II. She became the wife of her half-brother King Khafre (c.2558– c.2532 BC), and was about 50 years old when she died.

Her tomb lies below that of her mother and consists of a large, subterranean, rock-cut tomb chapel divided into three main sections. The doorway is inscribed with her name and titles, principally 'Daughter of the King' and 'Royal Wife of Khafre'. It also, unusually, records the time taken to mummify her body. The inscription states that 270 days elapsed between the dates of her death and burial, which is an unusually long time. The embalming process and associated ritual is generally thought to have taken about 70 days, so perhaps her tomb was not finished at the time of her death.

In the first section are scenes common to most tombs of the Old Kingdom (c.2686–c.2181 BC). As well as the usual offering scenes, they show farmworkers engaged in agricultural work, fishermen catching fish by various means, hunters in the marshes and fights between the boatmen. Meresankh and Hetepheres are depicted trapping birds in a net and sailing through the marshes in a papyrus boat, gathering lotus flowers.

▼ *Beyond the square pillars of the first large room is an extension containing statues in high relief of Meresankh III, her mother Hetepheres II and several young female members of the family.*

▲ *Meresankh and Hetepheres are depicted gathering lotus and catching birds with nets in the marshes. Both of these activities have religious significance, the lotus being a symbol of new life and the catching of birds representing the restoration of order over chaos.*

Immediately to the left of the entrance are scenes showing scribes, sculptors, goldsmiths and carpenters at work. The section showing the making of statues is particularly interesting because the names of two of the artists are recorded. Most Egyptian art is anonymous, and it is only very rarely that the names of individual artists come to light. One of the five panels shows Rehay painting a statue of Meresankh, while another shows his colleague, the sculptor Inkaf, at work on another statue of the queen.

The groups of actual statues are another unusual feature of this tomb. Further along from the scenes in the sculptors' workshop there are three niches containing six statues in officials' attire. Unfortunately, these are not inscribed, so their names are not known. Almost opposite, in the extension to this first room, is a huge niche with a group of ten large, female statues, who presumably represent Meresankh, her mother and her daughters, although, again, there are no inscriptions to identify them. The main room also has a false door stela, and offering lists are inscribed on the lintel over the door to the next room. Between the main room and the extension are two pillars decorated in painted, carved relief, with figures of Meresankh wearing a close-fitting dress of white linen. Her two young sons are also shown. One scene shows her father and mother in a papyrus boat.

Beyond the main room is the offerings chapel, decorated with agricultural scenes and others that depict the funerary banquet, where the guests are entertained by singers and musicians. On each side of a false door are two more statue niches. Each houses two statues, presumably of Meresankh and Hetepheres, her mother, placed there to receive offerings.

From the offerings chapel, a shaft leads down to the burial chamber, where George Reisner found a black granite sarcophagus in the course of his excavations in 1927. The mummy of the queen was inside, and this was taken to the Cairo Museum. ▶

▶ *A square pillar in the tomb of Meresankh III shows her dressed in an elegant, close-fitting gown of fine linen. Her two young sons are also depicted. Above her image are her name and titles.*

The mastaba of Qar

Qar lived in the Sixth Dynasty, probably some time during the long reign of Pepi II (c.2278–c.2184 BC). Although he was not an official of Khufu during the king's lifetime, he had responsibilities connected with Khufu's funerary cult and so merited a tomb close to the royal burial place. His titles included 'Overseer of the Pyramid City of Khufu and Menkaure' and 'Supervisor of Priests in the Pyramid of Khafre'. He was also 'Regent of the Pyramid' of Pepi I. His wife, Gefi, was a priestess of Hathor.

Qar's tomb is a stone-built mastaba consisting of a staircase passage, a large main room divided into two sections, and an offering chapel. Like the tomb of Meresankh, it has several interesting sculptures. In a niche in the wall to the left of the entrance is a seated statue of Qar, and on the south wall there is a whole series of statues representing Qar, his young son and other members of his family. The same room has well-preserved scenes showing the presentation of offerings and funeral ritual in painted, carved relief. On the pillar in the centre of this room are Qar's names and titles, together with scenes that show him with his sisters and sitting in a chair with his dog. In the offering chapel, which leads off to the right, is a false door stela.

▲ *The 6th-Dynasty official Qar and his young son are represented by two statues in his tomb. Qar was in charge of the funerary cult of Khufu, Khafre and Menkaure at Giza.*

▼ *Qar's tomb is located near to the pyramids of the kings whose cult he served. This view of the interior shows statues of Qar and his relations carved into the face of the rock.*

▲ *A detail of a painted relief of Idu before an offering table shows him wearing an official's wig and a wide collar, which he may have received as a reward for his services to the king.*

The mastaba of Idu

The tomb of Idu, who may be either the father or the son of Qar, is virtually next door. This stone-built mastaba is, in many ways, similar to that of Qar but is much smaller. Idu's tomb has one main room decorated with painted reliefs and rock-cut statues of the deceased and his family. On the jambs of the doorway at the entrance to the tomb are Idu's names and titles, which provide some biographical detail. From these it is clear that he also had duties relating to the funerary cults of the Fourth Dynasty kings. He was inspector of the *wab*-priests of Khufu and Khafre, as well as 'Scribe of the Royal Documents in the Presence of the King'.

The decoration of the tomb is funerary in character. There are few scenes of everyday life, which are otherwise common at this period. The false door stela, where offerings were presented, is in the middle of the east wall and is very unusual in design. A statue of the deceased shows him seated, his hands with upturned palms resting on his knees, as he waits to receive offerings. Above his head is a relief that shows him and his wife seated on each side of an offering table. On the opposite wall are niches containing the statues of Idu and his family. One of the most charming shows Idu wearing his short kilt and official's wig, standing next to his son.

The painted reliefs on the south wall to the left and right of the door are funerary scenes. They show Idu's home, a purification tent and the funeral procession. Facing these, on the back wall, are scenes depicting the preparation of food and drink, dancers and musicians, and the presentation of offerings. Idu oversees these sitting on his palanquin.

The Western Cemetery

Other officials are buried to the west of the Great Pyramid, where there is a whole pyramid 'town' with mastabas laid out in 'streets'. One of the most impressive of these tombs belonged to Iymery, a Fifth Dynasty official who was 'Prophet of Khufu' and 'Overseer of the Great House'. This is a large tomb consisting of an entrance, vestibule, first room, *serdab* (statue room) and offering chapel with a false door stela. Here are the familiar everyday-life scenes that decorate the walls of many of the Old Kingdom tombs. The vestibule has scenes showing carpenters, goldsmiths and sculptors at work. In the first room, there are scenes of cattle-breeding, fishing and fowling in the marshes. The offering chapel has scenes showing offerings being presented to the deceased, who is enjoying the company of his wife and family as musicians and dancers entertain them.

Although many of these tombs have been known for some time, several others have been discovered recently. One of these belongs to a priest called Kai, who remained in royal service from the reign of Sneferu (c.2613–c.2589 BC) to that of Khafre (c.2558–c.2532 BC). His tomb is decorated with elegant reliefs of the tomb owner and offering scenes, in which the colours look as if they were painted yesterday. ◆

False doors

In the offering chapel of a tomb, a stela (stone slab) resembling a door was erected to enable the spirit of the deceased to come out and partake of the daily offerings left in front of it. In some royal tombs, false doors were made of red granite, while in non-royal tombs they were of limestone, which was sometimes painted red in imitation of granite.

▼ *A painted carved relief from the false door of Idu's tomb shows the deceased and his wife at either side of an offering table.*

The Tombs of Pharaoh's Workers

The necropolis containing the tombs of the workers who built the pyramids has only recently come to light. It was found in 1990 when a horse ridden by a tourist stumbled over a low wall, which later turned out to be part of a tomb.

The tombs of this cemetery are very small and inferior in quality to the rather grand stone-built mastabas in the cemeteries of the high officials. They were constructed with odds and ends of different types of building materials left over from the building of pyramids and their associated temples. The first one to be explored was a long vaulted chamber with two false doors. Hieroglyphs in the tomb showed that it belonged to Ptah-shepsesu and his wife. There were three burial shafts at the back of the chamber, so perhaps their son was buried there too. Ptah-shepsesu may have been a supervisor of some sort as his tomb is larger than the others surrounding it. Altogether, about 600 of these small tombs have been found, as well as about 30 larger ones belonging to overseers. The tombs were constructed in all shapes and sizes, many of them appearing to imitate the plans of the tombs of high officials. One has a small ramp, perhaps in imitation of a royal tomb.

Later, an upper part of the necropolis was discovered. Here, the tombs were larger and inscriptions indicated that they were the tombs of the artisans, whereas the lower cemetery seems to have been where the labourers were buried. One of the more imposing tombs was a limestone mastaba with six burial shafts and two false doors carved on its eastern face. Attached to the mastaba was a rock-cut room. The burial was found to be intact, and a sealed niche was found to contain four statues of the deceased, whose name was Intyshedu

▼ *Metalworking processes are common themes in Old Kingdom tombs. Here, the workmen use bellows to increase the heat of the brazier, as depicted in the tomb of Mereruka.*

▶ *The dwarf Seneb and his family, from his tomb at Giza (c.2475 BC). Funerary statues project an ideal view of the deceased so Seneb's deformity has been disguised.*

and who styled himself 'Overseer of the Boat of the Goddess, Neith' and 'King's Acquaintance'. He was a carpenter who made ceremonial boats for the goddess Neith on behalf of the king, and the statues depict him at various stages in life, from youth to old age.

None of the workers' bodies had been mummified, and each had been laid in a small shaft in a foetal position. The skeletal remains, especially in the lower cemetery, showed signs of arthritis and joint injuries incurred during lives of hard physical work, and the lifespan of the workers seems to have been shorter than that of the officials and their wives buried in the officials' cemeteries.

The dwarf cemetery

Another important discovery of recent years is that of the dwarf cemetery. Dwarfs were respected members of society in ancient Egypt and often attained high positions at court. The dwarf Seneb, for example, who has been known for many years from his splendid statue in the Cairo Museum, was chief of all the dwarfs who were responsible for the royal wardrobe. He was also a priest involved in the funerary cults of Khufu and Djedefre. It is known from inscriptions on the false door of his tomb that he was a wealthy man who owned cattle. His statue depicts him sitting cross-legged in the position of a scribe, indicating that he was an educated man. Seneb's wife, Senetites, sits beside him with her arm affectionately around his shoulders, in typical Old Kingdom style. The sculptor has sensitively disguised his deformity, ingeniously compensating for his short stature by placing his two children where his legs would otherwise have been.

Among others, a further dwarf tomb was discovered a few years ago. It is of limestone and has two false doors on the east side, where the name of the dwarf, Prnyankhw, is inscribed. Three shafts were discovered, of which one contained his skeletal remains and the others the remains of two women. Statues of these women were found beside the false doors. Prnyankhw's statue is made of black basalt. He is seated on a chair and is shown as a strong and lively man. The only sign of deformity is that his lower left leg appears to be swollen, and it has been suggested that this might indicate the earliest known case of elephantiasis. Like Seneb, Prnyankhw was highly thought of. An inscription on his right leg describes him as 'One who delights his lord every day'. ◆

Memphis and Saqqara

Memphis, about 24km (15 miles) south of Cairo, was the first capital of the united land of Egypt and remained an important religious and administrative centre throughout the Pharaonic Period. It was the chief cult centre of the god Ptah, and in Egyptian mythology it was the place where he performed the act of creation. It was also where the goddesses Isis and Nephthys took the body of their brother Osiris from the Nile, after he had been murdered by his jealous brother Seth, and where Osiris entered the Underworld to become judge of the dead. The divine court, which finally decided that Horus should inherit the throne of Egypt from his father Osiris, was said to have sat at Memphis.

During the Ptolemaic Period (332–30 BC), the new city of Alexandria overtook Memphis in importance. Memphis never recovered its old status, and the ancient buildings were used as a quarry during the building of the new capital, Cairo, after the Arab invasion in the ninth century AD. Today, there is little to see of the ancient capital city. However, the remains of the tombs of kings and commoners at Saqqara, the cemetery site for Memphis, are spectacular.

◀ *Little remains of the ancient city of Memphis, first capital of Egypt and principal cult centre of the creator god Ptah.*

City and Cemetery

According to Herodotus, the city of Memphis was founded by Min, the legendary first king of Egypt, who would appear to be the Menes of the Egyptian kinglists. First, he prepared the site by building a dam to divert the River Nile. He then built the city and embellished it with the 'large and very remarkable temple of Hephaestus' (actually Ptah, the creator god of Memphis, whom the Greeks equated with their own god).

The name of Memphis may be derived from Men-nefer, the name of the pyramid town of Pepi I at Saqqara. It means 'Established and Beautiful'. Other names included 'White Walls', a reference to the city's fortifications, and 'Balance of the Two Lands', referring to its position at the meeting point of the Nile Valley and the Delta.

▲ *The head of the colossal polished-limestone statue of Ramesses II. Originally erected in front of the Ptah temple, today it is in the museum at Memphis. The statue stood 13m (43ft) high.*

Archaeological remains

In Memphis today, a museum housing a gigantic statue of Ramesses II and various other pieces from the New Kingdom (c.1550–c.1069 BC) and later periods are all the tourist usually gets to see of the ancient city. The remains of a Ramesside temple of Ptah are also visible. Material from earlier structures, including a lintel dating from the Middle Kingdom (c.2055–c.1650 BC), was reused in this building, suggesting the existence of previous temples on the site. However, these have not so far come to light as the high water table makes the site difficult to excavate. It is also possible that the city's location changed during the Pharaonic Period, corresponding to changes in the course of the Nile. Recent attempts to locate the most ancient city have been made by David Jeffreys and the Egypt Exploration Society using drill cores.

Close to the temple of Ptah in Memphis was the stall where the Apis bull, the living image of the god Ptah, was kept. On his death, the bull was mummified in the embalming house. The embalming tables used for this purpose remain on the site and the embalming house built by the Twenty-second Dynasty king Sheshonq I (c.945–c.924 BC) is currently undergoing excavation and reconstruction.

Saqqara

Saqqara was the main cemetery site for ancient Memphis, and was used by kings and/or their officials from the First Dynasty (c.3100–c.2890 BC) to the Christian era. Here are the great mastaba tombs of the First Dynasty élite, once thought to be the tombs of the kings of this period. Here, too, is the Step Pyramid of King Djoser (c.2667–c.2648 BC), the oldest stone building in the world. The officials' tombs of the Old Kingdom (c.2686–c.2181 BC) are grouped around the tombs of the kings they served. Most of the Middle Kingdom kings and their officials were buried further south at Dahshur, in the Faiyum, and at Thebes, but because Memphis continued to be the seat of government in the New Kingdom, many officials of this period were buried at Saqqara, although the kings themselves were usually buried in the Valley of the Kings.

Saqqara continued to be used for private burials from the Saite to the Ptolemaic Periods (664–30 BC). After this time the site was abandoned until the fifth century AD, when the Copts (Egyptian Christians) built a monastery here dedicated to St Jeremiah. The tombs of important Persian officials, dating from the Persian occupation of 525–404 BC, are currently being investigated.

The site is vast and extends for about 6km (4 miles) along the desert edge. ◆

▲ *A block carved in sunken relief from the pyramid complex of King Unas at Saqqara. The name of the king appears in the cartouches.*

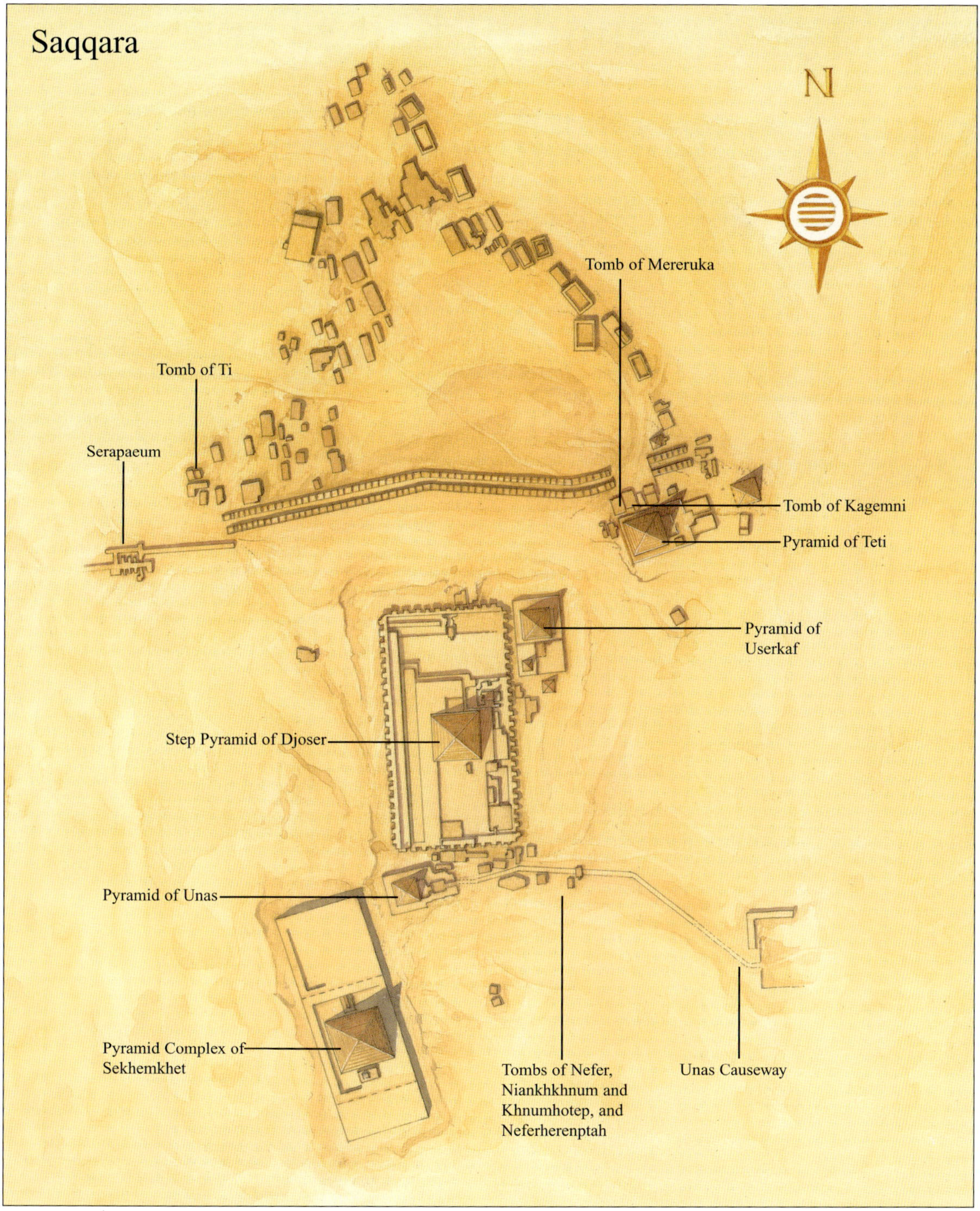
Saqqara
N
Tomb of Mereruka
Tomb of Ti
Serapaeum
Tomb of Kagemni
Pyramid of Teti
Pyramid of Userkaf
Step Pyramid of Djoser
Pyramid of Unas
Pyramid Complex of Sekhemkhet
Tombs of Nefer, Niankhkhnum and Khnumhotep, and Neferherenptah
Unas Causeway

The Step Pyramid of King Djoser

The buildings of the Step Pyramid complex of King Djoser (c.2667–c.2648 BC) are of two different types: some were designed for practical use, while the majority are dummy buildings. According to their excavator, Jean-Philippe Lauer, the latter appear to be primarily symbolic and represent the ancient city of Memphis, so that, just as the subterranean chambers of the pyramid were stocked with food and drink to supply the king's supposed physical needs, he was also provided with a capital city for the Afterlife. The functional buildings may have been used during the king's funeral and for the subsequent daily ritual of his mortuary cult.

▼ *The Step Pyramid of King Djoser, built on the desert plateau, is seen here across the date palm trees of the Nile Valley.*

Entrance to the complex

The complex covers a large area in the form of a rectangle 544 x 277m (1,785 x 909ft), 15 hectares (37 acres) in all, which is thought to be the size of a typical large town of the period. Boundary stelae, inscribed with the name of the king and his two daughters, Hetep-her-nebti and Int-ka-s, mark out the site, and it is entirely surrounded by a wall of fine-quality white Tura limestone. This may well have represented the walls of the city, which gave Memphis one of its epithets, 'White Walls'. Fourteen dummy doorways are set in the walls and the complex is entered on the south-eastern side through a doorway with a door carved in an open position. Inside the door is a small vestibule and a corridor composed of two rows of 20 half-engaged fluted columns, carved in imitation of bundles of reeds. The corridor leads into a small hypostyle hall (a chamber in which the roof is supported by columns) with eight columns arranged in pairs connected by limestone blocks. Beyond is the Great Courtyard in front of the Step Pyramid.

Djoser's pyramid

The Step Pyramid is a tower built in six stages, based on a mastaba 63m (207ft) square and about 8m (26ft) tall. This covers a shaft 28m (92ft) deep, leading to the burial chamber and a whole network of subterranean rooms and tunnels used for funerary goods. A further series of 11 shafts and chambers were constructed to the east, perhaps to accommodate the burial of the royal women. The mastaba seems to have been expanded to cover these extensions, and at some point

further stages were added. This produced a more imposing monument and perhaps represented a stairway to heaven, which, according to the Pyramid Texts found in the pyramid of King Unas (c.2375–c.2345 BC), the king expected to climb.

The Great Courtyard

On the south side of the court is a building called the Southern Tomb, which may have housed the king's internal organs (liver, lungs, stomach and intestines), the chamber being too small to take a body. Another theory is that it was intended for the burial of the king's *ka* statue, a representation of his spirit or vital force as his slightly smaller double. The walls are decorated with reliefs showing the king running his *heb sed* race and naming him as Horus Netjerikhet. The top of the tomb wall has a frieze of cobras, which represent the goddess Wadjet, the protector of kings.

The *heb sed*, or royal jubilee festival, usually took place after the king had been on the throne for 30 years and included a re-coronation ceremony, when the king was reinvested in his position and his royal power was renewed. It would seem that provision was made for this to happen in the Afterlife too, so that the king could be confirmed in his role eternally. In the centre of the Great Courtyard are a couple of semicircular blocks, two of the markers that once indicated the course to be run by the king during his *sed*-festival in the Afterlife. On the eastern side of the court is Temple T, a building that perhaps represents the pavilion where in real life the king would wait at certain points in the *heb sed* ritual. It contains a niche decorated with *djed*-pillars, which were associated with Osiris and symbolized stability, and the king is likely to have been represented here by a statue. ▶

▲ *This statue of King Djoser was found in the* serdab, *or statue room, of his pyramid. It is now in the Cairo Museum and a replica stands in its place on site.*

◀ *Distinctive columns carved to resemble bundles of reeds can be seen when looking east through the colonnaded entrance to Djoser's pyramid complex, which was built by Imhotep.*

◀ *A frieze of royal cobras decorates the top of the so-called Southern Tomb.*

The *heb sed* court

From Temple T the wall curves round, guiding the ceremonial procession into the *heb sed* court where the king would be recrowned, once as King of Lower Egypt and once as King of Upper Egypt. In this court, there is a platform approached by a short flight of steps. Here, there would have been a double canopy, under which the ceremony would have taken place. A tiny ebony label once attached to grave goods in an Early Dynastic tomb at Abydos depicts this ceremony and enabled archaeologists to reconstruct the platform and short flights of steps.The *heb sed* court is surrounded by dummy chapels with beautifully finished façades of dressed limestone, but entirely filled with rubble. They were designed to provide a suitable setting for the ceremonial. Several unfinished statues of the king have also been found in this area, but their precise intended location is not known.

The Southern and Northern Courts

Leading from the *heb sed* court is the Southern Court, the main feature of which is the House of the South. Although it is now restored only to doorway height, Jean-Philippe Lauer, the French architect who has restored the complex, thought that the building would originally have been more than 12m (40ft) high, with a façade embellished with slender, engaged fluted columns. Many of the capitals were found, almost complete, lying in the sand, carved in the form of pendant leaves. Set in a recess in the wall of the court, Lauer found the base of a small round column. He also found the uppermost part of the column, but unfortunately the capital seems to have disappeared. Lauer thought that it would have been in the form of a lotus, the symbol of Southern or Upper Egypt, hence the name given to the court.

Inside the House of the South are some interesting graffiti written by visitors during the New Kingdom (c.1550–c.1069 BC), expressing their admiration for the monument, which was by then about 1,500 years old. One of these is particularly informative because it mentions the name of Djoser, while the other inscriptions in the complex name King Netjerikhet as the owner. It is now recognized that they were one and the same (each king of Egypt having more than one name). This graffito reads:

▶ *The* heb sed *court in Djoser's Step Pyramid complex was meant to provide a setting for the king's celebration of the* heb sed *in the Afterlife.*

▲ *Papyrus-form pillar with a triangular stem and an open-umbel capital in the so-called Northern Court. The papyrus was the symbol of Lower Egypt.*

> *The scribe Ahmose, son of Iptah, came to see the temple of Djoser. He found it as though heaven were within it, Re rising in it. Then he said, 'Let loaves and oxen and all good and pure things fall to the* ka *of the justified Djoser; may heaven drip fresh myrrh, may it drip incense!'*

Next comes the Northern Court, the east wall of which has a recess with three slender triangular columns crowned with open papyrus umbels symbolizing Northern or Lower Egypt and emphasizing the dual nature of the complex. Another building, corresponding to the House of the South in the other court, completes this section.

At the north-eastern corner of the pyramid is the *serdab*, or statue chamber, which housed the *ka* statue of the king to which offerings would have been brought during the daily mortuary ritual. The original statue is now in the Cairo Museum and has been replaced by a replica. The mortuary temple was on the north side of the pyramid. It is largely in ruins now, but must have been imposing in its time and is the earliest example known. Also on the north side is the original entrance to the burial chamber, although this is no longer accessible to tourists. During the Saite Period (664–525 BC) another entrance was made on the southern side. ◆

► *The entrance to the Step Pyramid complex of King Djoser.*

Imhotep

The architect of the Step Pyramid of King Djoser was Imhotep, the king's vizier. He has been identified by an inscription on the base of a statue of the king. He was later also credited with medical knowledge, and his fame became so great that in the Ptolemaic Period (332–30 BC) he was deified and equated both with Thoth, the ancient Egyptian god of wisdom, and Asklepios, the ancient Greek god of healing.

The Asklepion, his cult centre, was visited by pilgrims who brought offerings of mummified ibises, many bearing the name of Imhotep on the wrappings. Pilgrims also left clay models of afflicted body parts in the hope that Imhotep would heal them. It was in the search for the actual tomb of Imhotep that the sacred animal cemetery at Saqqara was accidentally found.

The *Sed*-Festival

The *heb sed*, or royal jubilee festival, was a ritual during which the king's right to rule and his royal powers were renewed. In representations of this ceremony, he is usually shown running alongside the Apis bull, proving his fitness to rule, and then being recrowned as 'King of the Two Lands'. Officially, the *sed*-festival was held after the king had been on the throne for 30 years, but reliefs and inscriptions suggest that some kings, including those with relatively short reigns, celebrated earlier. Although this may sometimes have been the case, other kings may simply have been depicted symbolically fulfilling one of the obligations of kingship, just as Queen Nefertiti, for example, perhaps as co-ruler with her husband, Akhenaten (c.1352–c.1336 BC), is depicted smiting enemies.

The origins of the *sed*-festival are not known, although there is evidence that it was held from the very beginning of recorded history. On a small ebony label once attached to a jar of oil from the tomb of King Den (c.2950 BC) at Abydos, a tiny pin-man figure of the king is shown running around a clearly defined course and carrying the *heb sed* insignia. To the left, there is a platform approached by a short flight of steps, on which a double shrine has been erected. Inside the shrine, the king is shown again, sitting on a throne and wearing the Double Crown, having been recrowned twice, once as King of Upper Egypt and once as King of Lower Egypt.

The *heb sed* and the Afterlife

The Step Pyramid complex of King Djoser at Saqqara includes provision for this ceremony to be eternally re-enacted in his Afterlife. The markers in the Great Court that indicated the course the king would have to run perhaps represented the frontiers of Egypt and symbolized the extent of the king's dominion. The figure of the running king can be seen in low relief in the chambers below the Southern Tomb and beneath the pyramid.

▲ *Papyrus-form columns embellish the walls of the House of the North in the Step Pyramid complex, papyrus being the symbol of Lower Egypt.*

Evidence for the view that the king would expect to take part in this important ritual of kingship in the Afterlife is found in a beautiful alabaster

▶ *Queen Hatshepsut in her role as king of Egypt celebrates the* heb sed *by symbolically running around Egypt's boundaries accompanied by the Apis bull.*

vase that was discovered in one of the chambers beneath the pyramid itself. The vase is carved with the figure of a man with arms upraised, holding aloft a square object, perhaps a canopy, although Jean-Philippe Lauer suggests that it is the platform on which the double shrine and the two thrones would have been set up. The handle of the vase is decorated with reliefs of the thrones of the Two Lands. The figure represents the hieroglyph for millions of years and the thrones are those used by the king at his *heb sed*.

The *heb sed* in history

The ritual was practised throughout Pharaonic history. At Karnak, blocks from the reconstructed Red Chapel of Hatshepsut (c.1473–c.1458 BC) show her, as king, running with the Apis bull between the markers. Scenes from the inner walls of the hypostyle hall in the temple at Karnak show Ramesses II (c.1279–c.1213 BC) similarly engaged. Jubilees are also depicted in the mortuary temple of Amenhotep III (c.1390–c.1352 BC) at Thebes, although he seems to have altered the ritual and its usual setting somewhat. He celebrated three *heb seds* and descriptions of the ceremonies say that they took place on the great artificial lake he had created at Malkata. Here, the king and statues of the deities sailed along in barges, re-enacting the voyage of the sun god through the Underworld.

▶ *King Djoser, dressed in his* heb sed *costume, runs around the course markers that symbolized the boundaries of Egypt.*

Surprisingly, in view of the break with tradition during the reign of the Eighteenth Dynasty king Akhenaten, the *heb sed* was also depicted in the colonnaded court of the Temple of Aten at Karnak, although in this case Akhenaten's queen, Nefertiti, and the royal daughters also took part. The ceremony also took place very early in his reign, before the move to the new capital of Akhetaten. Another remarkable feature is that the Aten, the life-giving disc of the sun, is also seen taking part in a *heb sed* of his own. This is most unusual because the gods are usually seen to give *sed*-festivals to the king; they are never shown taking part in such a ritual themselves. Akhenaten seems to be pointing out that because the god is king, so the king is also a god.

The festival continued to take place in later times. This is confirmed by scenes from the temple of the cat-goddess, Bastet, at Bubastis, where the Twenty-second Dynasty king Osorkon II (c.874–c.850 BC) is shown seated in the *heb sed* kiosk, wearing the typical robe. At Kom Ombo, carved reliefs show Ptolemy VIII (170–116 BC) receiving *heb sed* symbols from the god Horus, showing that even foreign kings liked to depict themselves taking part in the traditional ritual of kingship. ◆

◀ *The* heb sed *court in the Step Pyramid complex makes provision for the king to renew his right to rule in the Afterlife for all eternity.*

The Pyramid of King Unas

▲ *A roofed causeway ran from the valley temple to the mortuary temple. Next to it were two large boat pits.*

The pyramid of King Unas (c.2375–c.2345 BC), the last king of the Fifth Dynasty, is located near the south-western corner of the Step Pyramid complex. Most of the outer casing has disappeared from this pyramid, revealing its inner core of loose blocks and rubble. It is the smallest of all the Old Kingdom pyramids, but also one of the most interesting as it has several unusual features. On the south side of the pyramid, for instance, there is an inscription of Khaemwese, son of the Nineteenth Dynasty king Ramesses II (c.1279–c.1213 BC), saying that he restored the pyramid on his father's instructions and replaced the name of King Unas because by that time it was missing.

The entrance is on the north side of the pyramid at ground level, and was originally closed with a limestone plug. A sloping passage only 1.4m (4ft 6in) high leads to a vestibule and a second corridor, where there are the remains of three granite portcullises. This corridor eventually leads to a small rectangular room with three niches, probably intended for the *ka* statues of the king. A passage leads to the burial chamber, in which Gaston Maspero of the Egyptian Antiquities Service found a basalt sarcophagus containing the remains of a mummy in 1881.

▼ *Although Unas' pyramid was repaired in antiquity, the outer casing has almost disappeared.*

Pyramid Texts

Both the rectangular antechamber and the burial chamber have ceilings made of two large, sloping limestone slabs decorated with gold stars on a blue ground. The walls of both chambers are covered with Pyramid Texts, and this is the earliest known appearance of these collections of spells, which were intended to enable the king to overcome hostile forces and powers in the Underworld, and so to join the sun god Re, his divine father. He would then spend his days in eternity, sailing with Re across the sky in the solar boat:

Re-Atum, this Unas comes to you,
A spirit indestructible...
Your son comes to you, this Unas comes to you,
May you cross the sky united in the dark,
May you rise in lightland, the place in which you shine!
(Utterance 217)

The sky's reed floats are launched for Re,
That he may cross on them to lightland...
The sky's reed floats are launched for Unas,
That he may cross on them to lightland, to Re...
(Utterance 263)

▲ *The causeway was decorated with scenes in carved and painted relief. Here, Unas is depicted smiting his enemies.*

Other spells describe the king climbing a ladder to heaven and joining the gods among the stars, or acting as Re's secretary:

Unas squats before him,
Unas opens his boxes,
Unas unseals his decrees,
Unas seals his dispatches,
Unas sends his messengers who tire not,
Unas does what Unas is told.
(Utterance 309)

The hieroglyphs of the texts are beautifully carved and filled with blue paste, so that they stand out boldly from the white background. Several kings of the Sixth Dynasty, Teti (c.2345–c.2323 BC), Pepi I (c.2321–c.2287 BC), Merenre (c.2287–c.2278 BC) and Pepi II (c.2278– c.2184 BC), also decorated their burial chambers in this way.

The pyramid complex

The mortuary temple of Unas was partly excavated by the Italian archaeologist Alessandro Barsanti in the early twentieth century, and more completely by Sir Charles Firth in 1929. It is almost completely destroyed, although it has been possible to trace the layout. The temple was similar to that of Sahure, although the floor was made of alabaster rather than basalt.

The plan of the temple is not known in its entirety as the remains of the building lie partly under a modern road. However, enough work has been done to show that the temple was embellished with beautifully made granite palmiform columns. There was a lake here, which made a harbour for the temple. The archaeologists also discovered the harbour, including quays and a slipway.

Linking the valley and mortuary temples is an impressive causeway, 750m (2,460ft) long and once decorated with brightly coloured reliefs. The scenes are amazingly varied. Some show agricultural work, others hunters pursuing lions, leopards, hyenas and a giraffe. Ships are depicted transporting granite palmiform columns, and craftsmen work copper and gold. Possibly the most intriguing are the famine scenes. The relief is not complete and it is not possible to identify the starving people with any certainty. Amelia Edwards surmised that they were foreigners to whom Unas probably sent aid, and that the scenes illustrated one of his good deeds that he wished to perpetuate for eternity. Others see them as Egyptian and read into the scenes signs of Egypt's decline towards the end of the Old Kingdom. ◆

◀ *The walls of the long, roofed causeway were also elaborately decorated with beautifully carved hieroglyphs .*

Tombs of Old Kingdom Officials

Alongside the causeway linking the mortuary and valley temples of King Unas (c.2375–c.2345 BC), there are several tombs belonging to officials of the Old Kingdom (c.2686–c.2181 BC). They chose to be buried near to the pyramids of their royal masters so that they could be on hand to continue to serve them in the Afterlife.

The tomb of Nefer

One of the best-preserved is that of Nefer, but it can be visited only with special permission. Nefer was 'Head of the Royal Singers' and 'Inspector of the Court'. He seems to have been close to the king because he calls himself 'keeper of the king's secrets'. Several members of his family were buried here, including his father, Kaha, who also held the position of 'Head of the Royal Singers', and his mother, Khons, who was a priestess of the goddess Hathor. In the tomb, Nefer's father is described as the 'controller of the beautiful voice' and 'unique among the singers of the funerary estate'. Nefer's three sons and his daughter were also musical and had positions as professional singers. The family is depicted in the tomb, which is noteworthy for a unique scene in which Nefer's wife and child are shown watching dancers.

The tomb is very beautifully decorated with lively scenes in painted relief. Some show work going on in a vegetable garden, where onions and lettuce are being planted and grapes are being gathered and pressed. A baboon is lending a hand. Papyrus is being gathered and prepared for transportation, cattle mate and calves are born. An interesting group shows the building of a wooden cargo boat, the construction of a canoe and a papyrus boat. Elsewhere,

▶ *Nefer, dressed in the leopardskin of a priest, sits in front of an offering table laden with loaves of bread. Above are jars of wine, beer and fruit.*

► *Papyrus plants are harvested and bound into bundles in preparation for transport. Papyrus was used for paper, making sandals and building boats.*

ships ply up and down the Nile. As usual, much attention is paid to hunting, fishing and the preparation of food.

A pit cut into the floor of the tomb houses one of the oldest mummies extant. It is about 4,500 years old and, even though the mummification process had not been perfected at this stage, it is virtually intact. It had been so carefully wrapped that the bandages bore the impressions of the fingernails and a callus on the sole of the foot. The body was naked apart from a bead collar. A false beard had also been added. When the body was discovered in the 1940s, the deceased was holding his long official's cane in one hand and a short staff in the other. It is not certain whether it is Nefer himself who is lying here, or a family friend called Waty. ►

The king's officials

The Narmer Palette, which dates from the beginning of the Dynastic Period, and labels attached to grave goods found at Abydos and Saqqara give the names of officials who held positions in the administration of Egypt. These make it clear that an organized central administration existed from the very beginning of the united land, c.3100 BC. Officials carried titles such as 'Sandal Bearer', 'Sole Companion' or 'Royal Seal Bearer'. The 'Chief of Scouts' organized trading expeditions to procure exotic goods for the king.

► *Nefer's tomb is one of the most beautifully decorated of the Old Kingdom. Here, a servant brings a deer to sustain Nefer in the Afterlife.*

◀ *Mereruka, vizier and son-in-law of Teti of the 6th Dynasty, receives a procession of offering bearers bringing food to the tomb.*

The tomb of Niankhkhnum and Khnumhotep

Niankhkhnum and Khnumhotep were brothers, probably twins. Like Nefer, they were high-ranking officials. Each held the position of 'Prophet of Re' in the sun temple of Niuserre (c.2445–c.2421 BC) and both were 'Overseers of the Manicurists of the Great House'. They are beautifully depicted, embracing each other, on the wall of the chamber leading to the offering room.

The superstructure of their tomb was almost completely destroyed in antiquity, because King Unas built his causeway over it. It has been reconstructed using the decorated blocks that were found during excavation, and is now open to the public. The part of the tomb that was cut into the rock is well preserved. The quality of the painted reliefs is excellent, especially in the first of the rock-cut chambers. The various scenes on the western side of the tomb include fishing and fowling in the marshes, stock breeding, papyrus gathering and fights among the boatmen. Opposite are agricultural scenes and scenes of sculptors and jewellers at work. There are also the usual offering bearers and banqueting scenes, where the guests are entertained with music and dancing.

The 'bird tomb' of Neferherenptah

Nearer to the boat pit of the pyramid complex of Unas is the mastaba of Neferherenptah, who was 'Head of the Hairdressers'. This tomb is unfinished, and it would appear that building was interrupted by the construction of the causeway of King Unas. However, it is decorated with simple designs of exceptionally high quality. The scenes depict agricultural work and the preparation of food and drink. There is also a fine fowling scene with a large flock of birds, from which the tomb gets its nickname.

The mastaba of Mereruka

Mereruka held office as vizier during the reign of Teti (c.2345–c.2323 BC), the first king of the Sixth Dynasty, and married the king's daughter. His tomb lies close to Teti's pyramid. It was excavated by Jacques de Morgan of the Egyptian Antiquities Service in 1892, and it is the largest of all the non-royal Old Kingdom tombs. There are 32 chambers in all: 17 are in the main suite, which accommodated the funerary arrangements of Mereruka himself, and the rest were used for the burials of his wife, Watetkhethor, and their son, Meryteti. Most of the rooms are decorated, and those that are not were used for stores.

▼ *Kagemni's tomb is decorated with scenes showing many types of fishing. Here, fish are being caught in baskets and nets from a papyrus boat.*

▶ *Lively scenes showing fights between boatmen in the marshes are common in later Old Kingdom tombs. This one comes from the tomb of Kagemni.*

Mereruka appears on the entrance to the tomb together with his name and titles. Just inside the vestibule he is shown hunting in the papyrus marshes, where birds, hippopotamuses and crocodiles are vividly portrayed. In the next room, Mereruka and his wife inspect a jeweller's workshop. All the processes are recorded, from the weighing out of the gold to the making up of the finished pieces. Several of the workers are dwarfs. Other scenes show sculptors, carpenters and makers of stone vases at work.

The main room, the funerary chapel, has a false door in which stands a life-sized painted statue of Mereruka, who appears to be striding forward to receive his offerings of food and drink. The roof is supported by six square pillars, and Mereruka appears on each face carrying his staffs of office. The walls are decorated with a variety of scenes in painted relief. To the right of the statue, another figure of Mereruka watches boys and girls playing boisterous games, while to the left there are some unusual scenes where animals, including hyenas, are being force-fed. Nearer to the entrance agricultural work is being carried out on Mereruka's estates, and on the opposite wall several large ships get ready to sail.

Although in poor condition, this tomb has some charming domestic scenes. The walls of Chamber 7 show Mereruka and his wife sitting together on a large couch, while she plays her harp to soothe him. Just to the left they are shown again, this time standing hand in hand while servants make their bed. On the opposite wall they receive offerings and are entertained by male and female dancers.

▼ *A detail of a beautifully carved relief from the tomb of Kagemni, showing cattle crossing a stream.*

In the area devoted to Mereruka's wife, she is shown being carried on a large sedan chair and receiving offerings in the company of her son and daughter. In another scene, she is portrayed with her three dogs and a pet monkey.

The mastaba of Kagemni

Kagemni was vizier, or chief minister, in the early part of Teti's reign. His large tomb also lies opposite Teti's pyramid, next door to that of Mereruka. Eight of its rooms are beautifully decorated in high relief. There are also five storage areas. The tomb has some unusual features. One is that the *serdab*, or statue chamber, which housed the *ka* statue, is completely sealed off from the rest of the tomb. (There is usually a 'window' from which the statue can see out.) There is also a stairway leading to the roof and two boat-shaped chambers reminiscent of the boat pits of King Unas.

Much of the decoration in Kagemni's tomb is taken up with offering processions, agricultural work and stock breeding. Some of the best scenes are of fishing, and show several different methods of catching fish, including the use of clap nets, trawl nets and a multi-hooked rod. Other scenes show birds trapped in a net and hippopotamuses speared with harpoons. Unusual themes include a piglet being fed and a mother feeding her baby on a boat. Kagemni himself is seen receiving offerings. ◆

New Kingdom Tombs at Saqqara

Saqqara continued to be used as a necropolis in the New Kingdom (c.1550–c.1069 BC). The necropolis was known in the mid-nineteenth century from the work of Carl Lepsius and from loose sculpted and inscribed blocks that had found their way into museums, but some of the most important discoveries of recent times have been made by the joint expedition of the Egypt Exploration Society and Leiden University, headed by Professor Geoffrey Martin.

The tomb of Maya

One of the tombs seen by Lepsius was that of Maya, treasurer of Tutankhamun (c.1336–c.1327 BC) and his two immediate successors in the Eighteenth Dynasty. Maya's tomb was found almost by accident when the EES–Leiden team were led astray by the inaccuracies in Lepsius' map of the necropolis. In 1986, while they were excavating in the tomb of Ramose, a contemporary of Maya and an officer in the Egyptian army, they noticed a shaft leading to the underground chambers of another tomb. Much to their delight it turned out to be the tomb of Maya, which they had been seeking and had so far failed to locate. The following year they began to explore the superstructure and soon found the tops of the mudbrick walls of the inner court and the main cult room with its adjoining chapels. These areas were cleared of sand and the reliefs revealed.

The tomb is decorated with painted, carved reliefs of the highest quality, and with texts that identify the owner and his wife, Meryt. Some that Lepsius had recorded were no longer there. These included some that he had taken to Berlin, but others seem to have been removed by local people and used to make lime. This also seems to have been the fate of several statues known to have been made for the tomb, although three, which were in perfect condition and are masterpieces of Egyptian art, had been acquired by the Leiden Museum in the 1820s and have thus survived. However, the statue group of Maya and Meryt, which Lepsius had noticed, was still there, albeit lying face downwards instead of standing upright against the wall. This revealed the fact that it had been made from a block taken from an Old Kingdom tomb. In fact, much of the material used in the building of this tomb had been 'recycled' in this way.

Some detail concerning the life of Maya was found in an inscription on the south wall of the entrance pylon, or gateway. He wrote about himself thus:

▲ *Prisoners from the city-states of Syria–Palestine are led by Egyptian soldiers into the presence of Tutankhamun.*

...the governance which came into being through me, [was] as something ordained by my god since my youth, the presence of the king having been granted to me since I was a child. I happily reached the end [of my career], enjoying countless favours of the Lord of the Two Lands...In the beginning I was good, in the end I was excellent, one who was revered in peace in the temple of Ptah. I carried out the

▲ *Nubian prisoners of war are very realistically portrayed awaiting transportation to a work camp.*

plans of the king of my time without neglecting anything he had commanded... [I made splendid] the temples, fashioning the images of the gods for whom I was responsible. I entered face to face to the August Image...

The tomb of Horemheb

Maya's great contemporary was the army commander Horemheb, who later became the last king of the Eighteenth Dynasty (c.1323–c.1295 BC) and was buried in the Valley of the Kings. In the earlier part of his career, he prepared a tomb at Saqqara. This tomb was also found by happy accident in 1975, when the joint EES–Leiden expedition was given permission by the Egyptian Antiquities Department to search for the tomb of Maya. Strangely enough, only a few days after starting work, the team came upon a column that bore the image, name and titles of Horemheb, who was already well known to scholars through inscriptions and reliefs in most of the major museums.

Horemheb's tomb is approached by an undecorated pylon, or gateway, leading to the first court. This is mainly decorated with scenes from his time in office and processions of offering bearers. One is a 'Window of Appearances' scene, which shows Horemheb being rewarded by the king for his services. On the west wall of this court there was originally a stela depicting Horemheb worshipping Re-Horakhty, the sun god, Thoth, the god of wisdom, and Maat, the goddess of truth. It was also inscribed with a long hymn in their honour. The original is in the British Museum in London, but a cast now replaces it on the site.

From inscriptions in his tomb, a great deal is known about Horemheb's career. He had a great many titles conferred on him, many by Tutankhamun, although his military career probably began under Akhenaten (c.1352–c.1336 BC). Among these titles are 'Hereditary Prince and Count', 'Deputy of the King in the Entire Land', 'Overseer of all Offices of the King', 'Generalissimo', 'King's Envoy', 'Overseer of Recruits of the King of the Two Lands', 'Chief of the Entire Land', 'Sealbearer of the King of Upper and Lower Egypt', 'Overseer of all Overseers of Scribes of the King', 'Overseer of all Works of the King in Every Place' and 'Overseer of All Divine Offices'. It was extremely important that all this was recorded so that Horemheb would be able to continue to serve the king in these capacities in the Afterlife. It was his wife Mutnodjmet, possibly the sister of Akhenaten's wife Nefertiti, who was buried here, while Horemheb enjoyed a royal burial at Thebes. ◆

▼ *Horemheb receives envoys from Libya and the Near East on behalf of Tutankhamun.*

▼ *Carved in delicate low relief, Maya adores Osiris. The hand of his wife, Meryt, also raised in adoration, is shown behind him.*

The Serapaeum

The Serapaeum was used for the burials and funerary cult of the Apis bulls, which were regarded as the living representation of the Memphite creator god Ptah during their lifetime and were identified with Osiris after death. Herodotus describes the birth and appearance of the Apis bull in Book Three of *The Histories*:

> *This Apis is the calf of a cow which is never afterwards able to have another. The Egyptian belief is that a flash of light descends upon the cow from heaven, and this causes her to receive Apis. The Apis-calf has distinctive marks: it is black, with a white diamond on its forehead, the image of an eagle on its back, the hairs of its tail double and a scarab under its tongue.*

The bulls lived for about 15 years, and when one died its body was taken to be mummified in the special embalming house at Memphis. It then went to the underground galleries of the Serapaeum for burial in a huge granite sarcophagus.

The Serapaeum was first discovered by Richard Pococke in 1738, and then rediscovered and excavated by Auguste Mariette in 1851. Mariette said that he had been led to the Serapaeum and the associated temple by a passage in the work of the Greek geographer and historian, Strabo, who described the avenue of sphinxes leading to it as being virtually buried by drifting sand, 'some having only their heads above the surface'. One day, as Mariette was walking in the desert, he came across the head of a sphinx just visible above the sand, and was immediately reminded of the passage in Strabo. He excavated the site, and found a vast complex of galleries that date from at least the early New Kingdom (c.1550 BC) and which were expanded in the Saite and Ptolemaic Periods.

▲ *The Apis bull, who represented the creator god Ptah while alive and Osiris after death, was kept in a stall outside the Temple of Ptah at Memphis.*

The catacombs

The galleries were extended during the time of Ramesses II (c.1279-c.1213 BC) and his son Khaemwese, who was High Priest of Ptah at Memphis. Another extension took place in the Saite Twenty-sixth Dynasty (664–525 BC) and they continued in use until the Ptolemaic Period (332–30 BC), when a further gallery was added. The galleries were cut into the solid rock and the burial chambers hewn out on both sides. These chambers house the enormous sarcophagi, which weigh up to 80 tons and measure about 4m (13ft) in length by 2m (6ft 6in) in width, with a height of 3.3m (11ft).

Altogether, 24 sarcophagi were discovered by Mariette, and all but one had been robbed. It seems this tomb had defeated the robbers because the lid was so firmly fixed that Mariette had to resort to dynamite to blast it off.

▼ *Large numbers of bronze statuettes of Apis have been found, indicating the popularity of the cult in the Late and Ptolemaic Periods.*

▲ *After death, the Apis bulls were mummified and placed in huge granite sarcophagi weighing up to 80 tons each.*

Inside he found the solid gold statue of a bull, now in the Louvre, Paris, and the mummy of the bull itself, which is now in the Agricultural Museum in Cairo. Elsewhere in the catacombs, Mariette thought that he had found the remains of the mummy of Khaemwese, although some scholars now think that the bones were actually those of a bull.

Mariette was obviously moved by his discoveries:

> *By some inexplicable accident one of the chambers of the Apis tombs, walled up in the thirtieth year of Ramesses II, had escaped the general plunder of the monuments, and I was so fortunate to find it untouched. Three thousand seven hundred years had had no effect in altering its primitive state. The fingermark of the Egyptian who set the last stone in the wall built to cover up the door was still visible in the mortar. Bare feet had left their traces on the sand…*

Votive tablets

What the robbers either overlooked or thought to be worthless were the 500 votive tablets dedicated in antiquity by pilgrims to the site. These, too, are now in the Louvre and, because they are dated, have proved invaluable for establishing the chronology of the Saite and Graeco-Roman Periods. Their use was demonstrated over a century ago. According to Herodotus, Cambyses (525–522 BC), one of the Persian rulers of Egypt, stabbed the Apis bull in a fit of jealous rage, after which 'Apis lay some time pining in the temple, but at last died of his wound and the priests buried him secretly'. Amelia Edwards, however, noted that one of the votive tablets stated that the bull did not die until the fourth year of the reign of Darius I (522–486 BC), the succeeding king. Herodotus may simply have used this tale to confirm his belief that Cambyses was mad, as this would have been considered such a heinous crime. ◆

▼ *Niches in the walls of the Serapaeum originally contained votive tablets set up by pilgrims to the vaults. These were taken by Mariette to the Louvre and are an invaluable source of information on chronology.*

The Valley of the Kings

From the beginning of the New Kingdom (c.1550–c.1069 BC), kings were no longer buried in pyramids in the north of Egypt but in tombs cut into the cliffs of the Valley of the Kings on the west bank of the Nile at Thebes. Throughout the New Kingdom, Thebes was an important religious and administrative centre. The kings were often in residence there, and the Valley of the Kings became the obvious location for their last resting place. During this period, the king was himself regarded as a god. The walls of royal tombs are covered with scenes depicting the pharaoh in the company of the gods on his journey through the Underworld and finally united with them in paradise. It was therefore natural that the Valley of the Kings should have been regarded as one of the most sacred sites of the Two Lands.

For the ancient Egyptians, death was not the end but the entrance to eternal life. Those who could afford to spent the greater part of their adult lives making preparations for it. Soon after his coronation, the king would instigate work on his tomb, where his transfiguration, resurrection and final union with the gods would take place. A suitable spot would be chosen, a plan drawn up, and the decoration of the walls decided.

◀ *From the beginning of the New Kingdom, royalty were buried in the remote Valley of the Kings on the west bank of the Nile.*

The Royal Burial Ground

The Valley of the Kings must have been wild and remote in ancient times. It is still possible to get the feel of the place by approaching the Valley along the mountain path from Deir el-Medina, as the craftsmen did 3,500 years ago on their way to work on the royal tombs. Even today, when motor coaches follow each other nose to tail along the approach roads and disgorge their passengers at the new rest-house, a sense of eternity pervades the site, defying the attempts of the little tourist trains plying their trade along the Valley to bring it into the twenty-first century.

The Valley of the Kings is actually two valleys. Most of the royal tombs are situated in the eastern valley, with the exception of those of Amenhotep III (c.1390–c.1352 BC) and Ay (c.1327–c.1323 BC), which are in the more remote western branch. The area seems to have been chosen because of its situation, remote from the city of Thebes and the village settlements down by the Nile, perhaps in the hope that the royal burials would be safe from the activities of the tomb robbers. If so, this proved to be a rather vain hope. When the tombs were excavated in the nineteenth and twentieth centuries, all were found to have been robbed except for that of Tutankhamun. That, too, had been entered, but was saved by the necropolis priests.

▲ *From the beginning of the New Kingdom, the kings were no longer buried in pyramids but in rock-cut tombs in the remote Valley of the Kings.*

However, there seems to have been another, perhaps more cogent reason for the location of the royal tombs. From a distance, the mountains of the west bank resemble the hieroglyph *akhet* (horizon). Since the sun set in the west, the ancient Egyptians associated it with the entry of the deceased into the Underworld. The *akhet* hieroglyph of the Theban massif, therefore, became the horizon below which the king entered the Underworld, just as the sun god, in the form of the setting sun, did each night. This belief was acted out each time a royal funeral procession wound its way over the mountain from the mortuary temple and down into the Valley of the Kings, sinking like the sun beyond the western horizon. ◆

◄ *Tutankhamun and his wife Ankhesenamun are seen here in an intimate scene from the gilded wooden statue shrine discovered in his tomb.*

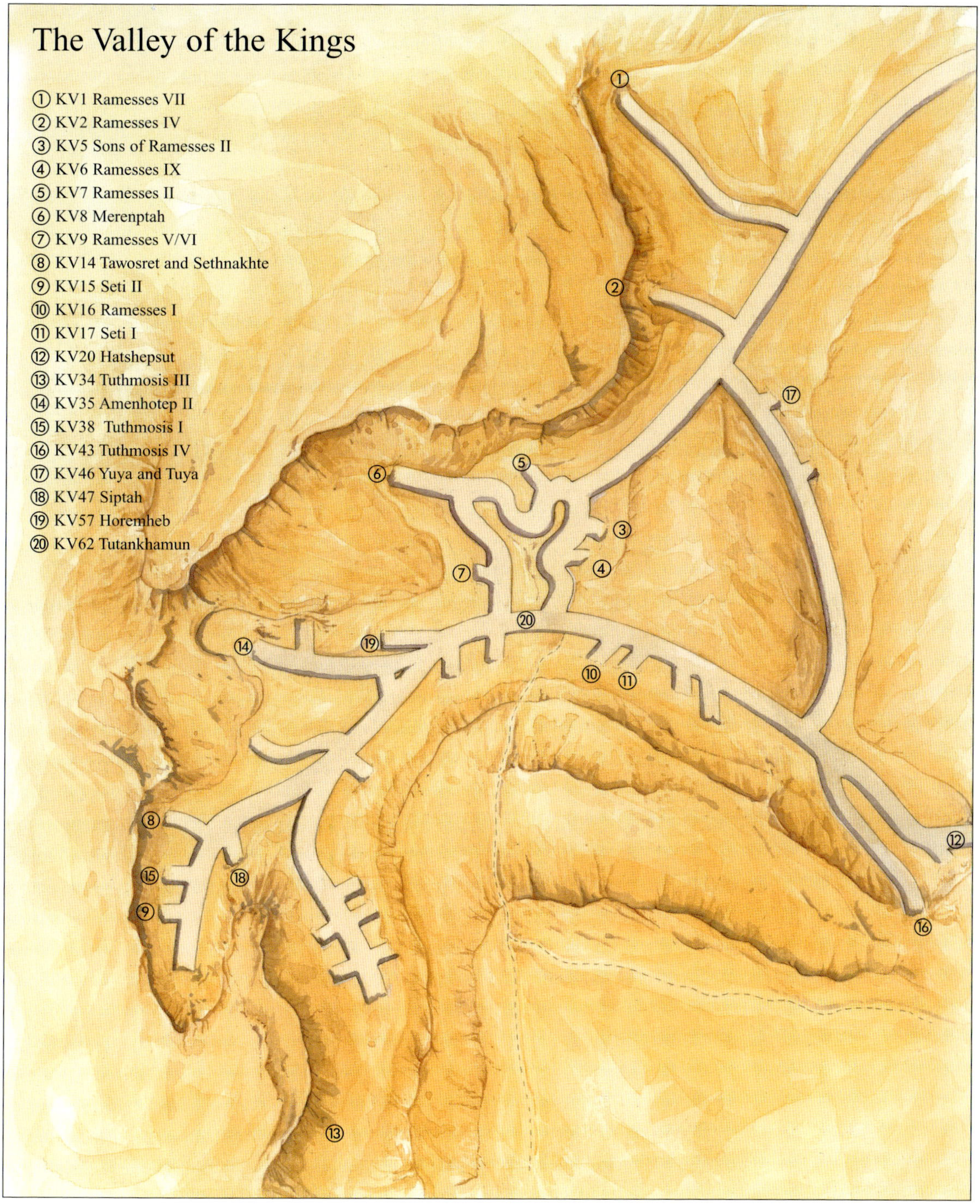
The Valley of the Kings
① KV1 Ramesses VII
② KV2 Ramesses IV
③ KV5 Sons of Ramesses II
④ KV6 Ramesses IX
⑤ KV7 Ramesses II
⑥ KV8 Merenptah
⑦ KV9 Ramesses V/VI
⑧ KV14 Tawosret and Sethnakhte
⑨ KV15 Seti II
⑩ KV16 Ramesses I
⑪ KV17 Seti I
⑫ KV20 Hatshepsut
⑬ KV34 Tuthmosis III
⑭ KV35 Amenhotep II
⑮ KV38 Tuthmosis I
⑯ KV43 Tuthmosis IV
⑰ KV46 Yuya and Tuya
⑱ KV47 Siptah
⑲ KV57 Horemheb
⑳ KV62 Tutankhamun

The Burial of the King

The tombs in the Valley of the Kings are radically different from those of the Pyramid Age. During the New Kingdom (c.1550–c.1069 BC) the royal tombs were not built of stone or mudbrick but were laboriously cut into the mountainside. Whereas the interior chambers of the pyramids had been relatively small and mainly undecorated, the passages and burial chambers of the rock-cut tombs were much larger and were brilliantly decorated with images of the king before the gods and with new texts that would ensure his safe arrival in the Afterlife and his union with both Re and Osiris.

Another distinguishing feature is that the mortuary temple, causeway and valley temple were physically separated from the tomb, although spiritually still connected. The temples now lay on the other side of the mountain, on the desert edge of the Nile Valley. The mortuary temples were grander than the earlier ones, while the valley temples were reduced to little more than landing stages, where the boats of the royal funeral procession would dock. The stone-built causeway was replaced in the later New Kingdom by a canal that led to a small harbour in front of the mortuary temple.

Concealed entrances

The location of the tomb and the basic plan, as well as the images and texts chosen for the decoration, varied from period to period. In the earlier part of the Eighteenth Dynasty (c.1550–c.1295 BC), the royal tombs were usually cut higher up the cliffs of the Valley than those of the later kings, and were often near a cleft in the rock. After the burial had taken place, these tombs were blocked with stones and plastered over. Debris deposited by rainwater pouring down the cleft would then conceal the entrance. Because the tombs of the later Eighteenth and Nineteenth Dynasties (c.1550–c.1186 BC) were built lower

▼ *A scene from the tomb of Ramesses I depicts the king flanked by the falcon-headed 'soul of Pe' and the jackal-headed 'soul of Nekhen' representing Upper and Lower Egypt respectively.*

down the valley, they have been subjected to damage by floodwater.

The latest group of tombs, those of the Twentieth Dynasty (c.1186–c.1069 BC), show no sign of any attempt having been made to seal or hide the entrance. These tombs were simply closed with wooden doors. They were often located at ground level at the ends of rocky spurs, and were protected to some extent by the water channels that ran down each side, although some have suffered from water seeping in through cracks in the rock or from storm damage.

Tomb layouts

The plans of the tombs, although basically consisting in each case of a series of descending corridors, an antechamber and a burial chamber, also varied. The typical tomb plan of the earlier Eighteenth Dynasty was perhaps derived from the general layout used in the pyramids of the Old Kingdom (c.2686–c.2181 BC), and follows a 'bent' axis: a flight of steps leads to three corridors, each known as one of the passages of the sun's nightly journey through the Underworld. This theme is later echoed in the decoration of the walls. Next comes a well or pit, which was perhaps intended to inhibit the activities of tomb robbers, or perhaps simply to drain off water and prevent damage to the tomb. Beyond the well is a small pillared hall. Then the tomb takes a right-angled turn, and a further flight of steps and a sloping ramp lead down into the burial chamber.

▲ *The sarcophagus of Tuthmosis IV is decorated with images of the funerary deities, who protect the royal body, and with magical spells, which ensure the king's safe arrival in the Afterlife.*

Over time, the plans became more complicated. More rooms and passages were added, and it could be that these echo the twists and turns seen in maps of the Underworld, which decorate the floors of the rectangular wooden coffins of officials during the Middle Kingdom (c.2055–c.1650 BC).

From the time of Horemheb (c.1323–c.1295 BC), the last king of the Eighteenth Dynasty, the bent-axis plan was abandoned in favour of the 'jogged-axis' or straight type. Although the passages leading to Horemheb's own burial chamber descend steeply, the general trend was for the inclines to become less acute in the tombs of the Nineteenth Dynasty and, later still, to slope only slightly in those of the Twentieth Dynasty. ◆

◀ *Tuthmosis IV is welcomed into the Afterlife by (from left) Hathor, Anubis and Osiris, in a scene typical of 18th Dynasty decoration of the well shaft and antechamber in royal tombs.*

The Tomb of Amenhotep II

The tomb of Amenhotep II (c.1427–c.1400 BC) is one of the most interesting in the Valley of the Kings. Not only is the decoration of the burial chamber extremely beautiful, but the story of the discovery of the tomb and its contents is also intriguing.

The tomb was discovered in March 1898 by the French archaeologist Victor Loret, then head of the Egyptian Antiquities Service. The previous month he had discovered and cleared the tomb of Tuthmosis III (c.1479–c.1425 BC) high up in the cliffs of the Valley of the Kings, and it was while he was still engaged in this work that he made his next exciting find. He had set his workmen to explore another area in the Valley, where no tomb had yet been discovered. They noticed a large area of loose pieces of cut stone piled at the foot of the cliff. When they cleared this away, they found the top of a tomb entrance. Eventually, Loret was able to enter the steeply descending corridors and cross the well by means of a ladder. He found himself in a small two-pillared hall full of smashed pieces of funerary furniture, including three broken wooden boats. On closer inspection one bore a rather grisly cargo. Loret described his find thus:

> *I went forward with my candle and, horrible sight, a body lay there upon the boat, all black and hideous, its grimacing face turning towards me and looking at me, its long brown hair in sparse bunches around its head.*

Loret had a fertile imagination, and in the heat of the moment he was convinced that he had found a human sacrifice or, at the very least, a tomb robber polished off during a fight over the division of the loot, or by the police interrupting the robbery. In fact, it turned out to be most likely that the body was that of Webensennu, the king's son, who in his lifetime had been in charge of the royal chariot horses. This is suggested by the find in the same room of a *shabti*-figure (or model servant) inscribed with his name.

▲ *The cartouche-shaped red sandstone coffin of Amenhotep II stands in a recess in his burial chamber. Isis and Nepthys guard his feet and head.*

The burial chamber

As Loret entered the burial chamber, he saw six square pillars decorated on each face with images of Amenhotep II, identified by the accompanying cartouches, in the embrace of the deities Anubis, Hathor and Osiris. In the sunken area at the end of the burial chamber there was a sarcophagus. Loret could scarcely contain his excitement as he went to examine it:

> *The sarcophagus was open, but was it empty? I did not dare to hope for the contrary as royal burials had never been found in the necropolis of the Valley, all of them having been moved in antiquity to a safe place. I reached the sarcophagus with difficulty being careful not to break anything underfoot. I could partially read the cartouches of Amenhotep II. I leant over the edge, bringing the light a little nearer. Victory! A dark coffin lay at the bottom, having at its head a bunch of flowers and at its feet a wreath of leaves...*

The journey of the sun god

The walls of Amenhotep II's burial chamber are decorated with a complete version of the Am Duat, or 'Book of What is in the Underworld'. This text describes the king's nocturnal journey with the sun god through the Underworld and his rejuvenation as the sun rises next day.

The work is divided into 12 'chapters', which represent the 12 hours of the night. Vertical borders define these, and each is divided into three horizontal registers. The middle one shows the King and the sun god sailing through the Underworld and overcoming the many hazards of the journey. Finally, the king's mummy is shown propped against the wall as his spirit soars to paradise. The ceiling is painted blue with golden stars.

Later, Loret was able to get a closer look at the coffin. To his relief the body was still inside, and was intact. 'It carried around the neck a garland of leaves and flowers, on the breast a little bouquet of mimosa, which hid the prenomen of Amenhotep II written on the sheet, the name which I later read.'

Apart from the mummy of Tutankhamun, that of Amenhotep II is the only one to have been found lying in his own tomb, albeit in what appears to have been a replacement coffin. Unlike the mummy of Tutankhamun, which still remains in his tomb, Amenhotep's was taken to the Cairo Museum later.

This was not the only surprise. Loret went on to clear the rooms that lay to the side of the burial chamber. The two left-hand ones were filled with storage jars, embalmed provisions, *shabti*-figures and other funerary goods. But on the right he found more mummies. The first chamber on the right contained a woman, a youth and a man. The second contained a further nine mummies, and turned out to be a cache of royal bodies removed from their tombs for safekeeping (see *The Fate of the Royal Mummies*). ◆

▼ *The starry ceiling of Amenhotep II's burial chamber is supported by six square pillars decorated with images of the king welcomed into the Afterlife by Anubis, Osiris and, shown below, Hathor, Mistress of the West. The figures are drawn in outline with only some decorative elements, such as Hathor's headress and the panel surround coloured in.*

The Tomb of Seti I

The tomb of Seti I (c.1294–c.1279 BC) is the longest and deepest royal tomb in the Valley of the Kings. Its decoration is also the most complete, although there are some unfinished scenes. The basic plan is of the 'jogged-axis' type, but here it is complicated by the addition of several extra chambers.

Original features

From the entrance, the three usual corridors lead to a well shaft and a pillared hall. Then a new feature appears in the form of a second chamber, designed perhaps to fool tomb robbers. The burial chamber also has additional pillared rooms and ritual niches. A further innovation is a passage leading down from the burial chamber in the main part of the tomb to another pit deeper down, near the level of the water table. This may have had some symbolic significance, linking the burial chamber to the primordial waters and uniting the concepts of creation and re-creation. In a similar way, the Osireion of Seti's temple at Abydos, built in honour of Osiris, is also sunk deep in the ground so that at times it would be surrounded by water, like the primeval mound.

▲ *Ceilings of the burial chamber are decorated with deities and stars. Below are funerary texts to aid the king on his journey to the Afterlife.*

◄ *Part of the astronomical ceiling in the burial chamber of Seti I showing the constellations.*

Tomb paintings

Another similarity with the Abydos temple is the quality of the decoration in the tomb. Most of it is embellished with beautiful figures of the king and the gods in painted raised relief.

Seti's choice of themes sets a precedent for all the later tombs in the Valley. For the first time, the first two corridors are decorated with texts from the Litany of Re, which praises the sun god under 75 different names. Scenes from the Am Duat are also present in the second corridor, whereas in earlier tombs these appeared only in the burial chamber. The well is decorated with images of the king before the gods, as in some earlier tombs. However, the pillared hall has scenes and texts from the Book of Gates and, again for the first time, an Osiris shrine marking the entrance to the lower part of the tomb. This style was followed in many later tombs. Seti's burial chamber is decorated with the earliest example of an astronomical ceiling, showing some of the constellations and a calendar with the 36 'decans', or groups of stars, into which the night sky was divided by the ancient Egyptians.

► *One of the masterpieces of ancient Egyptian art, this shows the goddess Hathor welcoming Seti I into the Afterlife.*

The mummy of Seti I

Giovanni Belzoni discovered the tomb in 1817. His most significant find at the site was the beautiful translucent calcite sarcophagus, also decorated with scenes and texts from the Book of Gates, now in Sir John Soane's Museum in London.

When Belzoni found the sarcophagus, it was empty. However, the mummy was found many years later by Emile Brugsch in the cache at Deir el-Bahri (see *The Fate of the Royal Mummies*). The body was quite well preserved, although the head had been detached from the body during one of several rewrappings by the high priests of Amun during the Twenty-first Dynasty (c.1069–c.945 BC). Inscriptions on the coffin, also restored by the priests, record Seti's removal from his own tomb in Year 10 of the reign of Siamun (c.978–c.959 BC), his reburial three days later in the tomb of Queen Inhapi, and his subsequent transfer to the cache in the reign of Sheshonq I (c.945–c.924 BC). There it remained until 1881 when it was removed with the other royal mummies to Cairo, where it is now on display in the Egyptian Museum. The tomb itself has been closed for restoration since 1991. ◆

The Book of Gates

This collection of magical spells, which decorated the pillared hall of Seti's tomb and his sarcophagus, was intended to enable the king to overcome the demons and powers of the Underworld. The spells provided him with the passwords he needed to get through the gates guarded by snakes and deities as he proceeded on his journey.

The Discovery of Tutankhamun's Tomb

Between 1903 and 1912, an American businessman, Theodore M. Davis, financed a series of excavations in the Valley of the Kings. One of those working for him was the experienced Egyptologist, Howard Carter (1874–1939). Together they made several important discoveries, including the (albeit robbed) tombs of Tuthmosis IV (c.1400–c.1390 BC) and Hatshepsut (c.1473–c.1458 BC), and the intact tomb of Yuya and Tuya, who may have been the great-grandparents of Tutankhamun (c.1336–c.1327 BC).

Davis also found various clues suggesting that the tomb of Tutankhamun might be in the vicinity. One was a robbers' cache containing items of Tutankhamun's funerary furniture. Another was a pit, discovered in 1907, containing seal impressions of Tutankhamun, linen bags filled with natron and other embalming materials, and the remains of his funerary feast. Finally, under a nearby boulder, Davis found a blue faience cup bearing the name of Tutankhamun. However, after several years of fruitless searching, Davis left the Valley convinced there were no more royal tombs to be found.

Howard Carter and his British patron, the fifth Earl of Carnarvon, gained the concession to dig and were ready to start work in 1914, but had to abandon the idea when World War I broke out. They started again in 1917, but had no more luck than Davis. After five unsuccessful seasons Lord Carnarvon was ready to give up, but Carter pleaded for just one more chance. Digging was resumed on 1 November 1921, the first job being to record and remove some ancient workmen's huts apparently used during the preparation of the tomb of Ramesses VI (c.1143–c.1136 BC). As they took down the old building, the top of a flight of steps was revealed.

▲ *Discovered in the antechamber of the tomb, this magnificent box shows Tutankhamun charging into battle against his enemies.*

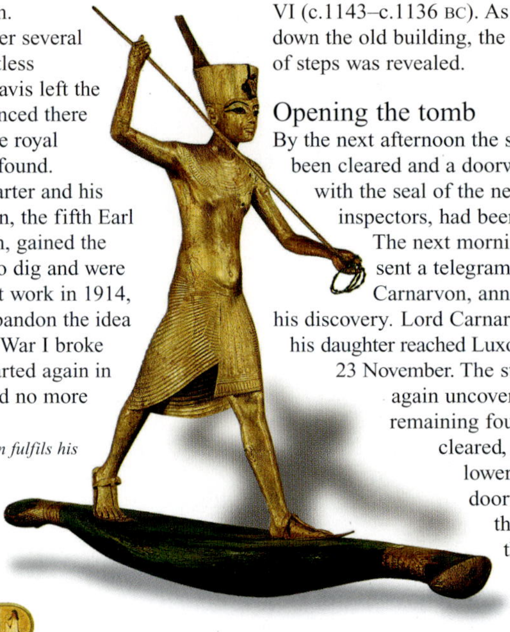

► *Tutankhamun fulfils his traditional role as Horus harpooning the evil Seth.*

Opening the tomb

By the next afternoon the stairway had been cleared and a doorway, fastened with the seal of the necropolis inspectors, had been found. The next morning Carter sent a telegram to Lord Carnarvon, announcing his discovery. Lord Carnarvon and his daughter reached Luxor on 23 November. The staircase was again uncovered and the remaining four steps were cleared, revealing the lower part of the doorway. Much to the delight of the excavators, this was stamped with the seals of Tutankhamun, proving that his long-sought tomb was found. The king's seals were on part of the original blocking of the tomb, while those of the necropolis inspectors referred to a resealing, which implied that the tomb might still contain some funerary equipment.

After entering and clearing the sloping tunnel behind the door, they came to another sealed doorway. Carter described the mounting excitement:

> *Slowly, desperately slowly, it seemed to us as we watched, the remains of the passage debris that encumbered the lower part of the doorway were removed, until at last, the whole door was clear before us. The decisive moment had come. With trembling hands I made a tiny breach in the upper left-hand corner. Darkness and blank space as far as I could reach, showing that whatever lay beyond was empty and not filled like the passage we had just cleared.*

▲ *Tutankhamun and his wife, Ankehsenamun, depicted on the back of a gilded wooden throne, which is decorated with glass paste and semi-precious stones.*

Candle tests were then applied as a precaution against foul gasses, and then, widening the hole a little, I inserted a candle and peered in, Lord Carnarvon, Lady Evelyn and Callender standing anxiously nearby to hear the verdict. At first I could see nothing, the hot air escaping from the chamber causing the candle to flicker, but as my eyes grew accustomed to the gloom, details of the room within emerged slowly from the mist, strange statues and animals and gold, everywhere the glint of gold. For the moment, an eternity it must have seemed to those standing by, I was struck dumb with amazement, and when Lord Carnarvon, unable to stand the suspense any longer, inquired anxiously, 'Can you see anything?' it was all I could do to get out the words, 'Yes. Wonderful things!' Then making the hole a little wider we inserted an electric torch.

Finds from the tomb

A painted wooden head of Tutankhamun emerging from a lotus flower was found among the rubble blocking the passage to the tomb. It shows Tutankhamun appearing as the sun god did at the time of creation from a lotus floating on the waters of the primordial ocean. It combines the idea of creation with the king's re-creation.

Three beds were found in the antechamber. One is in the form of a lion, representing the goddess Mehet, associated with Hathor, Sekhmet and Isis. Mehet is the deity responsible for the Nile flood. Another takes the form of a composite deity, part crocodile, part lion and part hippopotamus. She is Ammut, Devourer of the Dead. She stands near the scales in the Judgement Hall and devours anyone who fails to pass the test. The cow goddess depicted on the third bed is Mehet Weret or 'Great Flood'. She represents the primordial cow who rose from Nun, the primordial ocean, and bore the sun god Re, to the sky. She will raise Tutankhamun, too, so that he can join the sun god.

Tutankhamun's mummy was found in a gold coffin. It had been placed inside two more coffins, one inside the other. The innermost was made of gold and the second was of gilded wood covered with precious stones. These are on display in the Cairo Museum, along with the other treasures from the tomb. The body of Tutankhamun, now placed in the outermost coffin, still lies in his tomb in the Valley of the Kings.

◀ *The solid gold mask of Tuthankhamun was placed over the face of the mummy.*

Directly over the mummy's face was a solid gold mask. Tutankhamun is shown wearing the royal headdress, in which the blue stripes are made of glass paste in imitation of lapis lazuli. His eyes are inlaid with quartz and obsidian to make them sparkle and to emphasize that he is a living king. He wears a curved false beard to show that he has become Osiris.

The mummy of Tutankhamun was decorated with 150 pieces of jewellery, all of which are full of symbolism. The winged scarab is the sun god Khepri. He holds the lotus and papyrus, symbols of Upper and Lower Egypt, and *shen*-rings, symbols of eternity. At either side is the *uraeus*, the cobra that spits at Egypt's enemies, wearing a solar disc. Above is the solar boat carrying the *udjat*, or Eye of Horus (the moon). It is flanked by two more *uraei*, wearing moon discs. At the very top is the disc of the moon inside the lunar crescent. On the disc, Tutankhamun is crowned by Thoth and Re-Horakhty. The whole piece symbolizes the king's ascent to heaven and his rule throughout eternity. ◆

Texts from the Tomb of Ramesses VI

The tomb of Ramesses VI (c.1143–c.1136 BC) is a good example of the 'straight-axis' tomb plan. The floors of the first corridors slope only gently before descending to the lower passages and burial chamber. Inscriptions in the tomb state that it was prepared initially for Ramesses V (c.1147–c.1143 BC). There is no sign of Ramesses VI having usurped the tomb, so it is possible that both kings were buried here. Neither of their mummies was discovered in the tomb: both were found in the cache at Deir el-Bahri.

The choice of texts used for the decoration of this tomb is rather different from earlier ones, with a greater emphasis on the sun god Re and on astronomical texts. Unlike most tombs from the time of Seti I (c.1294–1279 BC), however, the Litany of Re does not appear, and is replaced by excerpts from the Book of Gates and the Book of Caverns. Apart from the text inscribed on the sarcophagus of Seti I, the most complete version of the Book of Gates appears in this tomb. The Book of Caverns is particularly concerned with rewards and punishments in the Afterlife, and especially with the annihilation of Re's enemies.

▲ *The magnificent tomb of Ramesses VI is one of the largest and most complete in the Valley of the Kings. The walls are covered with collections of spells to effect the king's resurrection.*

The first three corridors have astronomical ceilings and there are excerpts from the Books of the Heavens in the well room and first pillared hall. These books are a collection of texts that describe the sun's journey across the sky. They include the Book of the Day, the Book of the Night and the Book of the Divine Cow. Further extracts from these books decorate the ceilings of the lower passages and antechamber.

The walls of the corridors are painted with parts of the Am Duat or 'Book of What is in the Underworld', while the antechamber is decorated with images of the gods and sections of the Book of

◀ *The scenes from the Book of the Earth show the rebirth of the sun, which symbolizes the resurrection of the King.*

▶ *Boats in the retinue of the sun god accompany him though the Underworld. Above are avenging deities armed with knives to overcome Re's enemies.*

the Dead. This material is usually found inscribed on papyrus rolls in the tombs of commoners from the beginning of the New Kingdom (c.1550 BC). It is a collection of spells derived from the Middle Kingdom Coffin Texts and ultimately from the Old Kingdom Pyramid Texts, which were used exclusively in royal burials.

The magnificent ceiling of the burial chamber of Ramesses VI combines images of the sun god in the solar barque with the passage of the sun through the body of the sky goddess Nut.

The content of the texts

The funerary texts that decorate the walls of the royal tombs in the Valley of the Kings describe the voyage of the sun god, with whom the king is identified, through the Underworld. They enable the king to enter the Afterlife unmolested by the enemies of Re.

The earliest is the Am Duat. It tells of the sun god's journey through the 12 divisions of the Underworld, which are equated with the 12 hours of the night. Complete copies are found in the tombs of Tuthmosis III (c.1479–c.1425 BC) and Amenhotep II (c.1427–c.1400 BC). Portions decorate the walls of the lower passages of the tomb of Ramesses VI.

Nearer to the entrance are extracts from the Book of Gates, which also describes the sun god's journey through the hours of the night. The name of the book refers to the 12 gates through which the sun god passed and that divide one hour from another. One section of the Book of Gates depicts the Judgement Hall of Osiris where the hearts of the dead are weighed in the balance. The good are justified and wrongdoers condemned.

The Book of Caverns appears in the first three passages, the well room and the first pillared hall along with scenes from the Book of Gates. Osiris figures prominently in these texts where the sun god Re comes for him and punishes his enemies, condemning them to non-existence. In the pillared hall, Osiris wears a solar disc, which identifies him with Re so that they appear to be two aspects of one god. Elsewhere in the tomb, the sky goddess Nut carries the sun god on her hands. He is seen both as the disc of the sun and in human form with a ram's head. Four crocodiles on Nut's left are Re's enemies. On her right is the sun god in different forms.

The Books of the Heavens and a double image of the goddess Nut span the burial chamber. Here, the sun is shown as a disc being swallowed by the sky goddess and passing through her body to be reborn the next morning, and also as a ram-headed god sailing in the solar boat across the sky during the day. The king aspires to accompany the sun god through the Underworld, then to rise and sail with him upon the celestial waters throughout eternity. ◆

▼ *Depicted on the ceiling of the tomb, Nut swallows the sun in the evening whereupon it travels through her body during the night and is reborn at sunrise.*

The Fate of the Royal Mummies

In 1881, in the absence of Gaston Maspero, the then head of the Egyptian Antiquities Service, his assistant Emile Brugsch arrived in Luxor to investigate rumours concerning the discovery of a hitherto unknown tomb. For the previous ten years or so, objects such as funerary papyri, *shabtis* and canopic jars had been mysteriously appearing on the antiquities market from an undisclosed source. Brugsch's arrival in Luxor had, in fact, been prompted by the confession of the head of the Rassul family from Gurna on the west bank, who claimed that members of his family had been responsible for removing these artefacts from a tomb in the cliffs at Deir el-Bahri.

The cache of Deir el-Bahri

How the tomb came to be discovered in the first place is not known, although several romantic stories are told about it. Some members of the Rassul family acted as guides for visiting travellers, and it may be that their intimate knowledge of the area led them to it. The family had certainly been suspected of untoward dealings in antiques, and two of them had been interrogated and tortured by the local mudir, or governor, Daud Pasha. In spite of some brutal treatment they refused to give anything away and it was only in the face of great family opposition that the headman, Muhammad Ahmed Abd el-Rassul, decided to go to the authorities.

Although Brugsch realized that there would be more than one royal mummy in the tomb, he was astounded by the number that met his eyes when he entered the first chamber. In a further chamber, he found even more mummies. In his haste to clear the tomb before local treasure hunters could lay their hands on the contents, however, no proper records were kept.

An Egyptian film made in 1969, *The Night of the Counting of Years*, is based on the story of the discovery of the cache. In one of its most moving scenes, the procession of donkeys and mules bearing their precious burdens reaches the Nile and the royal mummies are put on a boat. Women from the villages come down to the river to wail in mourning for the long-dead kings as they sail downstream to Cairo.

On his return to Egypt, Maspero paid a visit to Luxor to see the tomb for himself, and was soon able to recognize two different groups of mummies. Those from the further chamber were carefully wrapped and placed in distinctive coffins, with their funerary goods around them. These were the mummies of a family of high priests of Amun descended from Herihor, who ruled the Theban area from the end of the Twentieth Dynasty (c.1069 BC). The mummies of the other group proved to be of kings, queens and officials previously buried elsewhere. They included Ahmose, Amenhotep I, Tuthmosis II, Tuthmosis III, Ramesses I, Seti I, Ramesses II and Ramesses III.

On examining the notes written on the mummy wrappings, Maspero discovered that many of the royal mummies had had a somewhat eventful career. The notes revealed that some of the mummies had been restored and rewrapped several times, and moved from one hiding place to another over a period of about 70 years. During this time several mummies had been taken to the tomb of Seti I and restored there before being moved again. The tomb of Queen Inhapi is mentioned many times in these notes, and at one time it was believed that the tomb in which the cache was found was hers. Recent research has shown that her tomb was yet another halfway house, and that the final hiding place was in fact the family tomb of Pinedjem II, High Priest of Amun. The family burials in the end chamber were orderly and intact, whereas the royal mummies seemed to have been pushed into the first chamber rather unceremoniously, Queen Inhapi's among them, suggesting haste.

Royal mummies in the tomb of Amenhotep II

A second cache of nine royal mummies was found in a side chamber in the burial suite of Amenhotep II (c.1427–c.1400 BC) (see *The Tomb of Amenhotep II*). At first, Victor Loret, who discovered the tomb in 1898, thought they must be members of Amenhotep's family. He changed his mind when he examined them more closely:

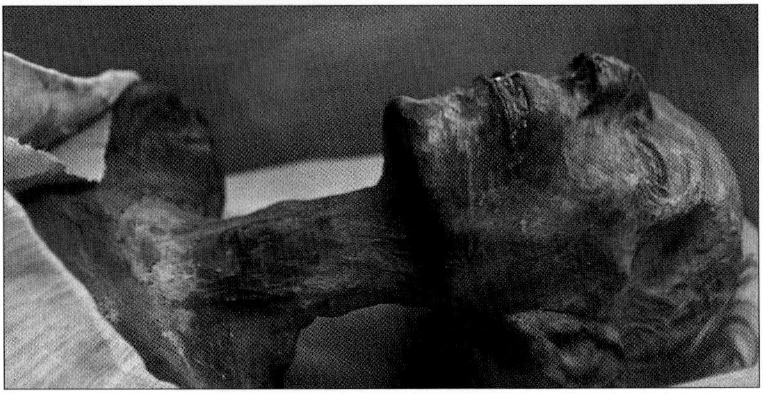

► *The mummy of Ramesses II demonstrates the skill of the embalmer and the degree to which the technique of mummification had been perfected.*

▲ *The lid of the coffin of Queen Maatkare, which was found in Deir el-Bahri. The daughter of the High Priest, she was installed as 'God's Wife of Amun', an important religious and political post.*

▲ *This wooden coffin, which housed the mummy of Ramesses II, found in the Deir el-Bahri cache, was possibly originally intended for Ramesses I.*

The coffins and mummies were a uniform grey colour. I leaned over the nearest coffin and blew on it so as to read the name. The grey tint was a layer of dust which flew away and allowed me to read the nomen and prenomen of Ramesses IV. Was I in a cache of royal coffins? I blew away the dust from a second coffin and a cartouche revealed itself, illegible for an instant, painted in matte black on a shiny black ground. I went over to the other coffins – everywhere cartouches.

He realized that he had indeed discovered a cache of royal mummies. The names of the kings proved to be every bit as illustrious as those in the tomb at Deir el-Bahri: Tuthmosis IV, Amenhotep III, Merenptah, Seti II, Siptah, Ramesses IV, Ramesses V, Ramesses VI and an unnamed female, perhaps Tawosret, wife of Seti II.

It is now thought that these mummies, and the various pieces of funerary equipment that were found with them, had been collected from other tombs and caches at the same time as the body of Amenhotep II himself had been rewrapped, since all the bodies bore a similar type of docket. This must have been some time after Year 12 of the Twenty-first Dynasty king Smendes (c.1069–c.1043 BC) because a note on the mummy wrappings of Amenhotep III states that the mummy had been restored that year in his own tomb.

Some of the mummies were in the 'wrong' coffins. Amenhotep III was in a coffin inscribed with the name of Ramesses III, while the lid had originally belonged to Seti II. Merenptah lay in the lower part of a coffin inscribed for Sethnakhte, while the female mummy was lying on the upturned lid.

Is there a third cache?

Not all the bodies of the kings of the New Kingdom have yet been found. The missing mummies include those of Tuthmosis I, Akhenaten, Horemheb, Ay and Hatshepsut. An inscription found by Sir Alan Gardiner at the entrance to the tomb of Horemheb may refer to the restoration of further royal mummies. This is supported by the fact that Theodore Davis found many dismembered skeletons, as well as funeral garlands of a type dating from the Third Intermediate Period (c.1069–c.747 BC), when he was working in the Valley of the Kings in 1908. ◆

The Craftsmen's Village at Deir el-Medina

The craftsmen who lived in the village known to the ancient Egyptians as the Place of Truth, now Deir el-Medina, were highly skilled sculptors and artists who worked on the royal tombs in the Valley of the Kings. Their village is one of the most interesting sites of ancient Egypt for two reasons: not only have very few other occupation sites been discovered but large amounts of written material, often inscribed on limestone chippings called 'ostraca', were found during excavation.

The village was laid out around a main street with side alleys leading from it. It originally consisted of 70 houses, and about 40 more were added during the Nineteenth Dynasty (c.1295–c.1186 BC). The houses were built of rough field stones and mudbrick, and consisted of four or five rooms: an entrance, a main room, two smaller rooms behind that and a kitchen with a cellar. A staircase led to the roof. The windows were high up on the walls, allowing light to enter while excluding the full glare of the sun. A feature of the main room was a mudbrick platform approached by a short flight of steps, which may have functioned either as a shrine or as a birthing bed. The village was about 3km (2 miles) away from the Nile Valley, apparently for security reasons. Bricks stamped with the name of Tuthmosis I (c.1504–c.1492 BC) suggest that the village was founded in his reign.

▲ *The interior decoration of the tomb of Pashedu, who was one of the highly skilled craftsmen who lived in the village.*

The craftsmen left the village at the close of the Twentieth Dynasty (c.1069 BC), as from that time the kings were buried in the Delta.

Organization of the workers

The workmen were divided into two gangs, called, like a ship's crew, the gang of the right and the gang of the left. Most lived permanently in the village, although the numbers varied according to the amount of work to be done. New workers were recruited from among the sons of the craftsmen. There were two foremen, one for each gang, who were appointed in the first place by the vizier on behalf of the king. Thereafter the position remained in the family unless something untoward happened, when a new appointment would be made. As well as being in charge of work on the tomb, the two foremen controlled the village and its activities.

Next in importance came the scribe of the tomb. His chief duty was to keep a register of work done and to note absentees. He also recorded the

◀ *The view from the surrounding hills of the village of Deir el-Medina, which housed Egypt's best artisans from the 18th to 20th Dynasties.*

▼ *Anherkhau and his wife depicted in his tomb at Deir el-Medina, where he was foreman.*

distribution of tools, materials and wages. The deputy foremen, usually the sons or near relatives of the foremen, sometimes undertook the supervision and distribution of supplies, while the guardians of the tomb controlled the royal storehouses where the tools and materials were kept. They were aided by doorkeepers, who worked in shifts to guard the entrances to the royal tombs, and the *medjay*, who were stationed outside the village. It was their job to preserve law and order and prevent unauthorized entry to the tombs in the Valley of the Kings.

The villagers were supported by the 'servants of the tomb', who lived outside the village but were sent by the central administration to supply the inhabitants with firewood, water, fish and vegetables. Some were potters and washermen. There were also slaves who ground flour for the villagers. All payment was in kind, and these goods formed part of the wages of the craftsmen. The workers also received monthly rations of emmer wheat and barley, as well as irregular payments of dates, cakes and beer. On special occasions, there were bonus payments of blocks of salt, natron (a salt used in the mummification process) and meat.

Generally, the rations seem to have been more than adequate, and there was usually something over that could be used for barter or even bribes. However, the payment was not always prompt and delays could mean hardship. When their wages did not materialize in Year 29 of Ramesses III (c.1184–c.1153 BC), the workers went on strike and demonstrated in front of the Ramesseum. The 'police' seem to have been sympathetic and arranged for them to be supplied with food to tide them over until they were paid. There were more strikes later in the year and in subsequent reigns.

The working week consisted of eight days, with rest days on the ninth and tenth, so the workers had six days off a month, although they seem to have taken longer 'weekends' quite frequently. They also had holidays on religious festivals. During the week, they may have camped-out near the Valley of the Kings. Otherwise they lived with their wives and children in the village.

Village life

On their days off, the villagers might set to work on their own and each other's tombs. The workmen who excavated and decorated the royal tombs were the best craftsmen of ancient Egypt. They included stonemasons, draughtsmen, sculptors, artists and carpenters. They trained their sons and passed on their skills to them. Consequently, their own tombs are some of the most beautiful on the West Bank. Those who had other skills did a brisk trade in coffins and funeral equipment.

Otherwise, their leisure time seems to have been spent reading, committing adultery or taking each other to court.

Local justice

The village had its own court, composed of the foremen and deputies, the scribe and some of the craftsmen. It is not known when it met, but it was a source of great entertainment. The village court had the authority to deal with all civil action and minor criminal matters. (Major crime was dealt with by the vizier's court at Thebes.) Most of the cases concerned non-payment for goods or services rendered, and were fairly trivial matters. The villagers conducted their own cases, so there were no fees to be paid to lawyers and arguments often dragged on for years. The craftsman Menna, for example, sued the chief of police over non-payment for a pot of fat and certain articles of clothing. The case lasted for 11 years. ◆

The register

The record of attendance kept by the scribe of the tomb shows that many of the craftsmen had days off due to illness. Scorpion stings and eye diseases are often mentioned. Some had time off for family reasons, often to do with funeral arrangements. Other much less reputable reasons were also noted: one man had had a row with his wife and another had been out drinking with his friend Khons and was in no fit state to work the next morning.

Tomb Robbery

The fact that most of the royal mummies were removed from their tombs in the Valley of the Kings and hidden elsewhere suggests that they had been in danger of violation by tomb robbers. There is also clear evidence of a break-in at the tomb of Tutankhamun.

Tomb robbery papyri

A great deal is known about the activities of tomb robbers, and the measures taken to deal with them, from a collection of papyri dating from the end of the Twentieth Dynasty (c.1069 BC). At this time there seems to have been a general breakdown in law and order, and the robbing of tombs was a symptom of these troubled times. The papyri contain the names of the tombs that had been robbed, the confessions of the robbers, and the results of the official inspections of the tombs undertaken in answer to allegations of theft. The discovery of the true extent of the tomb robbing was complicated by the rivalry of the two mayors of Thebes. Puwero, the mayor of West Thebes, was also chief of the necropolis police and particularly resented the implication that he had not been doing his job properly. Eventually, his resistance was broken down and the investigations began. A commission of high officials was set up to look into the reports of robberies in the necropolis and to inspect the tombs for damage.

Apart from the document now known as Papyrus Mayer B, which records the robbery of the tomb of Ramesses VI (c.1143–c.1136 BC), the papyri all refer to the plundering of tombs outside the Valley of the Kings. The royal tombs in question were situated at the nearby necropolis of Dra Abu el-Naga, where the kings of the Seventeenth Dynasty (c.1650–c.1550 BC) were buried. The commission extracted some extraordinary confessions from the accused, such as this one recorded in Papyrus Leopold-Amherst from the stonemason Amenpanufer in Year 16 of the reign of Ramesses IX (c.1126–c.1108 BC):

We went in accordance with our regular habit, and we found the pyramid of King Sobekemsef, this being not at all like the pyramids and tombs of the nobles which we habitually went to rob. We took our copper tools and we broke into the pyramid of this king through its innermost part. We found its underground chambers and we took lighted candles in our hands and we went down. Then we broke through the rubble that we found at the mouth of the recess, and found this god lying at the back of his burial place. And we found the burial place of Queen Nubkhaas, his queen, situated beside him, it being

▼ *The robbery of the tomb of Ramasses VI was documented in antiquity in Papyrus Mayer B. The entrance to his tomb can be seen below centre.*

▲ *A papyrus records the confession of robbers who entered the tombs of kings and commoners alike and stripped the mummies of their jewellery.*

protected and guarded by plaster and covered with rubble. This we also broke through, and found her there, resting in similar fashion. We opened their sarcophagi and their coffins in which they were, and found the noble mummy of this king equipped with a falchion; a large number of amulets and jewels of gold were upon his neck, and his headpiece of gold was upon him. The noble mummy of this king was completely bedecked with gold, and his coffins were adorned with gold and silver, inside and out and inlaid with all sorts of precious stones. We collected the gold we found on the mummy of this god, together with that on his amulets and the jewels which were upon his neck, and that on the coffin in which he was resting, and we found the queen in exactly the same state. We collected all that we found upon her likewise and set fire to their coffins. We took their furniture which we found with them consisting of articles of gold, silver and bronze, and divided it among ourselves. And we made into eight parts the gold which we found on these two gods coming from their mummies, amulets, jewels and their coffins, and 20 deben of gold fell to each of the eight of us, making 160 deben [14.5kg (32lb)], the fragments of furniture not being included. Then we crossed over to Thebes.

The confessions, from both men and women, were often extracted under torture. A certain Mutemwia, whose husband the measurer, Pawero, had been involved in robbing the tombs, was questioned concerning the whereabouts of the stolen goods, and denied all knowledge of them, but under torture 'with the birch and the screw' confessed that her husband had hidden his loot in the house of his brother-in-law.

The punishments meted out to the robbers are known from the oath that they were required to swear when they gave testimony: 'As Amun lives and as the ruler lives, if I be found to have had anything to do with any one of the thieves may I be mutilated in nose and ears and be placed on the stake.'

The tombs of priests and other commoners were not immune from violation by the robbers, who dragged the bodies out of their coffins to strip off their jewellery, and left them out in the desert. The commission also discovered that some of the workmen from Deir el-Medina were involved. Eight of the craftsmen were arrested, including the two deputy foremen. The stolen goods were found in their homes, and various members of other settlements on the west bank were named as receivers of stolen goods. A further investigation led to a complete purge of the village hierarchy, and new foremen and deputies were appointed. ◆

Queens, Princes and Officials

The pharaohs were not the only people to be buried in the Valley of the Kings. Other members of the royal family were buried there too. Tuthmosis III (c.1479–c.1425 BC) prepared a splendid tomb close to his own for his chief wife, Hatshepsut-Merytre, while Isisnofret, the wife of Merenptah (c.1213–c.1203 BC) was buried with him in his tomb in the Valley of the Kings. Royal sons buried in the Valley include the sons of Ramesses II (c.1279–c.1213 BC). Commoners of high rank could also be buried there, the most famous being Yuya and Tuya, the parents of Queen Tiye, and the chancellor Bay, who took charge in the unsettled period at the end of the Nineteenth Dynasty (c.1295–c.1186 BC).

Amenhotep III (c.1390–c.1352 BC) prepared places for two of his wives, Tiye and Sitamun, within his own tomb in the Western Valley. In the Ramesside Period, however, royal wives were usually buried in the nearby necropolis of the Valley of the Queens, although some of the royal children had been buried there since early in the Eighteenth Dynasty (c.1550–c.1295 BC). The most appealing of these tombs is that of Nefertari, Great Royal Wife of Ramesses II, and of the sons of Ramesses III (c.1184–c.1153 BC), Khaemwese and Amun-hir-khopshef. Most of the officials of the Ramesside Period are buried in beautifully decorated tombs in or near the modern village of Gurna.

◀ *This wall painting from the tomb of Nefertari in the Valley of the Queens shows the queen, identified in the cartouche, wearing the vulture headdress, which links her with Isis and Hathor.*

The Tomb of Nefertari

Nefertari was the favourite wife of Ramesses II (c.1279–c.1213 BC), the first of eight that he married during his long reign of 67 years. His other wives included two of his own daughters, his sister and two Hittite princesses. Nefertari seems to have belonged to a high-ranking family, but was not herself royal because she is never given the title of 'King's Daughter'. It is thought that she probably came from Thebes because she is always called 'Beloved of Mut', and Mut was an important goddess in the Theban area. Although she was given the title 'Mother of the King' and had several sons, they all seem to have died before their father. Merenptah (c.1213–c.1203 BC), the next king, was the son of Istnofret, Ramesses II's other chief queen.

Nefertari seems to have played a prominent ceremonial role on state and religious occasions. In the first year of Ramesses' reign she officiated at the investiture ceremony of Nebwenenef as Chief Prophet of Amun at Abydos. She also appears in Year 3 on the New Pylon, a ceremonial gateway, which Ramesses II built at the Luxor Temple, and in diminutive form among the royal statues with which he embellished the forecourt. Ramesses honoured her most of all at Abu Simbel in Nubia. He built two temples there, one for Re-Horakhty and the other state deities, including himself, and the other dedicated to the goddess Hathor and Nefertari.

▲ *Nefertari, the favourite wife of Ramesses II, is introduced to various deities in scenes from the vestibule of her tomb in the Valley of the Queens.*

Tomb paintings

Nefertari's tomb in the Valley of the Queens is the most beautiful of all the royal tombs. It is an absolute feast for the eyes, the bright colours used for the figures being enhanced by the white background and the dark blue of the ceiling. It was discovered in 1904 by Ernesto Schiaparelli, and was closed to the public shortly afterwards because the painted plaster was in such a fragile condition. It has recently been conserved by the Getty Conservation Institute and is now open to the public again for the first time in many years. However, the numbers of visitors to the tomb are strictly controlled, so that this treasure may be preserved for future generations.

Much of the decoration concerns the Heliopolitan creation myth, according to which Atum, the sun god, emerged from the primordial ocean to create Shu,

▶ *Wearing a diaphanous gown of fine linen and the vulture headdress, Nefertari plays* senet, *a board game similar to chess or draughts.*

the god of air, and Tefnut, the goddess of moisture, from his bodily fluid, which contained both male and female elements necessary for creation. Their union produced Geb, the earth god, and Nut, the sky goddess, who also married and produced Isis, Osiris, Seth and Nephthys. Linked to this is the myth of Osiris, in which he, as the highly esteemed king of Egypt, was murdered by his jealous brother Seth. After he had been restored to life he entered the Underworld to become the judge of the dead while his son, Horus, avenged his death to become the next king of Egypt. The upper section of the west wall of Chamber C shows Isis and Nephthys as kites at the foot and head of the dead Osiris. In the myth they beat the air with their wings to enable Osiris to breathe again and so be restored to life. Nefertari hopes to be restored in the same way.

Here, as in several later tombs in the Valley of the Kings, the sun god is assimilated with Osiris. On the west wall of Chamber G, Isis and Nephthys are depicted on each side of a god who takes the form of a mummy, as Osiris did, and is represented with the ram's head of the sun god. The text on the left reads, 'It is Osiris who sets as Re,' and on the right, 'It is Re who sets as Osiris.' Osiris and the sun god Re appear in various forms throughout the tomb, and Nefertari associates herself with both.

Elsewhere in the tomb, deities lead Nefertari into the presence of the gods. In Recess E, Hathor, the cow goddess, who was often depicted as the mother of the king, conducts Nefertari on her way through the Afterlife. She is also shown welcoming her on one of the pillars of Chamber K. ◆

▼ *The elegantly dressed Nefertari offers two* nu-pots *to Hathor; from the southern wall alongside the steps leading to the burial chamber.*

Conservation

The Getty Conservation Institute has cleaned the walls of the salt crystals that had formed over the centuries, and stabilized the plaster. It is adamant that the tomb has not been subjected to 'restoration', by which it means the addition of missing colour. No new paint was added – what can be seen is the original work. Where the original decoration has disappeared, blank patches of plaster, made from local materials, now cover the gaps.

The Tomb of Ay

Ay (c.1327–c.1323 BC) was an army commander who became king of Egypt after the death of Tutankhamun (c.1336–c.1327 BC). He may have been related to the royal family by marriage: there is evidence to suggest that he was the brother of Queen Tiye, wife of Amenhotep III (c.1390–c.1352 BC), while it is also sometimes mooted that he may have been the father of Nefertiti, the wife of Akhenaten (c.1352–c.1336 BC). He is shown on the walls of the burial chamber in the tomb of Tutankhamun, officiating at the young king's funeral, and thus staking his claim to the throne.

Whatever the truth about his relationship to the royal family, it is clear that Ay was a high official at the court of Akhenaten, where he held the title 'Superintendent of the Royal Horses'. Later, he rose to power as vizier and royal chancellor. Not unnaturally, he began work on a large and splendid tomb at Akhenaten's capital Akhetaten (Tell el-Amarna). This was left unfinished but is famous for its inscription of an extended version of the Hymn to the Aten, in praise of the sun disc, which was worshipped exclusively during Akhenaten's reign.

The Western Valley tomb

The tomb that was prepared for Ay as king lies in the wild and rugged Western Valley. Ay had a comparatively short reign of four or five years, and it appears that the tomb may previously have been intended for somebody else. Candidates include Tutankhamun or even Tuthmosis, the elder brother of Akhenaten who died before his father, Amenhotep III, who is also buried in the Western Valley. In any event, the decoration of the tomb is very similar in many ways to that of Tutankhamun's. It was discovered by Giovanni Belzoni in 1816 but was not fully excavated until 1972, when it was cleared by Otto Schaden.

The architecture of Ay's tomb is akin to that of the royal tomb at Tell el-Amarna, having a straight axis but with the burial chamber slightly to one side. A new feature is the slots cut into the walls of the first corridor, to accommodate a beam that was used to lower the sarcophagus into the tomb.

◀ *Ay was considered to be the last king of the Amarna period and consequently his tomb was badly mutilated. All images of Ay have been hacked away.*

▲ *The images of the gods and goddesses were left untouched. Here, the goddess Nut offers Ay the sign for water so he will not die of thirst on his journey to the Afterlife.*

Tomb decoration

The artistic style and the motifs of the tomb decoration so resemble those of Tutankhamun that it would seem that the same artist was responsible for both. In both tombs there are scenes showing the deceased king and his *ka*, or vital essence, being welcomed into the Underworld by Osiris and Hathor. Another scene shows 12 baboons, who represent the 12 hours of the night, while a further scene shows the boat of the sun god in his scarab beetle form, preceded by five deities.

A unique feature for this period is the scene of fishing and fowling in the marshes, in which Ay is shown hunting with his wife. This is a theme more usually found in the tombs of nobles,

although a similar scene appears in the much earlier mortuary temple of the Fifth Dynasty king Sahure (c.2487–c.2475 BC) at Abusir. There may even be another parallel with the tomb of Tutankhamun: although hunting is not part of the painted decoration there, it is perhaps reflected in the hunting scene on the small gilded shrine found among the grave goods. It is also echoed in two statuettes of Tutankhamun on a papyrus skiff, with a harpoon poised to thrust into his prey in the water.

A small room leading from the burial chamber is the canopic chamber, where the internal organs of the king would have been preserved. The entrance has been decorated with two pairs of figures who are sometimes identified with the Four Sons of Horus, the guardian deities of the viscera.

The images of Ay himself, although not those of his *ka*, were destroyed in antiquity, presumably because of his association with the heretical regime of Akhenaten. This probably happened

▲ *Ay performing the Opening of the Mouth ceremony in the tomb of Tutankhamun. Usually this is done by the son of the deceased. As Tutankhamun had no son, this scene indicates Ay as his successor.*

in the early Ramesseside Period, when steps were taken to obliterate the memory of Akhenaten from history. Ay's sarcophagus, also similar to that of Tutankhamun, was found in fragments, although it has now been restored. His mummy has never been found. ◆

The Tomb of Yuya and Tuya

Yuya and Tuya were the parents of Queen Tiye, the wife of Amenhotep III (c.1390–c.1352 BC). Because of their close connection with the king, they were allowed the honour of having a tomb in the Valley of the Kings, even though they themselves were not royal. They were very important people in their own right, however. Yuya was in charge of the king's chariotry and Tuya was 'Chief Lady of the Harem'. Yuya was also called 'God's Father', a reference to his relationship to the king.

The tomb of Yuya and Tuya was discovered in 1905 by James Quibell, and was found to contain the most spectacular collection of funerary goods that had yet come to light in the Valley of the Kings. This came as a complete surprise to the excavators, as it was obvious that the tomb had been broken into in antiquity. It had been resealed with a stone wall covered in mud plaster and stamped with the necropolis seal, and there was evidence to suggest that this had happened more than once.

The robbers had gone through the tomb feverishly searching for valuables. The mummy bandages had been ripped apart and the lids of boxes torn off in their haste. However, as was the case with the tomb of Tutankhamun, it appears that the robbers were disturbed just in time. A chariot yoke, a gilded wooden staff and a heart scarab had been abandoned in the corridor as they fled. Nevertheless, the robbers seem to have made away with all the smaller valuables. There was no jewellery in the tomb apart from that found on the mummies themselves. Other costly items such as oils and perfumes were also missing. The many treasures that remained are now in the Cairo Museum.

▲ *Tuya's jewel casket of gilded wood inlaid with elements made of ebony, pink-stained ivory and blue faience. The upper part is decorated with cartouches of Amenhotep III, her son-in-law.*

Quibell was working in the Valley under the auspices of Theodore Davis, who cleared the tomb in great haste while Quibell was away. Unfortunately, as time was at a premium, he did not take the trouble to record the finds properly, particularly their position in the tomb. It is not known whether Yuya or Tuya died first, and such information might have helped to answer that unsolved question.

▼ *The goddess Isis protects the mummy just as she protected Osiris in mythology.*

The mummies

The mummified bodies of Yuya and Tuya were found within the tomb. Although they had been partly unwrapped, they were very well preserved and are two of the finest examples known. Quibell wrote that Yuya's features were perfectly preserved, so that 'The powerful and dignified face of the old man strikes one as something human, as a face one would recognize in a portrait.' Yuya's mummy was placed in a nest of four coffins, one rectangular (but bottomless) and three anthropoid. Of these, the enormous outer one was covered in bitumen and bound with inscribed bands of gilt; the next had similar bands over a background of silver leaf; and the innermost was gilded all over and inlaid with glass hieroglyphs in imitation of jewels.

The faces of both mummies had been covered with masks. Royal mummy masks were usually made of beaten gold, but those of Yuya and Tuya were of gilded cartonnage (linen stiffened with plaster). Yuya's mask had been broken into fragments. That of Tuya was broken in two, but has now been restored. The

▲ *Gilded wooden side panels from a chair with images of the protector deities, Bes and Taweret.*

mask had been covered with a piece of very fine linen. When this was removed it revealed a beautiful portrait of Tuya. She has a charming smile and her eyes have been inlaid with blue glass and quartz, to which red touches have been added in order to give her a lifelike appearance. Her eyebrows have been inlaid and her eyes outlined with glass in imitation of lapis lazuli. She wears a long striated wig that is kept in place with a floral headband. Covering the upper part of her body is a huge collar composed of rows of leaf and petal shapes inlaid into a background of coloured glass, which imitates bands of lapis lazuli, turquoise and carnelian.

The four canopic jars of Tuya are particularly interesting. Each contains one of her internal organs wrapped up in a little mummiform parcel, and each miniature 'mummy' has been given its own small mummy mask.

The grave goods

The tomb was packed with all sorts of funerary goods, including several pieces of furniture, one of which was a beautiful jewel casket that had belonged to Tuya. It is made of gilded wood in the form of a little shrine and is inlaid with ebony, rose-tinted ivory and blue faience. The box is decorated with the cartouches of Amenhotep III, her son-in-law, and her daughter, Queen Tiye. A frieze running around the lower part of the casket is composed of the hieroglyphs for 'life' and 'prosperity', thus wishing the owner a blissful Afterlife.

Three beautiful chairs were also found in the tomb, one of which had belonged to Sitamun, the daughter of Amenhotep III and granddaughter of Tuya and Yuya. It is made of dark red wood and decorated with side panels covered in gold leaf. These show figures of the god Bes, protector of families and helper of women in childbirth, wielding knives and beating on drums to drive away evil spirits. The panel on the chairback shows Sitamun being presented with golden collars by Syrian princesses. There were also three beds whose headboards were decorated with images of Bes.

Yuya took his chariot with him to the tomb. It is made of gilded wood and is in remarkably good condition, being almost complete. It is decorated with spirals and rosettes in gilded plaster. Measures were also taken to ensure that Yuya and Tuya did not go hungry. Some of the boxes found in the tomb contained dried meat, geese and ducks to sustain them throughout eternity. ◆

▼ *The funerary mask of Yuya, father of Queen Tiye. His mummy is one of the best preserved ever found.*

▼ *The gilded plaster mask that once covered the head of the mummy of Tuya, mother of Queen Tiye.*

A royal seat

The Empress Eugénie, wife of Napoleon III of France, visited the tomb while Quibell was finishing its clearance. When he apologized for the fact that all the (modern) chairs had been packed away and there was nowhere to sit, the eye of the empress lit upon the chair of Sitamun and she decided that it would suit her very well. The archaeologists held their breaths as she sat down, but fortunately for both empress and chair it stood up to the strain.

The Tomb of the Sons of Ramesses II

Ramesses II (c.1279–c.1213 BC) had an extremely long reign of 67 years, and must have been over 90 years old when he died. He had several wives and concubines, and fathered a great number of children, many of whom he outlived. His successor, Merenptah (c.1213–c.1203 BC), whose own tomb is in the Valley of the Kings, was his thirteenth son, his older brothers having died before their father. Although they never inherited the throne, these brothers seem to have been given the privilege of burial in the Valley of the Kings (apart from Khaemwese, who may be buried near Memphis, where he was High Priest of Ptah). Other sons of Ramesses II may well have been buried there too.

Only 70m (77yd) from the tomb of Tutankhamun and almost opposite the tomb of Ramesses II, Dr Kent Weeks, an American archaeologist and director of the Theban Mapping Project, discovered an enormous enigmatic structure hailed by many as the most exciting archaeological discovery of modern times. It is thought to be the burial place of the sons of Ramesses II.

▲ *The names of many of Ramesses II's sons are known from inscriptions elsewhere, such as this relief from the Temple of Luxor. They include Meryatum (his sixteenth son) and Seti (shown here), who both died in their twenties as did several of their brothers.*

New discoveries

The existence of this tomb, known as KV5, has long been known, and it was partially explored as long ago as 1825 by the English Egyptologist James Burton. Howard Carter also examined the area around the tomb in 1902, but was not able to penetrate beyond the entrance. Kent Weeks and his team from the American University in Cairo relocated the tomb in 1985–6. As the first two chambers were cleared of debris it became obvious that a great deal of damage had been caused by the tourist coaches using the road above the tomb, and by a broken sewer. After the first season of work on the tomb, Weeks realized that the structure he had found was unique. He went so far as to claim that it was the tomb of at least two, and perhaps as many as eleven of Ramesses' sons. However, since then, many more chambers have been discovered. In May 1995 Kent Weeks made an exciting announcement:

Last February, excavating through the flood-borne debris that fills the tomb, my staff and I found a passageway leading past 20 chambers to a statue of the god Osiris. Two transverse corridors, each with another 20 chambers, extend beyond that. At the end of the corridors there are stairs and sloping corridors apparently leading to even more rooms on a lower level. The tomb could be the largest ever found in Egypt.

There are likely to be about 150 chambers and corridors in the complex, of which fewer than seven per cent have yet been cleared. In fact, Weeks has no intention of trying to complete the excavation himself. He wants to leave parts of the building to be explored by future generations, using new excavation techniques as they are developed. In the meantime, he and his team will concentrate on making the structure safe and recording, conserving and studying the wall decorations, inscriptions and artefacts that have already been discovered.

Tomb layout and decoration

The plan of the complex as a whole is unique, although there are some individual features that are similar to other tombs in the Valley. Some Eighteenth Dynasty tombs have a narrow entrance that leads directly into a chamber, rather than the more usual passage, while some of the chambers have vaulted ceilings like tombs of the Nineteenth Dynasty. In this tomb there are two chambers, which give way to a large pillared hall. Leading from the hall is a huge T-shaped area lined with many alcoves or small chambers. In the centre of the bar of the T is a statue of Osiris and, at each end, a stairway descends to a lower level where two passages slope, in the opposite direction to the upper level, towards the tomb of Ramesses II.

That this unique structure was intended as the burial place of Ramesses II's sons is indicated in the decoration of the first two chambers, where there are painted reliefs showing the king leading his sons into the presence of the funerary deities. These were originally similar to the scenes in the tomb of Amun-hir-khopshef (see *Tombs of the Sons of Ramesses III*), in the Valley of the Queens, but so much damage had been done by floodwater and sewage that the painted plaster had come adrift and lay in fragments among the debris. However, it has been possible, with the help of a skilled conservator, to preserve the south-western corner of the tomb. There, the name, titles and figure of another Amun-hir-khopshef, Ramesses II's eldest son, came to light. He is shown with his father, who introduces him to the goddess Hathor and the funerary deity Sokar.

Another son was 'discovered' on the south wall. He was named Ramesses after his father, who is shown leading him into the presence of Nefertem, the god of the lotus blossom. The name of a further son, Seti, was found on a fragment of a canopic jar in the

▲ *This rock-cut figure of Osiris, King and Judge of the Dead, was found in his shrine in the T-shaped tomb of the sons of Ramesses II.*

second chamber, and a fourth, Meryatum, on an ostracon found by Howard Carter. The names of a total of 52 sons of Ramesses II are known from other sources. It will be interesting to see how many eventually come to light in this tomb. The images of several more sons appear in the painted decoration of the tomb, but the inscriptions accompanying them have unfortunately been destroyed. Several skulls and a whole skeleton have been found, but there is, as yet, no clear evidence for their identification.

Another puzzle is that the entrances to the side chambers of the T-shaped section are too small to accommodate sarcophagi, so what was the purpose of these chambers? It is known that the main doorways of the tomb were widened at some time, as the alterations have cut into figures and texts already carved on the walls. This would have made it possible to bring sarcophagi inside the tomb itself. Perhaps they were then placed in parts as yet unexplored. ◆

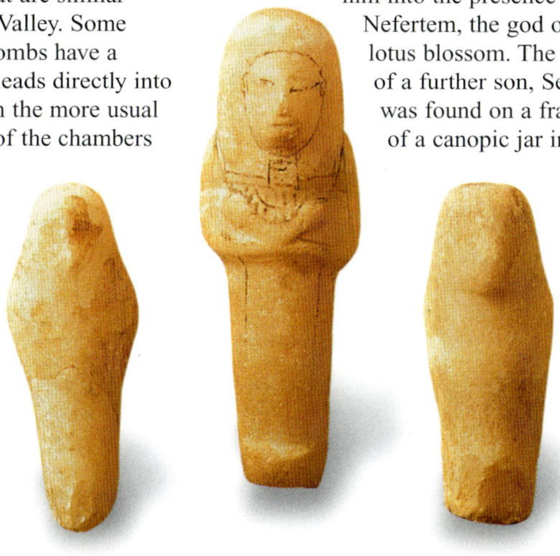

◀ *Inscribed* shabtis *were found among the funerary equipment.*

The Tombs of the Sons of Ramesses III

Of the five tombs prepared by Ramesses III (c.1184–c.1153 BC) for his sons, three were found by Ernesto Schiaparelli in the early 1900s. The most beautiful are those of Amun-hir-khopshef and Khaemwese, both of which were commissioned in Year 28, towards the end of the reign of Ramesses III. The tombs are decorated in painted carved relief.

Little is known of these two princes and nothing at all about the circumstances of their deaths, although the sequence in which the tombs were prepared can be worked out from developments in their decoration. Even the names of the princes are something of a mystery as they do not match up with a list of 13 sons in Ramesses III's mortuary temple at Medinet Habu. It is sometimes suggested that the princes suffered from some kind of congenital disease that led to an early death, and for this reason Ramesses made provision for them during his later years. Or were they perhaps carried off by some kind of epidemic? The ages of the princes are also uncertain. They are represented with the distinctive hairstyle known as the 'sidelock of youth', which suggests that they were very young, although it may simply indicate that they were sons. However, the fact that their father accompanies them into the Underworld and introduces them to the funerary deities seems to confirm their youth.

An unusual feature of these tombs is that it is the king, and not a god or goddess, who introduces his sons to the various deities. The main theme of the decoration in each tomb is that of the prince undertaking a ritual journey. Eventually, he finds himself alone in the Afterlife, which is symbolized by the tomb. By using the correct 'passwords' from the Book of the Dead he is able to proceed through the gates of the Underworld and join Osiris in paradise. Finally, he is reborn and becomes one of the 'imperishable stars'. ◆

◀ *Amun-hir-khopshef is depicted wearing the 'side-lock of youth' to show he is the son of Ramesses III; from his tomb in the Valley of the Queens.*

▲ *Ramesses III is received by Hathor, in her roles as Mistress of the West and as one of the main funerary goddesses.*

▼ *Ramesses III introduces his son Amun-hir-khopshef to the deities of the Underworld. The age at which he died is uncertain.*

The Tomb of Rekhmire

The vizier was the king's chief minister and the most important official in the land, and Rekhmire held this position under Tuthmosis III (c.1479–c.1425 BC) and Amenhotep II (c.1427–c.1400 BC). His tomb is one of the most attractive and informative of all the tombs of the New Kingdom (c.1550–c.1069 BC). It is located in the modern village of Gurna near the Valley of the Kings, the burial place of the rulers Rekhmire served during his lifetime.

Plan of the tomb

The tomb is cut into the rock and follows the usual plan of officials' tombs of this period. The doorway leads into an oblong chamber, with a long corridor leading from the centre of the back wall, opposite the entrance. The texts that form part of the wall decoration in this tomb are particularly interesting. They describe Rekhmire's installation as vizier and the wide-ranging nature of his work. As well as holding a number of priestly offices, he was also in charge of every government department and was also chief judge. His installation as vizier would have been the climax of an illustrious career.

One intriguing fact about this tomb is that there is no burial shaft, so it would seem that Rekhmire was eventually buried elsewhere. It is possible, as he was such an important person, that he was buried in the Valley of the Kings, although this is not known for certain.

The role of the vizier

The procedure followed in the court of the vizier is described in some of the texts inscribed on the tomb walls. The vizier sat on a chair wearing a cape and his chain of office, with an animal skin behind his back and another at his feet. He had his staff close by and 40 leather rods set out in front of him.

▼ *As vizier, part of Rekhmire's duties was to supervise activities in the state workshops. These carpenters are working on a fine chest.*

▲ *A scene from a jeweller's workshop shows gold being melted in the fire, possibly to be worked into a fine gold collar.*

Other senior officials and his scribes also sat with him in the court.

The vizier's other duties included reporting daily to the king about all the comings and goings in and out of the palace. He had to inform the king about the income and expenditure of the royal estates, the government finances and the border fortifications. He appointed officials and saw that the local governors were aware of the king's commands, and that they sent in their reports as required. The army was mobilized and the system of compulsory state labour (the corvée) was organized by the vizier, who also conducted land surveys, fixed local boundaries and fitted out ships. He was responsible for law and order, as well as reporting on the height of the Nile and the rise of Sirius, the dog star, the appearance of which heralded the Egyptian New Year.

The tomb's painted decoration includes many scenes depicting all sorts of agricultural operations and craft work. Farmworkers, sculptors, brickmakers and jewellers mingle on the tomb walls. The oblong hall has registers of gifts and shows tribute bearers from Nubia, Syria and Crete. They are all recognizable from the faithful depiction of the physical characteristics of the various ethnic groups and by the objects and animals they bring to the vizier. Other scenes show emissaries from the different regions of Egypt coming to present their taxes, while elsewhere in the tomb there are depictions of funerary and ritual scenes. ◆

▼ *Dancers and musicians entertaining guests at a funerary feast is a common theme depicted on the tomb walls of this period.*

The ship of state

During his long career, Rekhmire was close to the king. He served him well and helped him steer the ship of state, while as a judge he felt his conduct was impeccable:

I was the heart of the Lord, the ears and eyes of my Sovereign.
I was his skipper, and knew not slumber by night or by day.
Whether I stood or sat, my heart was set upon prow rope and stern rope, and the sounding pole was never idle in my hands...
I judged rich and poor alike.
I rescued the weak from the strong... I defended the widow.
I established the son and heir on the seat of his father... I judged great matters... I caused both parties to go away satisfied. I did not pervert the course of justice for reward. I was not deaf to the empty-handed. I did not accept anyone's bribe...

The Tombs of Eighteenth Dynasty Officials

The ancient Egyptians believed that the Afterlife would be very much like life on earth. They painted scenes on the walls of their tomb chapels recreating their current life to perpetuate it for eternity, and these scenes tell us a great deal about everyday life in ancient Egypt.

The tomb of Nakht

Although it is very tiny, the tomb of Nakht is one of the most charming in the Theban necropolis. Nakht was 'Chief of the Granaries', 'Keeper of the King's Vineyards' and 'Royal Astronomer' under Tuthmosis IV (c.1400–c.1390 BC). Both Nakht and his wife, Tawi, who was a chantress of Amun, were buried here.

On the left of the entrance to Nakht's tomb there are several scenes depicting life on an estate. Two farmworkers are planting seeds, while others plough with wooden ox-drawn ploughs. Farther along are scenes of harvesting, where the corn is cut with sickles and flax is pulled out by the roots. In the next section, the workers use wooden blades to scoop up the threshed grain to separate the grain from the chaff. Meanwhile, Nakht sits in his booth and oversees the work.

Opposite the agricultural scenes is a depiction of a funerary banquet. This is one of the most famous scenes in ancient Egyptian art. The guests are seated on elegant chairs and have cones of scented ointment on their heads. Young girls present bead collars to the ladies, who are dressed in glamorous diaphanous dresses and wear complicated wigs and enormous gold earrings. Musicians playing the harp, lute and some kind of flute entertain the guests. Under a chair, a cat is hastily devouring a stolen piece of fish.

To the right of the door, Nakht and his wife sit in front of an offering table. A similar scene is almost opposite. On the left side of the chapel is a false door, which supplies details of Nakht's life and implies that he hopes to enjoy this same rank and status in the next life. At the bottom, Hathor, goddess of the west, welcomes him into the Afterlife.

Just beyond there is a scene in which Nakht is fishing and fowling in the marshes with his wife and son. Nakht is shown twice, almost as a mirror image of himself, on a skiff in the papyrus marshes. To the left he is aiming a throwing-stick at a flock of birds, while to the right he is about to harpoon a fish.

Further along are two scenes showing the preparation of food and drink. In the top register, the workers are picking large bunches of grapes in the vineyard. Others are trampling the grapes, while another man catches the grape juice in jars and sets them up on a shelf to let the wine ferment. Below, a net is spread to catch birds. When the net is full, a cord is pulled tight and the birds are trapped. The sequel shows the birds being plucked and hung in preparation for cooking.

▲ *Part of a scene from the tomb of Nakht shows him catching wildfowl in the marshes. The other 'half' is a mirror image, which shows him fishing.*

▼ *These musicians, playing a harp, a lute and a double flute, entertain guests at a funeral banquet; from the tomb of Nakht.*

▲ *Sennefer, overseer of the gardens of the god Amun, and his wife in his Theban tomb, which is decorated with a trailing vine.*

The tomb of Menna

Menna was 'Scribe of the Fields of the Lords of the Two Lands of Upper and Lower Egypt' during the reign of Tuthmosis IV. Not surprisingly, a whole wall of his tomb chapel is devoted to agricultural scenes. The top register shows officials measuring the land and assessing the crop. Other sections depict the harvesters reaping in the fields. The grain is carried off to the granary in huge baskets. Scribes, perched on great heaps of grain, record the amounts harvested under the eagle eye of Menna himself, whose status is emphasized by the rather smart horse and chariot waiting to convey him to Thebes. Although such scenes were common to many tomb chapels of this period, the artist has included many details that make it an individual work. A mother is nursing her baby under a tree and two girls are quarrelling. Another vignette shows a girl taking a thorn out of her friend's foot.

The usual scene of hunting in the marshes is also included in this tomb. Like Nakht, Menna is shown in a papyrus boat with his wife and children. He is catching two fish and is about to hurl his throwing-stick in the direction of a papyrus thicket, which is full of nesting birds and small animals.

A different scene shows Menna on a voyage to Abydos, possibly recording a pilgrimage he made to the tomb of Osiris. However, below this are scenes showing the rites performed on the mummy before burial, so it is equally likely that the upper scene is connected with Menna's funeral. In the opposite corner at the far end of the chapel is a painting showing the ritual of the Weighing of the Heart.

The tomb of Sennefer

Sennefer was Mayor of Thebes and 'Overseer of the Granaries and Gardens of Amun' during the reign of Amenhotep II (c.1427–c.1400 BC). Judging from the decoration of his tomb chapel, he may also have been the king's chief vintner. One of the most delightful aspects of the tomb is the vine that is painted growing up the chapel wall and trailing across the ceiling. The surface of the ceiling is rough and the artist has made ingenious use of any raised areas by transforming them into bunches of grapes.

The wall paintings are equally charming. In the antechamber, Sennefer is brought offerings by his daughter and priests. Other scenes show Sennefer and his wife, Meryt, worshipping Osiris. In the main chamber, they are depicted entering the Underworld, sitting side by side on elegantly carved chairs, and accepting offerings. In one of the most attractive scenes, Sennefer is seated in front of an offering table holding to his nose a lotus flower (the symbol of re-creation). His wife sits at his feet, affectionately clasping his leg. ◆

► *Sennefer sails upstream from Abydos having completed his pilgrimage to the shrine of Osiris.*

The Tomb of Ramose

Ramose was governor of Thebes and vizier under Amenhotep III (c.1390–c.1352 BC) and Akhenaten (c.1352–c.1336 BC). His tomb is very grand and consists of a spacious hypostyle hall, internal hall and chapel. It is an extremely interesting tomb because both the traditional and the Amarna styles of carved relief are present. The tomb is unfinished, perhaps because the owner moved with Akhenaten's court to the new capital called Akhetaten (Tell el-Amarna), where he may have contemplated preparing another tomb.

The ceiling is supported by 32 rather squat papyrus-bud columns, which have been heavily restored. In the inner hall there are eight more. The inner hall is undecorated and the shrine in the chapel is empty. Two shafts lead down to burial chambers on a lower level, but no bodies were found there.

▲ *Women mourners raise their arms in grief at the passing of Ramose, vizier during the reigns of Amenhotep III and Akhenaten.*

▼ *Servants carry furniture into the tomb. A bed and headrest, four chests and a chair ensure Ramose's comfort in the Afterlife.*

Wall decorations

The carved relief in the traditional style is of the highest quality. Ramose apparently had no children, and his brother Amenhotep built the tomb for him. Amenhotep was an official in charge of the royal building works at Memphis, which may explain the high standard of the decoration. Just inside the hypostyle hall, on each side of the entrance, are funerary scenes. To the left of the door Ramose appears as vizier with his wife and relatives; priests make offerings, Ramose is purified, incense is burnt and three girls shake their *sistra*, the sacred instruments of Hathor, goddess of the west, who was believed to welcome the deceased into the Underworld. On the right is the funerary banquet. In this scene, the wigs, clothing and jewellery worn by the guests are the height of elegance. Ramose, his family and other guests are dressed in high-quality fine linen, which is very delicately portrayed, but the wigs

are particularly fascinating. A great variety are shown, composed of many different combinations of tiny plaits (braids) and curls, all obviously very expensive and the latest thing in fashionable Thebes.

On the opposite wall, to the right of the doorway to the internal hall, there is a typical Amarna-style scene known as the 'Window of Appearances'. Akhenaten and Nefertiti, the king and queen, stand at the palace window and reward Ramose for his services by decorating him with gold collars. Courtiers and fan bearers, who bow low in adoration of the king, accompany him. The royal pair stand below the Aten, the sun disc worshipped to the exclusion of all other deities by Akhenaten, and the rays of the Aten shine down on them. Several end in tiny hands that hold the ankh, the symbol of life, before the noses of the king and queen.

The next scene, further to the right on the west wall, is unfinished. The figures are merely sketched in, ready for carving, and vestiges of a grid remain on the wall. Ramose is shown wearing his gold collars and receiving representatives of foreign countries. Nubians, Libyans and 'Asiatics' are easily recognizable.

The funeral procession

This tomb also has scenes that were not carved but painted straight on to the walls of the tomb. These show Ramose's funeral procession progressing towards his tomb. On the lower register, food and drink, a bed and headrest, a chair, four chests with curved lids and personal possessions such as his sandals and scribal equipment, are carried to the tomb to ensure that his needs in the Afterlife will be catered for. The upper register shows three sleds, one carrying the coffin in a gilded wooden shrine, another carrying a canopic chest containing the internal organs of the deceased, and a third transporting a huge black object called the *tekenu*, the symbol of the 'sun in the form of a bull'. The procession is greeted by wailing women mourning the passing of Ramose. ◆

▲▼ *One wall of the hypostyle hall is decorated with finely carved reliefs depicting the funerary feast. Ramose, his family and guests are shown wearing fine linen clothing, which is beautifully portrayed. Their intricate wigs, their jewellery and facial features are also realized in exquisite detail. The reliefs are a fascinating insight into high Theban fashion of the 14th century* BC.

The Tomb of Sennedjem

The tomb of Sennedjem at Deir el-Medina is a small masterpiece. Every surface is brightly painted and the tomb is in perfect condition. The high quality of the tomb decoration is, perhaps, not surprising, as Deir el-Medina is the site of the 'Place of Truth', the village of the master craftsmen who worked on the royal tombs in the Valley of the Kings. Sennedjem was called 'Servant in the Place of Truth', a title that does not have any particular significance, so it is not known whether he had the special status in the village that the high quality of the work might suggest. It is not even known whether he was a draughtsman, sculptor or artist, so it is impossible to know if he did the work himself. As with most ancient Egyptian art, the work is anonymous.

▲ *Sennedjem and his wife plough the Field of Iaru where, according to the Book of the Dead, the deceased harvests crops of grain and dates.*

▼ *Their eldest son, wearing his priest's leopard skin, pours libations before his parents. Below the chair are younger members of the family.*

Dispersal of the finds

Most unusually, Sennedjem's tomb was found intact. It was discovered in 1886 by a local man who reported his find to the Director of the Egyptian Antiquities Service, Gaston Maspero, who was luckily in Luxor at the time. The tomb was found to contain the burials not only of Sennedjem, but also of his wife, Iineferti, their son, Khons, their daughter-in-law, Tameket, and a woman named Isis whose precise relationship to the others is not known. Coffins and funerary goods belonging to other members of the family were also found in the tomb, which had been used for at least two generations as a family vault.

Although the contents of the tomb were first taken to Cairo, they are now tragically dispersed. The mummy of Sennedjem remains in Cairo but the other members of the family were scattered, even their mummies and coffins ending up in different American and European museums. The mummies of Sennedjem's wife and son are in Cambridge, Massachusetts, while their coffins are in the Metropolitan Museum of Art in New York. His daughter-in-law is in Berlin, and the funerary goods are divided between the museums of Cairo, Moscow, Copenhagen and Paris. These include the sled that transported the coffins to the tomb, a bed, a table and two stools, loaves of bread, eggs, fruit, floral garlands and two pairs of papyrus sandals.

The tomb decoration

Virtually the entire end wall of the burial chamber is given over to a delightful scene showing Sennedjem and his wife working in the Field of Iaru, the ancient Egyptian version of the Elysian Fields. During their lifetime they would never have done agricultural work themselves; the purpose of the scene is to show them in paradise, a land of plenty, where they are enjoying the reaping of a bumper harvest.

At the opposite end of the tomb, Sennedjem and Iineferti worship Osiris, Re-Horakhty and other funerary deities. The upper registers of the side walls show Anubis, the god of mummification and the necropolis, preparing the mummy. This is matched on the opposite side by a scene showing Sennedjem as a mummy, having become Osiris. Isis, the wife of Osiris, and their sister, Nephthys, are depicted as kites. As in the Osiris myth, they beat the air with their wings to create the breath that would restore Osiris to life; here, they are doing the same for Sennedjem. Below this scene Sennedjem's family are shown at the funerary feast. Their eldest son performs the funeral rites in front of them, and the other children are shown as tiny figures below the chairs of their parents and the guests.

The vaulted ceiling has scenes from the Book of Gates, a collection of spells containing the passwords that enable the deceased to get through the gates of the Underworld. One charming vignette shows the goddess of the sycamore tree offering the couple refreshing drinks so they will not die of thirst in the Afterlife. Presiding over the entire event is Osiris, who is shown in a large scene immediately opposite the entrance. This ensures that Sennedjem will come back to life again, just as Osiris did in mythology. ◆

▲ *Osiris, god of the Underworld and King and Judge of the Dead, presides over the tomb of Sennedjem. The Eye of Horus and fetishes of Anubis ensure his resurrection.*

▶ *The elegantly dressed Sennedjem and his wife worship the gods of the Underworld who will protect them on their journey to paradise.*

Part Two: Religious Centres

From earliest times, Egypt has been the home of religious thought. There is evidence for belief in an Afterlife in the contents of graves from the Predynastic Period, when the gods seem to have been worshipped in portable shrines. The first permanent structures are those at the late Predynastic centre of Hierakonpolis and the Early Dynastic shrine at Elephantine by the First Cataract. Many ancient sites were built over by succeeding generations, so that a whole series of temples may occupy the same site. Very occasionally, as at Elephantine, excavations have revealed a succession of temples dating from the Early Dynastic to the Ptolemaic Periods (c.3100–30 BC).

In the Christian era, the ancient temples became churches. The Temple of Isis at Philae was converted to use as a church dedicated to the Virgin Mary. Many Jews settled at Aswan, where there is evidence of a Jewish temple. Egypt was largely converted to Islam in the seventh century AD, although the Christian Church continued to flourish in some areas.

Temples to the Gods

The ancient Egyptians built two main types of temple: mortuary temples, where rituals connected with the deceased kings were performed, and cult temples erected in honour of particular gods. Some, like the temple of the Nineteenth Dynasty king Seti I (c.1294–c.1279 BC) at Abydos, served both purposes.

The temples dedicated to the gods were not places of worship in the modern sense, since the Egyptian people did not congregate inside them to take part in religious ritual. Usually, only the priests seem to have been allowed into the temple to carry out the rites, which were centred on the statue of the deity housed in a shrine in the innermost part of the sanctuary. Only the outermost parts of the temple were accessible by other people, and only then at the time of the great festivals.

Most of the temples seen by visitors to Egypt today were built during the New Kingdom (c.1550–c.1069 BC) and later. This is generally because one of the most important duties of a king was the erection of temples to the gods, so earlier structures were frequently replaced by the buildings of later rulers. In addition, in the Delta, the earlier temples have disappeared because they were pillaged for building materials.

◀ *The First Pylon of the Luxor Temple, erected by Ramesses II, was originally embellished with six statues and two obelisks.*

Temple Architecture

Each temple built by the ancient Egyptians represented the Mound of Creation, which had risen from the primordial ocean at the beginning of time. In temple architecture, the mound was marked by a gradual rise in ground level between the entrance and the innermost shrine, while the columns of the hypostyle hall represented the first plant life to appear on the mound. Every temple had a sacred lake and was surrounded by an undulating mudbrick wall: it is thought that both these feaures were intended to represent the primordial ocean from which the mound arose.

The home of the god

A temple built for the worship of a god was regarded as 'the god's house', quite literally the place where he or she resided. The deity would be represented by a cult statue placed in the innermost part of the temple, in the sanctuary, which was the most secret and sacred area. Although the deities were often thought to possess creative powers, to represent parts of the universe and to embody natural forces, they were also seen in human terms, hence the god's need for a house, food and family.

In general terms, temple architecture provided for the physical needs of the god, and parallels can be drawn with the homes of private individuals. The pylon, or monumental gateway, formed the entrance, with the open courts representing the place where, in an ordinary house, visitors would have been entertained. The hypostyle hall, with its roof supported by tall columns, and the sanctuary were comparable with more private areas in the home such as bedrooms. Only the king, in his capacity as high priest, and other important functionaries would have been allowed to penetrate these inner chambers.

Temples did, however, provide dramatic settings for occasions in which the public could take part. These were the festivals of the gods, when sacred boats bearing the shrines containing the images of the deities were carried in procession along the banks of the Nile and from temple to temple amid scenes of great rejoicing, and even depravity, if we are to believe Herodotus.

▲ *Every temple had a sacred lake that represented the waters of chaos from which creation arose. This is the Sacred Lake at Karnak.*

Many of the places where temples stand today have been sacred sites since the dawn of history. Most of the remains

▲ *The Temple of Philae was said to be sited on the mound that appeared from the waters of chaos at the time of creation.*

► *The columns in the Hypostyle Hall at Karnak represent the plants that came into being on the Mound of Creation.*

that can now be seen, however, date to the New Kingdom (c.1550–c.1069 BC) or the Graeco-Roman Period (332 BC–AD 395), so are relatively modern in the context of the history of ancient Egypt. These buildings represent only the latest stage of a series of temples built over a long period of time. At Karnak, however, the development of the complex from the simple Middle Kingdom shrine of Senusret I to the prosperous New Kingdom and Graeco-Roman Periods can be clearly seen. ◆

The Temple of Satet at Elephantine

Elephantine is an island in the Nile, which lies opposite the modern town of Aswan near the First Cataract, where the river becomes unnavigable as it flows over a series of granite outcrops. The southern tip of the island is the site of an ancient settlement, also called Elephantine.

As it lay on the border with Nubia, the town was of great strategic importance and was fortified from the Early Dynastic Period (c.3100–c.2686 BC). Elephantine was also important commercially, and it was from here that expeditions set off into Nubia to procure gold, incense, precious oils, animal skins, ivory and other exotic goods for the Egyptian kings. The tombs of the governors of the South, who organized such expeditions, are carved out of the rocky hillsides on the west bank. Their autobiographies tell of the arduous nature of the trips they made to the south.

Successive buildings

During its long history, Elephantine was served by several temples dating back from the Ptolemaic Period (332–30 BC) to the Early Dynastic Period. A team from the German Archaeological Institute under Dr Günter Dreyer has recently brought the whole series of temples to light. In other places, later kings destroyed earlier buildings while erecting their own, but this was not the case at Elephantine. The earliest shrine was set up among the rocks of the cataract. Space was limited, so when later builders wanted to enlarge the shrine they filled it in, paved over it and built above it, thus creating a time capsule and providing a record of the earlier shrines, complete with votive offerings.

The shrine in the rocks

The earliest shrine was set in a niche formed by the granite rocks of the cataract. It is thought that the cult image would have stood here, but unfortunately it is no longer extant. In the later temples the goddess Satet, guardian of the cataract, was worshipped here, but it is not known if that was the case at this early stage. Many of the votive offerings found within the shrine are figures of children and it has been suggested that the shrine may have been frequented by mothers either hoping to give birth or bringing a thanksgiving offering for a newly born child. No texts have been found that throw light on the subject.

▼ *On the island of Elephantine is a series of temples dating back from the Ptolemaic to the Early Dynastic Period, when a simple shrine was set up among the rocks of the First Cataract.*

▲ *The New Kingdom temple of Tuthmosis III was built over the ancient shrine of earlier temples and dedicated to Satet.*

▲ *Alexander II worships Khnum, one of the deities of the cataract who protected royal expeditions.*

Whatever form it took, the cult image of the earliest shrine was protected by two small mudbrick rooms. In front of these was either a courtyard enclosed by more walls or possibly even a roofed hall. By the later Old Kingdom (c.2686–c.2181 BC) the small shrine had been replaced by a larger court or hall, in the centre of which was a pedestal made of layers of mudbrick and matting, with a wooden pole at each corner. This may well have been a stand on which to rest a portable tent shrine housing the image of the cult deity.

Among the votive offerings found at the shrine were objects inscribed with the names of some of the kings of the Sixth Dynasty (c.2345–c.2181 BC), perhaps produced in honour of their *sed*-festivals. Most were plaques bearing the names of Pepi I (c.2321–c.2287 BC) and Pepi II (c.2278–c.2184 BC) while one was inscribed with a squatting ape holding its young. Rock inscriptions of the kings Merenre (c.2287–c.2278 BC) and Pepi II were found on the walls of the niche.

Stone temples

In the early Middle Kingdom (c.2055–c.1650 BC), a completely new shrine was built, partly of mudbrick, but also using carved and painted stonework. This was in turn replaced in the Twelfth Dynasty (c.1985–c.1795 BC) by a temple built completely of stone. Both these structures were basically extensions of the Old Kingdom temple.

There was a dramatic change in the New Kingdom (c.1550–c.1069 BC), when the Twelfth Dynasty stone temple was dismantled and the ancient shrine filled in with blocks of stone to the level of the top of the boulders. The area was paved over and the Eighteenth Dynasty king Tuthmosis III (c.1479–c.1425 BC) built a new stone temple on top, although a shaft was constructed in the floor to connect it with the original shrine below. Further extensions or embellishment of the temple took place in later reigns until the Ptolemaic Period.

◀ *Reliefs recently restored by the German Archaeological Institute show Tuthmosis III and Satet wearing her distinctive headdress.*

▶ *Tuthmosis III adores the creator god Khnum, who was also worshipped at Elephantine.*

Satet, Khnum and Anuket

It is only with the building of the Middle Kingdom temples that the deity worshipped here is known with any certainty. The carved and painted stone blocks show the goddess Satet embracing the king. In mythology she was the wife of the ram-headed creator deity Khnum, who also had his cult temple at Elephantine from the Middle Kingdom, and the mother of Anuket, goddess of the First Cataract. All three deities were worshipped as guardians of the cataract area and protected the royal expeditions that had to pass Elephantine on their way to Nubia. The rocky island of Sehel, to the south of Elephantine, is covered with the inscriptions of the expedition leaders, who are shown making offerings to the deities of the cataract in the hope of gaining their protection. ◆

The Temple of Luxor

Luxor Temple lies in the centre of the modern town on the east bank of the Nile. It is connected by an avenue of sphinxes to the temple complex of Karnak, about 3km (2 miles) to the north. The ancient Egyptian name of the temple was *ipet-resyt*, which means 'southern harem'. It was dedicated to the cult of Amun in his fertility aspect, his wife, Mut, and son, Khonsu. The temple's main purpose was to provide a setting for the annual *opet*-festival, when the cult images of the gods were taken in procession by land and by boat from Karnak to Luxor.

Although blocks have been found that show that the temple was begun in the Middle Kingdom (c.2055–c.1650 BC), the buildings visible today date from the reign of Amenhotep III (c.1390–c.1352 BC), the great temple builder of the Eighteenth Dynasty (c.1550–c.1295 BC), a time when Egypt was very prosperous and powerful. On a black granite stela some 3m (10ft) tall, now in the Cairo Museum, his inscription records that he built the temple of:

> *...fine limestone, wide, very great, and exceedingly beautiful. Its walls are of fine gold, its pavements of silver. All its gates are worked with the pride of lands. Its pylons reach to the sky, its flagpoles to the stars.*

An ancient view of the temple façade, carved in miniature on the west side of the south wall of the Peristyle Court, gives some idea of what it was like. Ramesses II (c.1279–c.1213 BC), Alexander the Great (332–323 BC) and other later kings extended and embellished it, and the remains of the Roman town can still be seen.

The temple entrance

The complex is entered by the First Pylon, the great monumental gateway added by Ramesses II. On it is emblazoned the story of Ramesses' self-styled great victory over the Hittites at the Battle of Qadesh in 1274 BC. Ramesses is shown heroically taking on the Hittite army in the top registers, while scenes of life in the camp and preparation for battle are depicted below. Written accounts of the battle in both prose and poetry accompany the carved reliefs, which would once have been painted in bright colours.

Originally, there were two seated and four standing figures of Ramesses II, as well as two obelisks in front of the pylon. Only the seated statues, one standing statue and one of the obelisks are still in position. The rest are now in Paris, where the obelisk adorns the Place de la Concorde.

The First Pylon leads to the Peristyle Court, a large open area surrounded by a colonnade added by Ramesses II. Its squat papyrus-bud columns are in sharp contrast to the much more delicate versions seen in the sacred boat shrines of Amun, Mut and Khonsu in the north-west corner, built by the earlier rulers Tuthmosis III (c.1479–c.1425 BC) and Hatshepsut (c.1473–c.1458 BC). The court also sports numerous statues of Ramesses II, accompanied mainly by diminutive representations of Nefertari, his chief queen, between the columns.

▲ *Two seated statues of Ramesses II in front of the First Pylon of the Luxor Temple show him seated on the throne of the Two Lands.*

Above the eastern colonnade of the court is the Mosque of Abu el-Hagag, built in the nineteenth century on top of the accumulated debris. Until 1855, when the clearing of the temple was begun, there was also a village here.

The processional way

The entrance to the Great Colonnade of Amenhotep III is guarded by two further colossal statues of Ramesses II, with Nefertari tenderly embracing his lower

▶ *An avenue of sphinxes once connected the temples of Luxor and Karnak. It is currently being restored.*

leg. Each is seated on a throne decorated with the heraldic motif symbolizing the union of the Two Lands: lotus and papyrus plants tied to a windpipe and lungs. The defeated enemies are depicted underneath the feet of Ramesses.

The Great Colonnade is a processional way composed of 14 huge columns with open papyrus capitals. The sacred boats bearing the images of the gods would have been carried along this way at the time of the *opet*-festival. The inner walls of the court are decorated with scenes of the festival. The procession is shown leaving Karnak Temple, with the sacred boats carried by priests accompanied by musicians and soldiers carrying standards. Other boats are shown in the water, either rowed by energetic crews or towed by men on the banks. Nubian musicians and female acrobats entertain the crowd, and two royal chariots and horses are led by grooms. Finally, King Tutankhamun (c.1336–c.1327 BC) is shown making offerings to the gods. On the east wall, the gods are seen returning to Karnak.

At the southern end of the processional way there would originally have been a pylon, but today the Great Colonnade leads directly out into the Court of Amenhotep III. This too is surrounded on three sides with a double row of columns with papyrus-bud capitals, but the proportions here are much more harmonious. Originally, the colonnade would have been roofed over.

The inner sanctum

Behind the court is the Hypostyle Hall, with its 32 papyrus-bud columns. On the east wall, Amenhotep III is making offerings to Amun, Mut and Khonsu. Near the doors of the small chapels to the south are inscriptions of Ramesses II, indicating that he made some repairs to the temple.

The main Sanctuary, which lies behind the Hypostyle Hall, may have fallen into disrepair and was redesigned by Alexander the Great. The columns of one of the smaller rooms were removed to make room for a sacred boat shrine. Alexander is shown making offerings in the traditional manner of the pharaohs. However, in the Roman Period (30 BC–AD 395) the temple became a shrine to the imperial cult. An altar has been found dedicated to Emperor Constantine (AD 312–337), while the carved reliefs of Amenhotep III in the small court behind the Hypostyle Hall were plastered over and repainted with figures. These were once assumed to represent Jesus and his disciples but are now thought to show the emperor and his court.

A suite of rooms behind the sacred boat shrine represents the 'bedroom' of the god, where the secret rituals of the *opet*-festival took place. Reliefs in the birth room of Amenhotep III show the impregnation of Amenhotep's mother, Queen Mutemwiya, by the god Amun, while the ram-headed creator god Khnum forms the royal child on his potter's wheel. The queen is taken to the birth room by Khnum and Hathor. The child is born and presented to Amun. The last scene shows Amenhotep as an adult blessed by the gods and confirmed in his role as son of the sun god. ◆

◀ *The Court of King Amenhotep III is possibly the precursor of the open Aten temples at Amarna.*

The Temples of Karnak

The vast complex of temples at Karnak demonstrates the religious significance of the area in ancient times. The main Sanctuary is devoted to the worship of Amun, who rose from humble beginnings as a local god of Thebes to become a deity of national importance in the New Kingdom (c.1550–c.1069 BC), when his cult was linked to that of Re, the sun god of Heliopolis. However, the site is extremely complicated as it includes several temples dedicated to other gods. The Temple of Mut, the wife of Amun, lies to the south while the Temple of Khonsu, his son, is within it. Montu, a local war god, Ptah, the creator god of Memphis, and Osiris, the King and Judge of the Underworld, were also worshipped in their own temples inside the sacred area.

Unusually, the temple was built on two axes and spread outwards from the small shrine of King Senusret I (c.1965–c.1920 BC) as successive kings made their own contributions to the complex in the form of pylons, chapels and obelisks. Some buildings were dismantled by later kings and the blocks reused inside pylons. Some of these have now been removed and reconstructed in the Open Air Museum to the north of the main Temple of Amun. One such is the exquisite little shrine of Senusret I,

▲ *This statue of Ramesses II was usurped by Pinedjem, High Priest of Amun, and ruler of Thebes after the end of the 21st Dynasty.*

which was found in pieces in the foundations of the Third Pylon, having been removed from its original position at the heart of the Sanctuary.

Entering the complex

In antiquity, the temple was connected to the Nile by canal, and the remains of the landing stage and a small boat shrine of Amun can still be seen at the entrance to the complex. Leading to the First Pylon, which is thought to be the work of the Thirtieth Dynasty king Nectanebo I (380–362 BC), is an avenue of ram-headed sphinxes protecting the figure of a king. Some are inscribed for Ramesses II (c.1279–c.1213 BC) and Pinedjem, one of the high priests of Amun who ruled the South after the division of Egypt at the end of the Twenty-first Dynasty (c.1069–c.945 BC). However, it is likely that they were usurped from Amenhotep III (c.1390–c.1352 BC) or Horemheb (c.1323–c.1295 BC).

The First Pylon leads into the Great Court of the kings of the Twenty-second Dynasty (c.945–c.715 BC), whose achievements are recorded on its south side, next to the Temple of Ramesses III (c.1184–c.1153 BC). Both this temple and the sacred boat shrines opposite of Seti II (c.1200–c.1194 BC) once stood outside the main temple but were later incorporated into it, while the sphinxes of the avenue that linked the earlier temple to the Nile have been pushed unceremoniously to the side. In the centre of the court is an impressive open papyrus column of an even later king, Taharqo (690–664 BC), which was once part of a kiosk.

▼ *This view of the Karnak temples built by successive rulers from the Middle Kingdom to the Roman Period shows the scale of the complex.*

▲ *The Hypostyle Hall was originally roofed in by huge stone blocks. Clerestory windows let light into the building.*

A mudbrick ramp behind the First Pylon gives some insight into the way these huge structures were built. Another point of interest is the royal statue in front of the pylon. An inscription found under the base shows that it belonged to Ramesses II, while that on the statue itself shows that it was usurped by Pinedjem. The pylon was probably erected by Horemheb, who filled it with small blocks taken from the Temple to the Aten which the heretical Eighteenth Dynasty king Akhenaten (c.1352–c.1336 BC) built at Karnak before his move to Tell el-Amarna. Pylons Nine and Ten were also found to contain such blocks, known by the Arabic word *talatat*. It has been possible to use many of them to reconstruct one of the walls of the Aten Temple and this is now on display in the Luxor Museum.

The Hypostyle Hall

Between the Second and Third Pylons is the Hypostyle Hall, the most famous of the remains at Karnak. This was built in the early Nineteenth Dynasty (c.1295–c.1186 BC). The roof of massive sandstone blocks is supported by a forest of 134 columns, 122 in the closed papyrus-bud style and 12 open papyrus columns in the central aisle. This part of the building would have been completely dark but for the clerestory windows, which allowed shafts of light to penetrate and illuminate parts of the hall. The scenes carved by Ramesses II and his father, Seti I (c.1294–c.1279 BC), show the king worshipping the gods or being blessed and invested with royal authority by them. Those of Seti I are in delicate low relief and are highly superior to the deeply gouged work of Ramesses II. Traces of the original colour remain.

Eighteenth Dynasty monuments

Beyond the Third Pylon of Amenhotep III lies the area built by the kings of the earlier Eighteenth Dynasty. Here stood the alabaster shrine of Amenhotep I (c.1525–c.1504 BC), now in the Open Air Museum. Here, too, is the suite of Hatshepsut (c.1473–c.1458 BC), where the hacked image of the female pharaoh is seen running her *heb sed* race and, again virtually obliterated, being recrowned by Horus and Thoth. In the same area were her obelisks and those of her father. One of her obelisks still stands, while the upper part of the second is now by the Sacred Lake.

Just beyond the Sixth Pylon (also his work) Tuthmosis III (c.1479–c.1425 BC) built his Hall of Records, where the hieroglyphic accounts of his military campaigns are preserved. Somewhat incongruously, the sacred boat shrine lying slightly ahead was the work of Philip Arridaeus (323–317 BC), the half-brother and successor of Alexander the Great. This, however, replaced an earlier shrine, the Red Chapel of Hatshepsut, now also reconstructed in the Open Air Museum.

Royal records

One of the main duties of a king was to quell Egypt's enemies. His campaigns were undertaken at the behest of the gods, who granted him victory in battle. The king, in turn, dedicated the booty and prisoners to the gods, principally to Amun at Karnak. As a result, the temple became a vast storehouse of historical knowledge.

The outer walls of the Hypostyle Hall are inscribed with accounts of the campaigns of Seti I in Syria–Palestine and Ramesses II's triumph over the Hittites at the Battle of Qadesh. The terms of the consequent peace treaty are also inscribed. One of the small rooms adjoining the Festival Hall once contained an important list, now in the Louvre in Paris, of Ramesses' 57 ancestors. Other important documents include the Kamose Stela, an account of the attempt by King Kamose (c.1555–c.1550 BC) to free Egypt of Hyksos rule in the north, and the stela of Psamtek II (595–589 BC), which records his 591 BC Nubian campaign.

The original temple

The site of the original Middle Kingdom temple was in the open space between the Eighteenth Dynasty buildings and the Festival Hall of Tuthmosis III. Only a few vestiges of the early temple remain, but the Festival Hall is most interesting. The columns that support the ceiling are unique in temple architecture and are said to represent tent pegs, reflecting the fact that Tuthmosis III was the great empire builder of the New Kingdom and spent much of his reign on campaign. The columns are decorated with paintings of the heads of saints dating from the Christian era, when the hall was converted into a church. Behind the hall is a series of small rooms decorated in relief with exotic plants and birds, said to have been brought back by Tuthmosis III from his travels. ◆

Temples to the Aten

During the reign of the Eighteenth Dynasty king Akhenaten (c.1352–c.1336 BC), the emphasis of religion changed radically. Akhenaten, who began his reign as Amenhotep IV, attempted to elevate a single deity, the Aten, from the vast Egyptian pantheon to the status of sole god. Old traditions of worship, ritual and art were swept away, and a new capital was built. But neither Akhenaten's new religion, nor his city, survived him.

Sun deities

The sun, with its life-giving properties, had always been worshipped as a god who appeared in many different forms. Khepri, represented as a scarab beetle, was the rising sun; Re, in the guise of a hawk, was the noonday sun; and Atum, depicted as an old man leaning on a stick, the setting sun. Horus, the falcon god, was also sometimes seen as a sun god, as was another falcon god, Re-Horakhty. The Aten, another manifestation of the sun god, was always represented as the sun's disc, without any human, bird or animal form.

The most important of these deities was Re, the sun in the sky and the creator of life. During the day he was thought to sail across the sky in his boat and at night, in his ram-headed form, to sail through the Underworld shedding his recreating light as he went. Suti and Hor, two important officials in charge of the building works of King Amenhotep III (c.1390–c.1352 BC), wrote two hymns in praise of the sun god in all of these different forms, which are inscribed on a black granite stela now in the British Museum, London.

Akhenaten's new religion

Amenhotep III's son and successor, however, preferred the Aten to all the other forms of the sun god. All the other manifestations of the deity were abandoned and only worship of the Aten was allowed. Changing his name to Akhenaten ('Beneficence of the Aten'), in the fifth year of his reign, the king founded a whole new city dedicated to the deity and called Akhetaten ('Horizon of the Aten'). The new capital was built on a virgin site in Middle Egypt now known as Tell el-Amarna, and Akhenaten set up 14 boundary stelae in the cliffs around it, three on the west bank of the Nile and eleven on the east.

▲ *Akhenaten and Nefertiti worship the Aten whose rays shine down on them in blessing. The king links himself with Aten as a creator god.*

The earliest of these stones records that the king had been led to the site by the Aten himself, who had chosen it as his special city, and points out that no other deity had been worshipped there previously. It mentions the temples and palaces, which were to be built on the east bank, and also the agricultural land and the villages on the opposite bank, which were all to be included in the new city. The city was also to include harbours and several suburbs. A year or so later the king revisited the city and drove round it in his 'great chariot of fine gold, like Aten when he dawns in

▲ *A typical scene from the officials' tombs at Amarna shows the royal couple at worship.*

lightland and fills the Two Lands with his love'. He promised never to alter the boundaries and celebrated the occasion with 'a great offering of bread and beer, large and small cattle, fowl, wine, fruit, incense and all good herbs'. At the top of each stela, Akhenaten, his wife Nefertiti and two of their small daughters are shown before a great offering table. As they worship, the disk of the Aten shines down on them in blessing. The rays of the sun end in little hands and each of those nearest to the noses of the king and queen holds a tiny *ankh*, thus infusing them with life.

The Great Temple

The design of the temples of the new city was completely different from traditional ancient Egyptian temples, the inner parts of which were roofed over. The Amarna temples lay open to the sun. Although Akhenaten's city was destroyed after his death and the building blocks removed and reused elsewhere, it is still possible to gain some idea of what these temples looked like. Fortunately, officials like Panhesy, who moved with the royal court to Akhetaten, prepared tombs in the cliffs surrounding the city, and in these they showed the royal family worshipping in the temple.

The Great Temple was enormous. The temple enclosure measured 229 x 730m (750 x 2,400ft). As so much of the interior seems to have been an empty space, it is assumed that the temple was unfinished. To provide a setting for worship, the buildings were initially put up rapidly using mudbrick, which was then gradually replaced in stone. Even so, only two main parts seem to have been completed, the House of Rejoicing and the Gem Aten ('Aten is Found'). Entrance to the temple was by way of two pylons, leading to a series of offering tables in open courts. The Gem Aten was at the back of the building and was similar in layout to the rest. In these sections of the temple, ceremonies celebrating the daily rising of the sun took place at dawn. Beyond this was the main Sanctuary, with a raised platform on which Akhenaten and Nefertiti made offerings to the Aten, as shown in the scene from the tomb of Panhesy. There were 772 offering tables in the temple itself and about 900 in the sacred area around it.

▼ *These scenes show the king and queen playing with their little daughters, and are unique to the Amarna period. Such displays of affection are otherwise never depicted in royal art.*

Royal temples and shrines

There was also a smaller temple in the city centre called the Mansion of the Aten. This was a scaled-down version of the Great Temple and resembled a chapel royal. As it is in line with the Royal Wadi, the site of the royal tomb, it has been suggested by the excavator, Barry Kemp, that it may also have doubled up as a mortuary temple where the cult of the king would have been perpetuated. Within this temple is a small building, which Kemp feels might have contained a robing room and a 'Window of Appearances', both features of the royal funerary temples at Thebes.

Elsewhere in the city were shrines that housed the king's statue as an object of veneration, and some of these have been found in the gardens of private houses. A further group of buildings beyond the main city was called the Maru Aten and was composed of two walled enclosures containing lakes and gardens, pavilions, shrines and 'sunshades' (platforms reached by steps). Recently, another complex to the south of the city has been excavated, although its ancient name is not yet known. Here, the main temple building was surrounded by a garden and was served by a bakery and other workshops within the temple enclosure. ◆

Abydos

Abydos was one of the most sacred sites in ancient Egypt. According to one tradition, it was where Osiris himself was interred; in another myth his head, after his murder and dismemberment by his brother Seth, was buried here. Temples were built on the site from the Predynastic Period to Christian times – from about 4000 BC to AD 641.

Because of its association with Osiris, the Judge of the Dead and King of the Underworld, Abydos was also an important cemetery site. The kings of the earliest dynasties were buried here: Flinders Petrie found and identified the tombs of the kings of the First Dynasty (c.3100–c.2890 BC), and some of those of the Second Dynasty (c.2890–c.2686 BC). More recently some even earlier royal tombs have been found, belonging to the period now known as Dynasty Zero. Later, when the kings were buried elsewhere, they often built cenotaphs at Abydos to identify themselves with Osiris. Private individuals also set up chapels and commemorative stelae in the hope that they would receive divine blessing and be restored to life again, as Osiris was.

Khentamentiu

Osiris was not the first god to be worshipped at Abydos. He was preceded by Khentamentiu, whose name means 'Foremost of the Westerners', signifying that he was a god of the dead. His cult was identified with that of Osiris when the latter came to prominence, and Osiris used the name Khentamentiu as one of his epithets.

There was a city on the site from the Predynastic Period, the most important feature of which was the temple. It stood on the mound today called Kom es-Sultan, which is surrounded by a huge mudbrick wall dating from the Thirtieth Dynasty (380–343 BC). Very little remains of the early temple itself as it was built mainly of mudbrick, but the finds from the site cover a long period of time and suggest that it remained in use until the Graeco-Roman Period (332 BC–AD 395).

▲ *The temple of Seti I at Abydos has the best account of daily ritual in ancient Egypt. Seti I as High Priest is seen here offering incense to Horus.*

▼ *The Abydos temple built by Seti I is dedicated not only to Osiris, his wife Isis and son Horus, but also to the national gods, Amun-Re, Ptah and Re-Horakhty, and to the dead king himself.*

◀ *Horus is shown pouring a libation for Seti I and offering him the hieroglyphs* djed, ankh *and* was, *symbolizing the king's resurrection and confirmed wellbeing in the Afterlife.*

Temples of Seti I and Ramesses II

Today, visitors to Abydos can explore the New Kingdom temples of Seti I (c.1294–c.1279 BC) and his son, Ramesses II (c.1279–c.1213 BC), which lie to the east of the site. That of Seti I is the better preserved. The temple has a deceptively conventional appearance from the outside, although the interior is highly unusual, reflecting the fact that it was dedicated to several gods rather than a single deity. It also combines the functions of a temple built in honour of the gods and a mortuary temple (in this case a duplicate mortuary temple).

The plan is L-shaped. Two pylons, now virtually destroyed, lead into open courts with pillared porticoes. Then come two hypostyle halls and seven chapels, standing side by side and dedicated to the main deities of New Kingdom Egypt. Seti I is also honoured as a god, probably in order to underpin his right to rule, as his dynasty was newly established. His chapel is at the opposite end of the row to that of Horus, perhaps a reminder that as king he embodies Horus. The seven chapels are each reached by their own individual processional way from the First Hypostyle Hall. Originally there were seven entrances from the portico but, except for the central one, they were all blocked by Ramesses II, who completed the building of the temple after his father's death.

Reliefs and inscriptions

It is easy to tell the parts of the temple decorated by Seti I and those by Ramesses II. As at Karnak, Ramesses' reliefs are cut deeply into the stone, whereas Seti's are in delicate raised relief. These are considered by many to be the best work of the sculptors of ancient Egypt.

In the Second Hypostyle Hall, Seti is famously seen offering a figure of the goddess Maat to Osiris, Isis and Horus. Maat represented the perfect world order, based on truth, righteousness and justice, and Seti was thus depicted as the ideal king whose reign was the epitome of these concepts. As the temple doubled as a cenotaph to the deceased king it was important that his reign was seen in this light, so that he would not only spend eternity in the presence of Osiris but become Osiris himself. The funerary aspect of the temple is emphasized by the false doors that occupy the end wall of the shrines and by further suites of rooms dedicated to Osiris and to Ptah-Sokar and Nefertem, the funerary gods of Memphis.

Leading from the Second Hypostyle Hall is the Gallery of Kings, where a list of the predecessors of Ramesses II is carved on the walls.

The Osireion

Behind the temple is the Osireion, which at one time was held to be the burial place of Osiris, but is now thought to be a duplicate tomb of Seti I. The granite structure representing the burial chamber is approached from the desert by a long sloping decorated corridor, which imitates the royal tombs in the Valley of the Kings. It is the most elaborate of all the cenotaphs that kings of different periods built at Abydos to stress their devotion to Osiris and their hope of resurrection. ◆

▲ *Seti I offers to Amun. In Seti's cartouches, the Isis knot hieroglyph replaces the usual Seth animal to avoid any association with the murder of Osiris.*

The Myth of Kingship

Abydos was very important to the kings of ancient Egypt. It was here that their divinity, through their identification with the gods Horus and Osiris, was most clearly expressed. Basic to these concepts is the myth of Osiris. There are allusions to the myth in the Pyramid Texts inscribed in tombs of the Old Kingdom (c.2686–c.2181 BC) and odd episodes are mentioned in works such as the Great Hymn to Osiris, the Memphite Theology and, at greater length, in the complicated story of The Contendings of Horus and Seth. However, for a full version of the story we must look to the work of the second-century Greek writer, Plutarch.

The death of Osiris

In his essay Peri Isidos kai Osiridos, Plutarch states that Osiris was once a real king of Egypt. He was a great king who taught his people all the skills of civilization and was so popular that his wicked brother Seth became jealous of him and planned to get rid of him and take the throne for himself. Seth invited Osiris to a banquet, where he produced a beautifully carved and painted box, which he said he would give to anyone who could fit inside exactly. Everyone tried, but they were either too tall or too short. Then Osiris tried his luck. As soon as he was inside Seth slammed down the lid and threw the box into the Nile. According to the Memphite Theology, Osiris was drowned and his body was taken from the river by Isis and Nephthys (his wife and sister) at Memphis, the place where he entered the Underworld. Plutarch, however, claims that the body was washed right down the Nile and out into the Mediterranean Sea, where the current swept it up the coast until it came to rest at Byblos, in modern Lebanon. There it caught against a sapling, which proceeded to grow at a rapid rate until it completely enveloped the box containing the body. The king of Byblos had the tree cut down and used it to support the ceiling in a room in his palace.

Isis's quest

According to Plutarch, Isis, mourning the loss of her husband, travelled the world searching for him. Eventually, she heard the story of the tree. She arrived at Byblos and begged the king for the body of Osiris. Returning to Egypt she lay down to sleep in the Delta marshes. Unfortunately, Seth came upon the sleeping goddess, snatched the body, cut it up into 14 pieces and scattered them throughout the land.

When Isis discovered what had happened she and her sister set off to recover the various parts of the body. They found all except the penis, which had been eaten by an oxyrhynchus fish. Anubis and Thoth, the funerary deities, helped them to embalm and restore the body, and Isis replaced the lost penis with a clay model by which Osiris was able to impregnate her. She then gave birth to Horus. Isis and Nephthys turned into kites and beat the air with their wings to create breath that Osiris could inhale and so be restored to life. Osiris became King of the Underworld and Judge of the Dead. Isis and Nephthys are often shown at the foot and the head of royal coffins, beating the air with their wings to help restore the dead king to life.

This was not the end of the story, however. The throne of Egypt was now vacant: who would be king next? The wily Seth claimed the kingship but was challenged by Osiris's son, Horus. The matter was angrily debated in the divine court for over 80 years. At one point it was decided to divide the kingship between them. Seth was to be king of the South and Horus, king of the North. Eventually, this decision was overruled and Horus became king of the Two Lands.

▲ *Seti I is suckled by Isis, mother of Horus, thus demonstrating that he is the living Horus.*

▲ *This selective list of the kings of Egypt is carved on the walls of the Gallery of Kings at Abydos. Ramesses reads the same names from his scroll.*

Royal identification with Horus

The story explains much about ancient Egyptian ideas concerning kingship. From earliest times, the records show that the kings regarded themselves as Horus, the rightful heir of Osiris. Grave markers found by Petrie outside the tombs of the First Dynasty (c.3100– c.2890 BC) show Horus as a falcon perched above the *serekh* (a device carved in imitation of a niched palace façade) containing the name of the king. The 'Horus name' of the king was always the first of the five by which the king was known in the fully developed titulary. The title *nesw bity*, King of Upper and Lower Egypt, is a further reference to this myth. It literally means 'He of the Sedge and the Bee', the sedge being an emblem of the Nile Valley and the bee of the Delta.

On the walls of the Sokar Chapel at Abydos is a scene of special significance. It shows the posthumous conception of Horus as the deceased Osiris impregnates Isis, who hovers above him as a kite. As the temple is dedicated to Seti I (c. 1294–c.1279 BC) as well as the Abydos triad (Osiris, Isis and Horus), it neatly identifies the king with Horus and substantiates his claim to be the son and heir of Osiris. When the king died he was said to fly off on his falcon wings to join the sun god or to take his place among the stars. In other texts the king became Osiris while his son became the next living Horus.

Horus played an important part in his father's resurrection. Many of the Pyramid Texts refer to the fact that Horus restored Osiris to life by giving him his Eye. In one episode in the dispute between Horus and Seth, Seth was turned into a hippopotamus and was harpooned by Horus. An inscription of Ramesses II (c.1279–c.1213 BC) details all the many good deeds he has done on his father's behalf, claiming to have done as much for his father as Horus did for Osiris. ◆

▼ *Ramesses II makes an offering of two* nu-*pots to the gods.*

The kinglist

In the temple at Abydos, an important description shows Seti I (c.1294–c.1279 BC), with a youthful Ramesses, reading from a scroll bearing the names of all his royal ancestors. It thus purports to be a complete list of all the kings of Egypt down to Seti I. It is, however, selective, and includes only 'approved' kings, or those who adhered to the concept of *maat* (justice and order). There are therefore no kings of the Intermediate Periods, when Egypt sometimes had several rulers. This contravened the ideal of a single king who ruled a united country. Female rulers were also excluded, as were the kings of the 'heretical' Amarna period – Akhenaten, Smenkhkare, Ay and Tutankhamun. The Nineteenth Dynasty kings seem not to have been related to those of the previous dynasty and were anxious to prove that they were 'proper' kings of Egypt and the true heirs of Osiris. They therefore had their claim to legitimacy carved on the walls of Osiris' main sanctuary.

Pilgrimage and Pageant

From at least the Middle Kingdom (c.2055–c.1650 BC) the tomb of the First Dynasty king Djer (c.3000 BC) in the royal cemetery at Abydos was held to be the actual burial place of Osiris. When it was first excavated by Emile Amélineau at the end of the nineteenth century it contained a statue of Osiris lying on a funerary couch. This has parallels with the Pyramid Texts, which refer to him 'lying on his side', a subtle allusion to his murder by Seth. The tomb became a place of pilgrimage and many people aspired to visit the site, either in this life or the next. In the New Kingdom (c.1550–c.1069 BC), a common scene in the tombs of officials at Thebes shows two boats, one with sails down sailing downstream and the other coming upstream against the current with the sails raised. This is often interpreted as the 'pilgrimage to Abydos', which the tomb owner had either made during his lifetime and hoped to continue in the Afterlife, or planned to do then if he had failed to do it before his death.

From the end of the Old Kingdom (c.2181 BC), people who came from different parts of Egypt were either buried at Abydos near Osiris himself or, if this was not possible, they erected a chapel or commemorative stela to themselves in his presence, hoping in this way to share in his resurrection. Hundreds of *ka* statues (representing the spirit of the deceased), offering tables and stelae have been recovered from the site and are now in museums all over the world. Some of the stelae shed light on the nature of the festivals that were held at Abydos and make it possible to imagine what the shrine of Osiris and the cult statue, gilded and decked out in jewellery, looked like.

▼ *This painted carved relief from the Osiris temple at Abydos shows the god's sacred barque with its statue shrine, which was carried in procession during the annual pageant to commemorate his death and resurrection.*

◀ *After Isis retrieved the scattered remains of her husband's body, she turned herself into a kite and uttered spells so that Osiris was able to impregnate her.*

Ikhernofret's pilgrimage

One of the most important stelae belonged to Ikhernofret, a high-ranking official of the Twelfth Dynasty king Senusret III (c.1874–c.1855 BC). Ikhernofret was commanded by Senusret to go to Abydos to make a portable shrine and to gild the cult statue of Osiris with Nubian gold. On his stela (now in Berlin) he describes what he did:

I did all that His Majesty commanded [regarding] his father Osiris, Foremost of the Westerners, Lord of Abydos…I acted as 'his beloved son' [a priestly title for those concerned with this work] for Osiris, Foremost of the Westerners. I furnished his great barque, the eternal everlasting one. I made for him the portable shrine that carries the beauty [statue] of the Foremost of the Westerners, of gold, silver, lapis lazuli, bronze, sandalwood and cedarwood. The gods who attend him were fashioned, their shrines made anew. I set the hour-priests to their tasks. I made them know the ritual of every day and of the feasts of the beginnings of the seasons. I directed the work of the neshmet-barque, I fashioned the cabin. I decked the breast of the Lord of Abydos with lapis lazuli and turquoise, fine gold and all costly stones which are the ornaments of a god's body. I clothed the god with his regalia in my rank of master of secrets…I was pure of hand in decking the god, a priest whose fingers are clean.

Ikhernofret was also in charge of the great festival of Osiris. This seems to have been an annual pageant when Osiris's murder by Seth and his subsequent revival were acted out:

I conducted the Great procession, following the god in his steps. I made the god's barque sail, Thoth steering the boat. I equipped with a cabin the barque 'Truly is Risen the Lord of Abydos'. Decked in his beautiful regalia he proceeded to the domain of Peqer. I cleared the god's path to his tomb in Peqer. I protected Wen-nofer on that day of great combat. I felled his foes on the shore of Nedyt.

In this part of the proceedings the shrine of Osiris was carried on another boat in a procession that wended its way from the temple of Osiris at Abydos to his symbolic tomb in the desert. The focal point of the drama was the fight against the enemies of Osiris and their defeat at a place called Nedyt. This was the place where, in mythology, Osiris was killed by Seth. Finally, the procession came back in triumph to Abydos by boat, and the god returned to his temple.

I made him enter the great barque. It bore his beauty. I gave joy to the eastern deserts; I caused rejoicing in the western deserts. They saw the beauty of the neshmet-barque as it landed at Abydos. It brought Osiris, Foremost of the Westerners, Lord of Abydos to his palace. I followed the god to his house. His purification was done: his seat made spacious… ◆

◀ *This gilded wooden statue of Tutankhamun may be similar to that of Osiris that Ikhernofret restored at Abydos.*

Temple Ritual

One of the duties of the king was to see that the temple ritual was carried out and the festivals celebrated properly. By doing this he was trying to ensure that *maat*, the perfect world order, was maintained. The king of Egypt was officially high priest in every temple in the land, though of course it was not physically possible for him to carry out the ritual everywhere on a daily basis. Other priests must have substituted for him most of the time, although he probably took part personally on special occasions. However, only the king is ever shown on temple walls officiating in the cult. Of all the temples of the New Kingdom (c.1550–c.1069 BC), that of Seti I (c.1294–c.1279 BC) at Abydos has the most complete record of the daily ritual. All the stages are depicted in beautiful painted relief.

The morning ritual

Each morning, before the king took part in the cult, he was purified by two priests acting the parts of the gods Horus and Thoth. Dressed in a very simple manner to show his humility before the god, the king approached the sanctuary bearing a censer. The sanctuary contained the sacred boat and a shrine housing the god's statue. As it was dark in the sanctuary, the king would light a lamp. He sprinkled incense on the censer to perfume the air. Reaching the shrine he broke the seal and removed the bolt, called the 'Finger of Seth'. Echoing the myth of Osiris, the king told the god he had brought him the 'Eye of Horus' to restore him to life. He then opened the doors of the shrine, which are described as the 'Doors of Heaven', and gazed on the face of the god. He bowed twice before the god, rose again and sang hymns of praise. The king then anointed the god and burnt incense before him.

Entering the shrine the king embraced the statue and restored him to life by offering him the Eye, just as Horus did for Osiris in the myth. He repeated this part of the ritual in his capacity as king of

▲ *Seti I assists Isis in the ceremony of 'Raising the* Djed*-pillar', which symbolically re-enacts the resurrection of Osiris.*

▲ *Detail of a raised relief in the Hypostyle Hall at Karnak. Seti I offers flowers to the Theban triad, Amun, Mut and Khonsu.*

▲ *A painted carved relief of Seti I in the Osiris temple of Abydos. He stands before an offering table and sprinkles incense.*

the Two Lands. At the end of the repeat ceremony, the king offered a tiny figure of Maat, the goddess of truth and justice.

In the next part of the ceremony, the king took the god's statue from its niche and set it up on a mound of sand. Next, he presented four baskets containing linen, precious ointments and incense. After this, he walked four times round the statue and purified it with water and incense. He then dressed the statue, decked it in jewellery and anointed it with perfumed oils and ointments. Wine and bread were offered. Finally, the statue was put back in its shrine and the doors were bolted and sealed. The king then withdrew, sweeping away his footprints with a broom.

Raising the *Djed*-pillar

One special festival depicted on the walls of the Abydos temple is that of 'Raising the *Djed*-pillar'. The origins of the *djed*-pillar are uncertain, although it is thought by some to represent a pole with grain tied around it. At first it was associated with Ptah-Sokar, a funerary god of Memphis, but by the New Kingdom it represented the backbone of Osiris. The ceremony referred to the resurrection of Osiris and the *djed* motif is often found painted on the bottom of coffins so that the backbone of the deceased would rest on the image of the backbone of Osiris. Its restorative power would then ensure that the dead would return to life, just as Osiris had in mythology. The ceremony of 'Raising the *Djed*-pillar' was also part of the king's *heb sed* or jubilee festival, when he was rejuvenated and reinvested with his royal power. The *djed* symbolized stability and continuity so the ceremony linked the reign of the king with the rule of Osiris in the Underworld. ◆

▶ *The inner walls of the Hypostyle Hall at Karnak are decorated in raised relief scenes showing Seti I offering to Amun and his wife Mut.*

Temples of Hathor

Hathor was one of the most commonly worshipped goddesses in ancient Egypt, beloved of royalty and commoners alike. She was principally a mother goddess and was often regarded as the mother of the king. Her name means 'House of Horus', signifying the womb that sheltered Horus. Hathor was believed to enable women to conceive, and she also helped them in childbirth. In another capacity, as Mistress of the West, Hathor figured in both royal and private tombs as the deity who welcomed the deceased into the Afterlife. She was also Mistress of Foreign Lands, Mistress of Turquoise, and a goddess of music, dance and sexual love.

As early as the Fourth Dynasty (c.2613–c.2494 BC) there is written and archaeological evidence for temples dedicated to Hathor, and the wives of high-ranking officials are known to have been her priestesses. She was also revered by the kings of the New Kingdom (c.1550–c.1069 BC). The Eighteenth Dynasty female ruler, Hatshepsut (c.1473–c.1458 BC), added a small shrine dedicated to Hathor to her mortuary temple at Deir el-Bahri and Ramesses II (c.1279–c.1213 BC) built the lesser of his two temples at Abu Simbel for Hathor and his principal wife, Nefertari. Hathor retained her popularity until the Ptolemaic Period (332–30 BC), when the great temple at Dendera was built in her honour.

◀ *The Roman* mammisi *(birth house) is part of the temple complex at Dendera, where Hathor was worshipped as the mother of kings.*

Hathor in Art and Architecture

Hathor, the cow goddess, seems to have been popular at all periods of ancient Egyptian history. A cow goddess appears on the Narmer Palette, which dates from about 3100 BC. She is not named but may well be Hathor. Even earlier, in the Predynastic Period, vases were painted with pictures of cows and dancing women holding up their arms in imitation of cows' horns. They are thought to be performing 'cow dances', as the women of the southern Sudan do today. These ancient dances were possibly in honour of Hathor.

▲ *The head of Hathor is often used to decorate the capitals of columns in temple architecture. The goddess has a human face and cow's ears.*

The nurturing mother goddess

Hathor was often represented entirely as a cow. In the Egyptian Museum in Cairo there is a famous statue of her in this form. King Amenhotep II (c.1427–c.1400 BC), portrayed as an adult, stands in front of Hathor under her protection. He is also shown as a child kneeling down to drink from her udders. Hathor was otherwise depicted as a beautiful, slender woman wearing a headdress of a pair of cow's horns with a sun disc between them, or in human form with cow's ears. Very occasionally, she was represented as a woman with the entire head of a cow. She thus represents divine motherhood.

One of the most beautiful depictions of Hathor comes from the tomb of Seti I (c.1294–c.1279 BC) in the Valley of the Kings. This was removed at the beginning of the nineteenth century by Giovanni Belzoni, and is now in the Louvre, Paris. It shows Hathor lovingly holding Seti by the hand and welcoming him into the Afterlife. The delicacy and tenderness of the carving are unique, and the way in which the king's diaphanous linen clothing reveals the fine modelling of his limbs is unsurpassed in the art of ancient Egypt. Hathor wears a dress embroidered with a design based on the king's name and titles. She holds out her *menat*-necklace to him. This is made of dozens of strings of tiny metal beads,

◀ *Hathor as depicted in the Book of the Dead, where she appears as a cow emerging from the Mountain of the West to welcome the deceased into the Afterlife. The papyrus plant is sacred to her.*

▶ *A delicately carved and painted raised relief, originally from Seti I's tomb in the Valley of the Kings, shows Hathor embracing Seti.*

which jingle when shaken; it is a sign of rebirth, so the scene reflects the re-creation of the deceased king.

Mistress of the West

Another scene from the royal tombs in the Valley of the Kings shows Horemheb (c.1323–c.1295 BC) making an offering of wine to Hathor. Here she wears a different headdress which is the hieroglyph for 'west'. It identifies her as the Mistress of the West, and signifies that she was goddess of the necropolis on the west bank of the Nile, the place of the setting sun where the dead entered the Underworld. In this form, Hathor offered the deceased protection on their hazardous journey to the next world. In the text accompanying the relief, she assures Horemheb that she will give him protection and guarantees him 'the throne of Osiris forever'.

Sekhmet the lioness

Usually Hathor was a benign goddess. However, in the myth The Destruction of Humankind she was sent by her father, the sun god Re, to punish the Egyptians for their disloyal murmurings against him. She changed from her maternal cowlike self and became a raging lioness, Sekhmet. She was diverted from devouring all in her path by a trick. The people brewed hundreds of jars of beer dyed with red ochre, which Sekhmet took to be blood and greedily drank. She fell into a drunken stupor, forgetting when she awoke what she had been sent to do. Her motherly aspect returned and the Egyptians were saved.

The symbols of Hathor

In the Book of the Dead of Ani, Hathor is depicted as a cow emerging from the western mountains wearing her *menat*-necklace, welcoming the dead to the Afterlife. In the text she is also associated with the papyrus plant, since thickets of papyrus were the habitat of the wild cow. Another of her symbols was the *sistrum*, a musical instrument which, when shaken, made a noise like a tambourine. The instrument was decorated with the head of Hathor and priestesses played it in temple rituals. As Hathor was a goddess of love and beauty, the shape of the *sistrum* was also used as a handle for mirrors. The *sistrum* was also used as a decorative motif in architecture. It was carved on the sides of square columns, while round columns represented the handle of the *sistrum*, with Hathor's head as the capital, surmounted by the instrument itself. ◆

The Temple at Dendera

Dendera, which lies about 60km (37 miles) north of Luxor, was the capital of the Sixth Nome of Upper Egypt and Hathor's chief cult centre. The ancient Egyptian name of the town was Iunet, which the Greeks translated as Tentyra. The antiquity of Hathor's link with the city is suggested by the discovery of an ancient cemetery there that included some cow burials. Her husband, Horus of Edfu, or Horus the Elder, and their son, Ihy, were also worshipped at Dendera. Their son is also identified as Hor-sema-tawy, the Younger Horus, whose name means 'He Who Unites the Two Lands'.

Early temples

A shrine to Hathor existed at Dendera from the Predynastic Period (c.5500–c.3100 BC) when she was worshipped as She of the Pillar, a reference to the fetish associated with her. This shrine was rebuilt in the Pyramid Age by the Fourth Dynasty king Khufu (c.2589–c.2566 BC) and was dedicated to Hathor, Lady of the Pillar, and her son Ihy, the *Sistrum* Player. Ihy was depicted as a child, that is naked, wearing the sidelock of youth and pointing to his mouth with his index finger, playing the *sistrum*, the musical instrument sacred to his mother. The Sixth Dynasty king Pepi I (c.2321–c.2287 BC) presented a gold statue of Ihy to the temple, and the interest of the Old Kingdom kings is further attested by a fragmentary inscription of Pepi II (c.2278–c.2184 BC).

The Middle Kingdom kings also paid their respects to the goddess. Mentuhotep III (c.2004–c.1992 BC) added a limestone *naos*, or raised shrine, to the temple, while the name of Amenemhat I (c.1985–c.1955 BC) has been found on a granite lintel. An incense altar was presented by one of the Thirteenth Dynasty kings.

The temple was extended and embellished by several of the New Kingdom kings. Inscriptions on some of the columns indicate that Tuthmosis III (c.1479–c.1425 BC) rebuilt the temple at Dendera and revived the ritual. Amenhotep III (c.1390–c.1352 BC) presented a gold statue of Hapi, the god of the Nile inundation, offering stalks of papyrus. Ramesses II (c.1279–c.1213 BC) is shown in relief on a block recovered at the site, presenting two *sistra* to Hathor.

The crypts

An interesting feature of the temple is the existence of crypts below the floor and built into the thickness of the walls. Some of these can be visited and, uniquely, they are very beautifully decorated with carved relief. Strangely, in view of this artistry, they seem to have been used as storage spaces rather than for secret ritual. The lavish decoration is, perhaps, a comment on the valuable nature of the ritual vessels and cult statues that would have been stored there. The carved reliefs include Horus in falcon form, wearing a gold collar with counter-poises decorated with heads of Hathor.

The temple site

The building that the visitor can see today was built during the Graeco-Roman Period (332 BC–AD 395). It is difficult to be precise about its dates as many of the cartouches of the kings have been left blank or simply say 'pharaoh'. However, it is likely that building began during the reign of Ptolemy XII (80–51 BC) and was abandoned during the first century AD.

The temple is vast and largely intact. The site is entered by a Roman gateway, the work of Domitian (AD 81–96) and Trajan (AD 98–117). The former is shown on the outer face making offerings to Hathor, Horus the Elder and Ihy. The temple is unfinished so there is no pylon or open court in front of the main part of the building, the Hypostyle Hall.

◄ *Hathor's chief cult centre was at Dendera, where a shrine or temple stood on the site from the Predynastic to the Roman Periods.*

▲ *A figure of Bes, a dwarf-like god, who was believed to aid mothers in childbirth. Images of the god are used on the pillar capitals of the* mammisi *(birth houses) of the king at Dendera.*

▲ *A carved relief of Hathor and her son Ihy on the rear wall of the Dendera temple (shown here) is balanced by the figures of Cleopatra and her son Caesarion at the opposite end.*

The temple halls

The façade of the Hypostyle Hall dates from the reign of the Emperor Tiberius (AD 14–37). The screen wall is decorated with relief panels and the design incorporates six columns decorated with heads of Hathor. Much of the original colour remains. Inside the temple, the roof of the main hall is supported by massive columns, 15m (49ft) high, representing *sistra* and carved with offering scenes and mythological texts. They are topped with square capitals, on each side of which is a head of Hathor, in human form but with cow's ears.

The ceiling is divided into seven bands. The central one shows the vulture goddess Nekhbet, wearing the crown of Upper Egypt, and winged sun discs with the crown of Lower Egypt. These symbolize the union of Hathor and Horus. The other bands are decorated with astronomical scenes. At each end is an elongated figure of Nut, the sky goddess, along which sail the boats of the gods who represent the stars. On the bands inside these, the gods represent the hours of the night, the signs of the zodiac and the planets. The bands on either side of the centre show the daily course of the sun and the moon.

Beyond is a second hall, a Hall of Appearances, where the walls are decorated with scenes depicting the temple foundation ritual. The approach to the Sanctuary is through the Hall of Offerings and the Hall of the Gods, where the statues of the gods were brought on festival days when they were carried in procession to the roof. The Sanctuary itself originally contained a shrine that housed the statue of the goddess. Unfortunately, this is now missing but it appears in the carved reliefs on the Sanctuary walls, as does the sacred boat, which once a year took Hathor to visit her husband, Horus, whose temple was at Edfu, where a sacred marriage took place before the boat returned to Dendera.

The public shrine

Generally, the public were not allowed into the temple proper: this was the prerogative of the king and the priests. At Dendera, some provision was made for those otherwise excluded. In the centre of the outside wall at the back of the main temple was a small shrine to Hathor. It took the form of a carved relief of the goddess, which was originally protected by a gilded wooden canopy. Here, the public could approach the goddess and offer their prayers and petitions.

This wall is also decorated with a rare, clearly identifiable representation of the famous Queen Cleopatra (51–30 BC). She is shown here with Caesarion, her son by Julius Caesar. Together they are making their own offerings to the gods.

Behind the main temple is the smaller, ruined temple of Isis, probably destroyed by the early Christians. From the New Kingdom (c.1550–c.1069 BC), the mother goddesses, Isis and Hathor, were closely associated, Isis frequently adopting the iconography and attributes of Hathor. ▶

◀ *The statue of Hathor was carried each year to the Chapel of the Union with the Sun's Disc, to be exposed to the re-creative powers of the sun.*

Union of Hathor with the sun

The walls of the temple contain stairways leading to and from the roof, which are decorated with carved reliefs depicting the processions that took place here annually. The figures of priests, some of whom wear masks, are shown carrying shrines of Hathor and other offerings to the little chapels on the flat roof of the temple. The most important festival took place at the New Year, when the statue of Hathor was taken to the roofless Chapel of the Union with the Sun's Disc, so that the sun could shine in on her to reinvigorate her.

A scene showing this ceremony is used to great effect on the ceiling of the Nut Chapel near the foot of the stairway that leads up to the roof from the Hall of Offerings. Here, the sun, swallowed by the sky goddess, Nut, passes through her body during the hours of the night and re-emerges at dawn. As Nut gives birth to the sun it shines down on to an image of Hathor in her shrine. She is then rejuvenated for another year.

The temple roof

Other chapels were used to celebrate the resurrection of Osiris, and they show scenes of the posthumous impregnation of Isis. One is decorated with a copy of the Zodiac of Dendera (the original is in the Louvre, Paris). This is a map of the sky with the constellations divided into 36 decans, or sections, which were used by the Egyptians to tell the time at night. Each decan was visible for ten days at a time (hence the name). The point at which it appeared above the horizon indicated the hour.

From the flat roof it is possible to climb up to an even higher level. A procession of gods and goddesses is carved into the temple wall alongside the ancient flight of steps leading upwards. (Visitors now climb an iron staircase.) From the topmost level there are superb views over the surrounding countryside and the rest of the temple buildings.

The birth houses

From the roof of the main temple many other buildings associated with the cult of Hathor can be seen. To the west are two birth houses or *mammisi*. One of these was built in the reign of Nectanebo II (360–343 BC), the last of the Egyptian pharaohs, and is decorated with carved reliefs, which depict his divine birth. Hathor is shown as his mother and Amun (not Horus) as his father. As they sit together on a bed, Amun gives Hathor the *ankh*, or sign of life, and so impregnates her. Thoth announces the

▶ *This detail of the ceiling of the Hypostyle Hall at Dendera shows the nocturnal passage of the sun, which shines down on Hathor as it is reborn.*

▲ *A large Coptic church lies between the two* mammisi *(birth houses) and is one of the earliest Christian churches in Egypt.*

▲ *A detail from the Roman* mammisi *(bath house) shows the emperor offering to the mother goddess. The building was dedicated to Hathor and her son Ihy.*

birth to the assembled gods and goddesses, and the ram-headed god Khnum creates the divine child on his potter's wheel, while the frog goddess Heket holds out the *ankh*. In a double scene on the rear wall the goddess is shown suckling the child while Thoth and Seshat, deities of writing, record the years of his life. These scenes are very similar to the ones at Luxor and Deir el-Bahri, which depict the pharaohs Amenhotep III (c.1390–c.1352 BC) and Hatshepsut (c.1473–c.1458 BC) as children of the god Amun.

Nearer to the temple gateway is the Roman Birth House, begun in the reign of Augustus (27 BC–AD 14) with decoration completed by Trajan (AD 98–117) and Hadrian (AD 117–38). Here, the scenes relate to the birth of Hathor's divine son rather than the king, who is shown presenting offerings. The outer screen walls also show the king adoring the goddess and her son. Above the capitals are *abaci* (slabs supporting the stone beam, which in turn supports the roof) carved with images of Bes, the god who helped mothers in childbirth.

Between the two *mammisi* is a large Coptic church. It dates to the late fifth century AD and was largely built of reused material removed from the Roman Birth House. It is a very good example of the layout of an early Egyptian church, consisting of three main parts: narthex, nave and apse.

Surrounding buildings

Between the temple proper and the Birth House of Nectanebo is a collection of mudbrick rooms and a bath. This complex has now been recognized as a sanatorium. Pilgrims came from near and far to be cured by spending some time in this famous centre of healing. The patients either drank or bathed in water that had been poured over a divine statue inscribed with magical texts, which was considered to have healing properties. Others slept in the cubicles and hoped to receive a dream that would restore them to health.

To the south-west is the Sacred Lake, which represents the primordial ocean. The complex is surrounded by a massive mudbrick wall built in a wavy design, which reflects this symbolism. ◆

Hathor as healer

In mythology, Hathor had healing powers. At one point in The Contendings of Horus and Seth, Seth gouged out the eyes of Horus. Hathor found him weeping in the desert. She caught a gazelle and milked it, and by pouring the milk into Horus's eye sockets she restored his sight.

The Temple of Philae

Hathor was honoured with a shrine at Philae, the main sanctuary of Isis, just as Isis was worshipped at Hathor's cult centre, Dendera. In later ancient Egyptian history, the two deities were often regarded as one because they were both principally mother goddesses. From the New Kingdom (c.1550–c.1069 BC), both were depicted wearing the same headdress – a pair of cow's horns with a sun disc between them. The two goddesses often look so much alike that it is difficult to tell them apart if there are no hieroglyphs to distinguish them. Where there are, Isis is identified by a small throne and Hathor by a square containing Horus as a falcon.

Both Isis and Hathor were important in relation to the king, although in different ways. As far as the succession was concerned, the legitimate king regarded himself as Horus, the heir of Osiris, while his other identity as Horus,

▲ *A view of the approach to the Temple of Philae from Lake Nasser shows the outer walls and two pylons.*

▼ *Images of Hathor decorate the pillars of the First Court at Philae, principally a temple of Isis. Both goddesses were mothers of the kings of Egypt.*

▲ *Bes, a dwarf-like god who helps mothers in childbirth and is often associated with Hathor in this capacity, plays the harp in her honour.*

▲ *An ape plays the lyre, an instrument often shown in 18th-Dynasty tomb paintings being played by female musicians at a banquet.*

son of Hathor, emphasized his divinity. Both aspects of divine motherhood are represented at Philae. On the First Pylon of the Temple of Isis, Ptolemy XII (80–51 BC) is shown smiting his enemies while Isis, Horus of Edfu and Hathor look on. Beyond the First Pylon is the *mammisi* (birth house), where the walls are decorated with scenes depicting the birth of Horus in the Delta marshes. In this myth, his mother was Isis. Nonetheless, the screen walls of the surrounding ambulatory are linked with columns, whose capitals are heads of Hathor.

Musicians and dancers

Outside the Temple of Isis, Hathor has a charming little chapel all to herself. This, like the main temple, was built by the Ptolemies, with later additions by Augustus (27 BC–AD 14). Here, Hathor is commemorated as a goddess of music and dance. The columns of the vestibule are decorated with lively and humorous carved reliefs of musicians of various kinds, including flute players and harpists. There are even some monkeys playing the lyre. The protective god Bes, who often aided Hathor in her capacity as goddess of childbirth, is seen here playing a tambourine. Elsewhere, he is dancing and playing a harp. On the screen walls separating the columns, the emperor Augustus is shown making offerings to various personifications of Hathor. Kings sometimes worshipped Hathor with music and dancing as well as with offerings of food and wine.

The worship of Isis at Philae continued long after the introduction of Christianity. It was not until the reign of the emperor Justinian (AD 527–565) that the temple was closed and a Christian church, dedicated to the Virgin Mary, established on the site. ◆

▲ *Another pillar is decorated with an image of Bes playing a tambourine resembling those often depicted in ceremonial scenes.*

▲ *A priest plays a double flute before a clump of papyrus, a plant sacred to Hathor in her form as a wild cow.*

The king dances

The King, Pharaoh, comes to dance,
He comes to sing;
Mistress see the dancing,
Wife of Horus, see the skipping!

He offers it to you,
This jug:
Mistress see the dancing,
Wife of Horus, see the skipping!

His heart is straight, his inmost being open
No darkness is in his breast:
Mistress see the dancing,
Wife of Horus, see the skipping!

O Golden One, how good is this song!
Like the song of Horus himself;
Re's son sings as master singer,
He is Ihy, the musician!

O beauteous one, O cow,
O great one,
O great magician, O splendid lady, O queen of gods!
The King, Pharaoh, reveres you,
grant that he live!
O queen of gods, he reveres you,
give that he live!

(Extracts from Ptolemaic hymns at Dendera)

Hathor at Deir el-Medina

In the New Kingdom Period (c.1550–c.1069 BC) Hathor was very popular among the inhabitants of Deir el-Medina, the village occupied by the craftsmen who built the tombs in the Valley of the Kings. Some of the village women had the title 'Songstress of Hathor'.

There were several chapels dedicated to Hathor in the village. The Nineteenth Dynasty king Seti I (c.1294–c.1279 BC) built a chapel dedicated to her, as did his son, Ramesses II (c.1279–c.1213 BC), who endowed it with offerings from his own mortuary temple nearby. This was replaced in the Ptolemaic Period (332–30 BC), long after the village had been abandoned, by the rather grand temple surrounded by a massive mudbrick wall that still dominates the site today.

Excavation of the temple revealed the statue of a snake goddess, Mertseger, who was regarded as another form of Hathor. She was often depicted as a cobra and was associated with the peak, covered with shrines, that dominated the west bank. A beautiful head from a statue of Hathor in the form of a cow also came to light. It was made of calcite and the eyes had been inlaid with rock crystal and lapis lazuli.

The craftsmen's stelae

Several of the craftsmen set up stelae in honour of the goddess. The stela of Nefersenut shows him kneeling in front of Hathor, holding a brazier containing an offering. Below, his sons join him in adoration of the goddess. Nefersenut's stela shows Hathor in the form of a woman, while on the stela of Khabekhenet she is shown as a cow emerging from the mountains of the west.

The heartache of a childless couple can be seen in the prayers of another

▶ *A Hathor column from the interior of her temple at Deir el-Medina is decorated with snakes, representing the goddess Mertseger, with whom Hathor is associated.*

► *The Ptolemaic temple to Hathor at Deir el-Medina was built long after the craftsmen's village had ceased to exist.*

craftsman, Ramose. He set up two stelae to the deities of fertility and childbirth, probably in a shrine to Hathor, and also dedicated a stone phallus to her. Inscribed on it was his plea to the goddess to send him a son, expressed in these words:

> *O Hathor, remember the man at his burial. Grant a duration in thy House as a rewarded one to the scribe Ramose...cause me to receive a compensation of thy house as a rewarded one.*

Unfortunately his cries fell on deaf ears and he had to be content with an adopted son.

▼ *A rare representation of Hathor, from the Ptolemaic temple at Deir el-Medina, shows her with a complete cow's head rather than the more usual human head with cow's ears.*

Hathor in literature

The craftsmen of Deir el-Medina appear to have been avid readers, if the amount of ancient Egyptian literature found in the village is anything to go by. Hathor appeared in The Contendings of Horus and Seth when her father, the sun god Re-Horakhty, was angry because the other gods wanted to give the throne of Egypt to Horus while he favoured Seth. He was lying sulking in his tent when Hathor restored his good humour by hitching up her skirts and 'revealing her nakedness'. In a later episode in the same story, she restored the sight of Horus after he had been blinded by Seth.

Hathor also appeared in love poetry, where she was called the 'Golden One' and was regarded as instrumental in bringing lovers together:

O Golden One,
I worship her majesty,
I extol the Lady of Heaven;
I give adoration to Hathor,
Praise to my Mistress!
I called to her, she heard my plea
She sent my mistress to me:
She came by herself to see me,
O great wonder that happened to me!
I was joyful, exulting, elated,
When they said, 'See, she is here!'
As she came the young men bowed,
Out of great love for her.
I make devotions to my goddess,
That she grant me my sister [the girl he loves] as a gift
Three days now that I pray to her name
Five days since she went from me. ◆

▼ *This limestone chipping shows the snake goddess Mertseger adored by one of the craftsmen at Deir el-Medina. Mertseger was one of the aspects of Hathor.*

Serabit el-Khadim

Hathor was the goddess most often associated with foreign countries and desert areas. She was particularly closely linked with the Sinai region, where she was known as *nebet mefkat* ('Mistress of Turquoise'). Turquoise was highly prized in ancient Egypt and was used in jewellery from the Predynastic Period. One of the most beautiful early examples of royal jewellery was found by Flinders Petrie in the Abydos tomb of the First Dynasty king Djer (c.3000 BC). It was a bracelet formed of tiny *serekhs* (plaques bearing the king's Horus name) surmounted by a Horus falcon. The 13 gold plaques and 14 of turquoise were used alternately to make a stunning piece of jewellery. It is now in the Cairo Museum.

Expeditions to Sinai

Sinai was the most important source of turquoise for the Egyptians throughout the Pharaonic Period. Inscriptions from Wadi Magara and Serabit el-Khadim show that from as early as the beginning of the Old Kingdom (c.2686 BC) the kings mounted expeditions to obtain turquoise from those areas. At Serabit el-Khadim a temple was built in honour of Hathor, whose blessing was sought by the leaders of the expeditions.

A wealth of information on the expeditions to Sinai comes from the stelae set up by the leaders along the approach to the Temple of Hathor. Most of these date from the Middle Kingdom (c.2055–c.1650 BC). Many are badly eroded but it has been possible to use all the available information to build up a more or less complete picture. They describe the numbers of men involved in such an expedition, what part they took in the proceedings, what the transport arrangements were and even when was the best time to go.

The expedition leaders were usually called 'Seal-bearer of the God (meaning the king) and Director of Gangs'. There was also an official in charge of transport. He arranged for boats to bring men and supplies to the nearest accessible point on the coast and organized the donkeys for the rest of the journey. An expedition would need about 500 donkeys, each of which had to carry the food for one man for five days, as well as its own fodder and water. Most of the workforce were quarrymen and stonecutters but the party also included quartermasters, donkey-men and a scorpion-magician.

The best time for the expeditions was in the cooler weather, after the inundation had receded and the sowing had been done. One inscription reads:

> *By the time the hot weather came on, all this body of men were on their way back to Egypt accompanying the bags full of the precious gifts of the Mistress of Turquoise.*

Not all expeditions were so fortunate, however. The expedition leader, Horrure, at first had difficulty locating the turquoise, and had to toil in the scorching sun, having been forced to travel 'when it was not the proper season for coming to this mining region'.

The Temple of Hathor

The original shrine of Hathor was a sacred cave, and seems to have been founded by the Fourth Dynasty king Sneferu (c.2613–c.2589 BC). Although there is no direct link between Sneferu and the Sanctuary, the form of hieroglyphs on an inscribed hawk found in it was thought by Petrie to be contemporary with him, and later kings mention him in terms that suggest that they considered him to have been the founder. The throne of a statuette of the Twelfth Dynasty king Senusret I (c.1965–c.1920 BC) bears a dedication to Sneferu and a stela of Amenemhat III

▼ *Hathor's temple at Serabit el-Khadim contains many inscribed stelae recording successful royal expeditions to Sinai to procure turquoise for the Egyptian kings.*

▲ *This stela was dedicated to Hathor by an expedition leader and names her* nebet mefkat *('Mistress of Turquoise'). Her blessing was thought to bring success to the mission.*

(c.1855–c.1808 BC) refers to himself as 'Beloved of Sneferu'. Sneferu is also the only king from before the Twelfth Dynasty to be named in the Hall of Kings by Hatshepsut (c.1473–c.1458 BC), when she extended the Sanctuary in the New Kingdom. A stela belonging to a Middle Kingdom expedition leader mentions that he had mined more turquoise than anyone else since the time of Sneferu.

The Sanctuary was extended in the Middle Kingdom by the Twelfth Dynasty king Amenemhat III. He enlarged the sacred cave, set up altars and began the building of a portico. The New Kingdom kings were also very active here. Several vases and *menat*-necklaces were dedicated to Hathor by Ahmose-Nefertari, wife of Ahmose (c.1550–c.1525 BC), the first king of the Eighteenth Dynasty, and by their daughter, Merytamun. However, the most enthusiastic builders were Hatshepsut and Tuthmosis III (c.1479–c.1425 BC). Their most important addition to the Sanctuary was a court surrounded by four great columns with Hathor heads on the capitals. There was a basin for ablutions in the centre. At least a partial remodelling of the cave was carried out at this time, and the main hall of the temple was built.

► *A fallen capital from a column in the Hathor temple shows her, in typical style, with a human face, a bouffant hairstyle and cow's ears.*

Hatshepsut also built the Hall of Kings, which contains a relief showing the queen making offerings to Sneferu and depictions of King Amenemhet III and the deities Hathor and Sopdu. The work of Hatshepsut and Tuthmosis III was completed by a Great Pylon. Other rooms were added by later Eighteenth Dynasty kings and some major reconstruction work was done in the Ramesside Period (c.1295–c.1069 BC). However, the kings of later dynasties do not seem to have had much interest in the shrine and it was eventually abandoned.

The temple remains

Today, the temple can only be reached on foot after an exhilarating climb. The views across the mountains are stupendous and well worth the effort. On your return you may well be rewarded by a cup of tea provided by local people, but only after you have bought one of the fragments of turquoise, which is all the mines produce today.

It is also a humbling experience to clamber up the hillsides as the donkey caravans of the expeditions did so long ago. As you survey the bleak ridges of mountains that roll away to the Red Sea, it is easy to imagine their heartfelt need of the goddess's blessing, especially when they were forced to come at the 'wrong' time of year, and their great joy when she led them to stones of 'a good colour', as she eventually did for Horrure, who returned with more turquoise 'than any who had come before':

Offer, offer, to the Lady of Heaven!
May you propitiate Hathor!
May you do this, it is good for you!
Increase this, it will be well for you! ◆

A prized turquoise

A story about King Sneferu tells that he was feeling bored one day and was advised to take some young court ladies out on the palace lake to cheer himself up. He ordered them to change their usual dresses for bead-net versions and apparently 'his majesty's heart was happy seeing them row'. After a while the boat started drifting around in circles, because the women on one side of the boat had stopped rowing. Their leader had dropped her turquoise hair ornament into the water and was so distressed that she refused to go on. The king offered to get her another but she refused. Eventually the king had to send for a magician to roll the water back and retrieve her precious jewel for her.

Hathor, Mistress of Foreign Lands

Foreign lands were regarded as the personal property of Hathor, and the goods that the Egyptians obtained from these countries were said to be her 'gifts'. Temples were erected in her honour in such countries. In the Middle Kingdom (c.2055–1650 BC) she was worshipped at Byblos in Lebanon. Egypt had trading connections with this city that went back at least to the Pyramid Age. The Palermo Stone, on which the annals of the first five dynasties are recorded, notes the arrival from Byblos of 40 shiploads of timber in the reign of King Sneferu (c.2613–c.2589 BC). Excavations have revealed evidence of a cult to Hathor in this ancient commercial centre, where she was called Lady of Byblos.

Imports from Nubia

Egypt had longstanding trading relations with Nubia. In his famous autobiography engraved on the façade of his tomb at Aswan, Harkhuf, a governor of the South, described the expeditions that he undertook on behalf of the king to fetch exotic goods such as incense, ebony, ivory and panther skins. The king was especially pleased about the pygmy that Harkhuf had brought to dance for him, and wrote to congratulate him. Harkhuf was very proud of this letter and had it carved on the front of the tomb next to his autobiography:

> *The King's own seal: Year 2, third month of the first season, day 15. The king's decree to the Sole Companion, Lector-priest, Chief of Scouts, Harkhuf. You have said in this despatch of yours that you have brought a pygmy of the god's dances from the land of the horizon-dwellers, like the pygmy whom the god's seal-bearer Bawerded brought from Punt in the time of King Isesi. You have said to my majesty that his like has never been brought by anyone who did Yam previously.*

The writer of the letter was Pepi II (c.2278–c.2184 BC) who would have been a child of about eight at the time.

▼ *The smaller of the two temples built by Ramesses II at Abu Simbel was dedicated to Hathor of Abshek, a local form of the goddess.*

◀ *The Kiosk of Qertassi, now reconstructed at New Kalabsha, originally stood at the entrance to the sandstone quarries further south.*

Nubian sanctuaries

Temples were built in honour of Hathor in Nubia. One of the most charming is the little Kiosk of Qertassi, which today stands close to the Temple of Kalabsha. It was one of several temples moved to higher ground to save it from the rising waters of Lake Nasser after the building of the Aswan High Dam. Originally, the kiosk stood at the entrance to the old sandstone quarries about 40km (25 miles) further south. As at Serabit el-Khadim in Sinai, Hathor was regarded here as a patron goddess of miners and quarrymen, so it is not surprising that the capitals of the two columns on either side of the entrance are in the form of Hathor heads.

Hathor was also worshipped at Faras, where Queen Hatshepsut (c.1473–1458 BC) founded a sanctuary to her at the time when Egypt was bringing Nubia under direct control. The British Museum's collection includes several figurines of Hathor that were brought to the shrine as votive offerings by the workers of this desert region. She is represented in the Temple of Ramesses II at Wadi es-Sebua, where she appears, unusually, in human form but with the head of a cow. Hathor is one of the most frequently depicted deities in the Ptolemaic Temple of Dakka and was also honoured in the New Kingdom shrines at Qasr Ibrim.

Abu Simbel

Hathor's most important Nubian shrine is at Abu Simbel, where Ramesses II (c.1279–1213 BC) built two temples. In the larger of the two, Ramesses is shown worshipping himself as one of the gods honoured in the temple. The smaller temple he dedicated to Hathor of Abshek, a local goddess of beauty, love and motherhood, and also to Nefertari, Ramesses' principal wife, who was identified with Hathor. It should be remembered that the New Kingdom rulers built temples in Nubia to demonstrate their power and control over the area, and the monuments also served as storehouses for the precious commodities the ancient Egyptians extracted from the area. So Hathor's role as Mistress of Foreign Lands is in evidence here, as she protects the king's dominions on his behalf. However, it is her gentler aspects that are emphasized at Abu Simbel, where the square columns of the rock-cut temple are decorated with the *sistrum*, the sacred instrument that identifies her as a goddess of music and sexuality. ◆

▶ *The Temple of Dakka is dedicated to 'Thoth of Pnubs', Pnubs referring to the sycamore tree where Thoth waited for his wife Tefnut, associated with Hathor, to persuade her to return to Egypt.*

Hathor, Mistress of the West

In her capacity as Mistress of the West, Hathor welcomed the dead into the Afterlife. She is shown in many of the royal tombs, especially on the pillars around the burial chamber, where she is depicted embracing the king and holding out to him the *ankh,* or sign of life, used here as a symbol of the new life that awaits him. On the walls of private tombs and on stelae and funerary papyri of the Ramesside Period (c.1295–c.1069 BC), Hathor appears most commonly as a cow emerging from the western mountain. She comes to protect the deceased in the Underworld and grant them safe passage to the Afterlife.

Beautiful Feast of the Valley

Every year, in the second month of Shomu, there was a special festival connected with this aspect of the goddess. It was called the Beautiful Feast of the Valley. The images of the gods Amun, Mut and Khonsu were carried in their sacred boats from Thebes and were taken to the various Hathor sanctuaries at Deir el-Bahri and the royal mortuary temples on the west bank. Inscriptions in the temples make reference to this festival. The best source of information on the subject comes from the mortuary temple of Hatshepsut (c.1473–c.1458 BC) at Deir el-Bahri, where the reliefs show soldiers and standard bearers taking part in the procession.

The festival was extremely important to private individuals as well as to royalty. Local people would use the opportunity to visit the tombs of their ancestors, where there would be a reunion of past and present members of the family and the sharing of a meal. This idea lingers on in a Muslim context today.

Deir el-Bahri

The association of Hathor with Deir el-Bahri is evident in the number of shrines and chapels dedicated to her in the area. The most important is the chapel to Hathor attached to the mortuary temple of Hatshepsut. It lies on the second level and consists of a vestibule and hypostyle hall and a rock-cut sanctuary. The columns are topped by Hathor-head capitals and the walls are decorated with offering scenes and episodes from the festivals held in her honour. Hathor is represented as a cow standing on her sacred boat. The most secret parts of the ceremonies took place in the rock-cut

◄ *This statue shows Hathor in cow form protecting King Amenhotep II. He is also seen as a child being suckled by the goddess in the Chapel of the Sacred Cow of Tuthmosis III at Deir el-Bahri.*

Sanctuary. Here, Hathor is depicted as a cow who both suckles and protects Hatshepsut. At the very back of the Sanctuary, Hathor and Amun are shown consecrating Hatshepsut as king.

The association of Hathor with this area was probably one of the reasons that the first king of the Middle Kingdom, Mentuhotep II (c.2055–c.2004 BC), built his mortuary temple at Deir el-Bahri, on what was then a virgin site. The princesses who were buried near the temple were priestesses of Hathor.

Between this temple and that of Hatshepsut was the Temple of Tuthmosis III (c.1479–c.1425 BC). A small chapel, a subsidiary shrine of this temple, was found quite by chance after a fall of rock by the Swiss Egyptologist Edouard Naville in 1906. Both the chapel and the statue it contained of Hathor as a cow, suckling and protecting a king, were in an excellent state of preservation and are now in the Cairo Museum. Although the chapel was built by Tuthmosis III, the name of the king depicted turned out to be his son Amenhotep II (c.1427–c.1400 BC). The walls of the chapel are decorated with scenes showing Tuthmosis III making offerings to Hathor in the form of a woman.

Until the death of Hatshepsut her temple was the final destination of the procession of the sacred boats during the Beautiful Feast of the Valley. Later, the Temple of Tuthmosis III took over this function. According to inscriptions found in the area, the cult of Hathor was maintained here until the Ramesside Period, when earthquakes caused the destruction of the main temple and the entrance of the little Chapel of the Sacred Cow was blocked. ◆

▲ *A painted relief from the chapel dedicated to Hathor at Deir el-Bahri shows festivities held in her honour, including a running race and a falconry competition.*

▼ *A vignette from the Book of the Dead shows Hathor, in the form of a cow, emerging from the western mountain to welcome the deceased into the Afterlife.*

Mortuary Temples

Mortuary temples were often called 'House of Millions of Years', and this helps to explain their function. The ancient Egyptians believed that the spirit of an individual, called the *ka*, came into existence at birth and was intimately linked to the physical body during life and after death, when it continued to need sustenance in the form of offerings of food and drink. In a royal mortuary temple, offerings were presented daily for the king's *ka*, and in theory this was to continue in perpetuity.

In the Old Kingdom c.2686–c.2181 BC), mortuary temples were usually built against the east side of the pyramid itself. In the New Kingdom (c.1550–c.1069 BC), when the kings were buried in the Valley of the Kings, mortuary temples were physically quite separate from the tombs, although they were still part of the concept of a funerary complex. They were built on the edge of the desert, just beyond the cultivation, and were separated from the royal tombs by a steep range of cliffs. The layout of the interior was usually the same as that of a cult temple.

The mortuary temples were served by priests who officiated in various capacities. While some presented the *ka* statue of the deceased king with offerings to satisfy his physical needs, others were involved in the running of the temple estates or engaging in trade to finance the mortuary cult.

◀ *The mortuary temple of Hatshepsut at Deir el-Bahri was built in the great bay of the cliffs next to the funerary complex of Mentuhotep II, in an area sacred to Hathor, as Mistress of the West.*

Western Thebes

In ancient times, Thebes was a significant religious centre, with the city of the living and the temples to the gods situated on the east bank of the Nile while the west side was devoted to the dead. Although kings had been buried there since the Eleventh Dynasty (c.2055–c.1985 BC), western Thebes was especially important in the New Kingdom (c.1550–c.1069 BC) when the royal tombs were in the Valley of the Kings. Even in the Ramesside Period (c.1295–c.1069 BC), when the kings ruled from their northern capital of Per-Ramesses, they continued to be buried in western Thebes. The royal mortuary temples, such as Medinet Habu and the Ramesseum, which served the *ka* of the kings buried in the valley, are strung out along the desert fringe. ◆

▲ *This Hathor column, with the capital in the form of a* sistrum, *is from the mortuary temple of Queen Hatshepsut at Deir el-Bahri.*

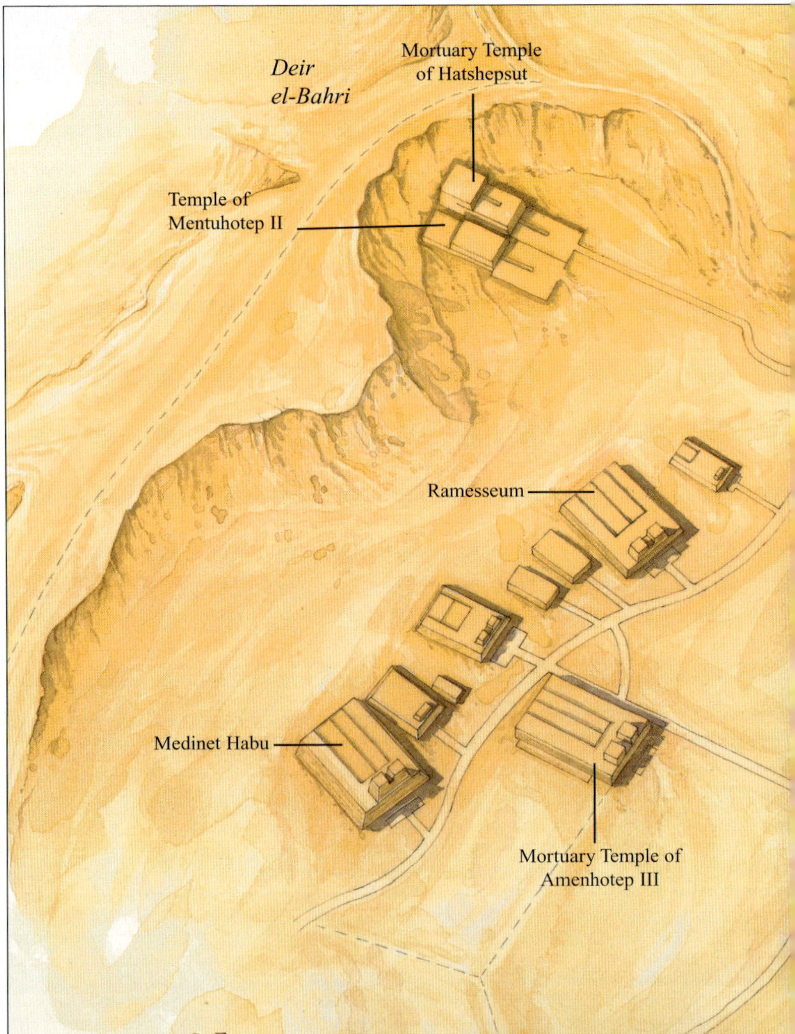

▲ *The statues of Ramesses II as Osiris as seen in the Second Court of the Ramesseum.*

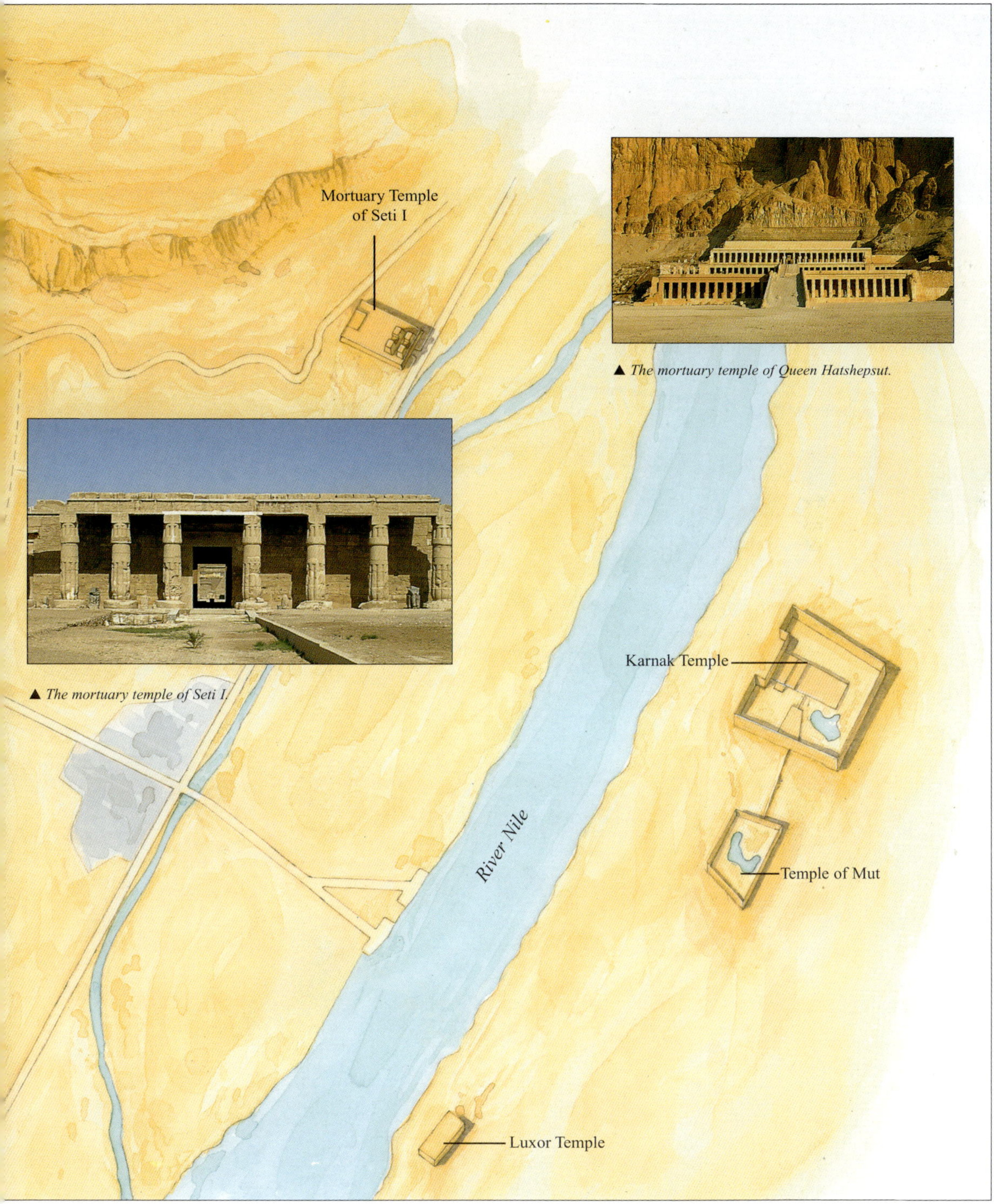

▲ *The mortuary temple of Queen Hatshepsut.*

▲ *The mortuary temple of Seti I.*

Deir el-Bahri: The Funerary Complex of Mentuhotep II

Mentuhotep II (c.2055–c.2004 BC), the Eleventh Dynasty king who reunited Egypt at the beginning of the Middle Kingdom, built a very unusual funerary complex. His mortuary temple was built on different levels in the great bay of cliffs at Deir el-Bahri. It was approached by a 46m (150ft) wide causeway leading from a valley temple, which no longer exists.

The mortuary temple itself consists of a forecourt, enclosed by walls on three sides, and a terrace on which stands a large square structure that may represent the primeval mound that arose from the waters of chaos. As the temple faces east, the structure is likely to be connected with the sun cult and the resurrection of the king. From the eastern part of the forecourt, an opening called the Bab el-Hosan ('Gate of the Horseman') leads to an underground passage and an unfinished tomb or cenotaph containing a seated statue of the king. On the western side, tamarisk and sycamore trees were

▲ *The remains of Mentuhotep's funerary complex can be seen cut into the cliffs at Deir el-Bahri. Facing east, it celebrates the sun cult and the resurrection of the king.*

▼ *A painted carved relief of Mentuhotep II from his mortuary temple at Deir el-Bahri reveals the hieroglyphs for 'one thousand' and 'duration', wishing him eternal life.*

planted beside the ramp leading up to the terrace. At the back of the forecourt and terrace are colonnades decorated in relief with boat processions, hunts and scenes showing the king's military achievements. Statues of the Twelfth Dynasty king Senusret III (c.1874–c.1855 BC) were found here too.

The inner part of the temple was actually cut into the cliff and consists of a peristyle court, a hypostyle hall and an underground passage 150m (492ft) long leading to the tomb itself. The cult of the dead king centred on the small shrine cut into the rear of the Hypostyle Hall.

The royal princesses

The mastaba-like structure on the terrace is surrounded by a pillared ambulatory along the west wall, where the statue shrines and tombs of several royal wives and daughters were found. The princesses were priestesses of Hathor, one of the main ancient Egyptian funerary deities. Although little remained of the king's own burial, six sarcophagi were retrieved from the tombs of the royal ladies. Each was formed of six slabs held together at the corners by metal braces and carved in sunk relief.

The sarcophagus of Queen Kawit, now in the Cairo Museum, is particularly fine. She is shown as the picture of elegance, her slender form set off by a close-fitting dress and simple jewellery. One of her attendants arranges her hair, while others present offerings of perfumed oils and milk. Another sarcophagus belonged to Ashait. When found, her mummy was still lying in a wooden inner coffin, brightly painted with scenes of palace life. Similar scenes were carved on the limestone sarcophagus.

Ashait is shown as a young woman sniffing a lotus flower and seated before an offering table. To the right of her, workers hurry to the granary with sacks of grain, thus ensuring a plentiful supply of food for her in the next life. ◆

▶ *This painted sandstone figure of Mentuhotep II was found in what was probably the original tomb below the terrace of the mortuary temple. His black skin, curved beard and crossed arms identify him with Osiris.*

Mentuhotep's statue

The seated statue of Mentuhotep II was discovered accidentally when the horse on which Howard Carter was riding trod on the paving stone over the entrance to the cenotaph. This caused the covering to collapse, and horse and rider fell into the tomb. The statue had been ritually interred. It was wrapped in a linen cloth and it is thought that the flesh was painted black just before it was buried. The king is wearing the red crown of Lower Egypt and the jubilee robe. His arms are crossed and he would once have carried the crook and the flail, the symbols of kingship. This stance, his curved beard and black flesh identify him with Osiris, with whom he hoped to become assimilated after death.

Deir el-Bahri: The Temple of Hatshepsut

Next to the mortuary temple of Mentuhotep II (c.2055–c.2004 BC) at Deir el-Bahri is that of Hatshepsut (c.1473–c.1458 BC), the female pharaoh of the Eighteenth Dynasty. For a woman to rule Egypt for over 20 years was extremely unusual. Other royal women had ruled as king previously, but only when there were apparently no male heirs to the throne. Their reigns were short and generally came at the end of a dynasty. Women were usually omitted from the kinglists, as the idea of a woman on the throne did not fit in with the Egyptian concept of *maat*, the correct order of things as laid down by the gods at the time of creation.

Hatshepsut's succession

Hatshepsut's father was Tuthmosis I (c.1504–c.1492 BC) and she was married to her half-brother, Tuthmosis II (c.1492–c.1479 BC). On his untimely death, his heir was his son by a secondary wife, but as the young Tuthmosis III (c.1479–c.1425 BC) was still a child, Hatshepsut became regent and ruled on his behalf for about seven years, before proclaiming herself king and ruling jointly with him for a further 14 years.

In the past, Hatshepsut has often been portrayed as a ruthless, scheming woman, hated by her stepson, who had her done away with as soon as possible and subsequently had her name and image removed from her monuments. In the light of modern scholarship, however, this does not seem to have been the case. Rather, Hatshepsut and Tuthmosis III seem to have enjoyed a highly successful and prosperous joint reign, with Tuthmosis undertaking military campaigns while Hatshepsut maintained the royal authority at home. The later obliteration of her name and image from monuments was in any case partial and seems to have had more to do with the concept of *maat* than with the jealousy and hatred of Tuthmosis III.

▲ *The head from a painted statue of Hatshepsut. Although she was a woman, she projected her official image as that of a king, and even wore the royal false beard.*

Hatshepsut's mortuary temple

Like the temple of Mentuhotep II, that of Hatshepsut is partly free-standing and partly rock-cut, and imitates the terraced layout of its predecessor. In antiquity the building must have been a very impressive sight, embellished with sphinxes and statues, as well as trees and flowerbeds.

A monumental causeway led from the valley temple, which has now vanished, although its location is known from foundation deposits. An avenue of sphinxes

▲ *The mortuary temple of Hatshepsut, the female pharaoh, at Deir el-Bahri was built next to the funerary complex of the first Middle Kingdom king, Mentuhotep II.*

lined the causeway and there was a sacred boat shrine in the temple forecourt.

The temple itself is laid out on three terraces, each approached by a ramp. At the rear of each terrace is a portico protecting the lively reliefs carved on the rear wall. On the lowest level, these show barges bringing Hatshepsut's famous obelisks from Aswan to Karnak, while in the middle section there are scenes depicting her divine birth to the right of the ramp, and scenes of the expedition to the land of Punt on the left. At the entrance to the topmost level were Osiris pillars and colossal statues of Hatshepsut. At this level, vaulted rooms on both sides of the court were dedicated to Hatshepsut and her father, Tuthmosis I, and to the gods Re-Horakhty and Amun. There were further statues of the queen on the back wall of the hall around the original entrance to the Sanctuary, although the sanctuary seen by modern visitors to the temple was cut by Ptolemy VIII (170–116 BC) over 1,000 years later.

As well as maintaining the king's cult, mortuary temples were usually also dedicated to the cults of various gods. On the south side of the main complex is a small chapel dedicated to the goddess Hathor, where the columns are topped with Hathor-head capitals. Hathor was paramount on the west bank and is particularly significant here. Another chapel is devoted to Anubis, the god of embalming and funerary rites.

Hatshepsut's mortuary temple was intended to be closely connected with her second tomb in the Valley of the Kings (the first having been located in a remote valley to the west). The original idea seems to have been to excavate a passage from the tomb entrance in the Valley of the Kings to a burial place under her sanctuary in the temple of Deir el-Bahri. However, the tomb builders struck bad rock and had to make a great loop backwards in the direction of the entrance. ◆

▼ *This column is in the form of a* sistrum, *the musical instrument sacred to Hathor. The column is the 'handle' and is decorated with a Hathor head. Above the head, the metal loop of the instrument itself is depicted.*

The Colonnades of the Queen's Temple

In the Southern Colonnade to the left of the ramp are scenes depicting Hatshepsut's celebrated expedition to the land of Punt, the prime object of which was to obtain incense for the cult of her 'father', the god Amun. The accompanying text reveals that a wide variety of exotic goods was obtained, including fragrant woods, ebony, ivory, gold, spices, eye paint, panther skins, apes, monkeys, dogs and native people. Punt is thought to be either modern Somalia or Eritrea.

Some of these reliefs remain clear, colourful and lively, while others, such as the birth scenes, are extensively damaged. Among those that are less easy to see are the scenes showing Hatshepsut (c.1473–c.1458 BC) dedicating the fruits of the expedition to Amun, where the image of Hatshepsut has been obliterated. Another scene shows gold being weighed, with Horus in charge of the scales. Seshat, the goddess of writing, keeps account of the weight, while Thoth, the god of wisdom and patron of scribes, records the amounts of incense obtained. Hatshepsut is shown in the presence of Amun, while Tuthmosis III (c.1479–c.1425 BC) offers incense to the sacred boat.

The birth scenes of Hatshepsut

In spite of her female form, Hatshepsut was in every respect a king. She had herself depicted on her monuments as pharaoh, wearing male dress and with the royal regalia. She undertook the customary activities of a king: building temples, sending expeditions to foreign countries and taking part in the *heb sed*, or jubilee

▲ As well as incense resin, incense trees in baskets were carried on board ship for transport to Egypt, where they were planted on the terraces of Hatshepsut's temple at Deir el-Bahri.

▼ This relief from the South Colonnade shows the King and Queen of Punt receiving Hatshepsut's expedition. The queen appears to suffer from elephantiasis.

▶ *This carved relief shows the journey to Punt, which involved sailing down the Red Sea to Punt, which is equated with present-day Eritrea or Somalia.*

festival. As other kings before her, she regarded herself as divinely appointed and took the title 'Son of Re'. Going further than this, she had her divine birth recorded on the walls of her funerary temple at Deir el-Bahri. These painted reliefs should not be interpreted as a political ploy to uphold a doubtful claim to the throne, but as Hatshepsut following in the royal religious tradition. They are now very difficult to see and interpret. The god Amun, disguised as Tuthmosis I (c.1504–c.1492 BC), impregnates her mother, Queen Ahmose. The accompanying text describes the scene:

Amun made his form like the majesty of her husband, Aakheperkare [Tuthmosis I]. He found her as she slept in the palace. She was woken by the god's fragrance. She smiled at his majesty. He went to her immediately, his penis erect before her. He gave his heart to her...his love passed into her limbs. The palace was flooded with the god's fragrance and all his perfumers were from Punt...Khenmet-Amun-Hatshepsut shall be the name of this daughter I have placed in your body. She shall exercise kingship over the whole land. ◆

▶ *The pregnant queen is led to the birth chamber by gods concerned with childbirth. After the birth, the child is presented to Amun.*

The Rameseum

The mortuary temple of the Nineteenth Dynasty king Ramesses II (c.1279–c.1213 BC), known as the Ramesseum, is one of a string of such temples that lay along the desert edge a short distance from the tomb of the king to whom the temple was dedicated. The Ramesseum was also dedicated to Amun, the chief god of the state pantheon. Much of the temple has been destroyed, but the remains are nonetheless impressive.

The victorious king

The decoration of the temple records the military successes of Ramesses and otherwise depicts him as a pious ruler, worshipping the gods and taking part in religious festivals. The reliefs and related texts are thus a sort of justification of the king's reign. Although the kings held that they were appointed by the gods, they also believed that they were responsible to them for the wellbeing of the people. From the kings' accounts of their campaigns it can be seen that they considered military action to be one of their chief duties. The gods, especially Amun in the New Kingdom (c.1550–c.1069 BC), instigated the campaigns and frequently proposed the strategy. They came to the king's aid in battle and rewarded him with victory.

Ramesses recorded his Syrian campaigns on the Great Pylon at the entrance to the temple. The Syrian fortresses he destroyed in the eighth year of his reign are depicted on the North Tower. There are also scenes from his much vaunted war against the Hittites, including depictions of the Egyptian army on the march, and the Egyptian camp surrounded by a 'fence' of shields, within which the soldiers prepare to do battle. To the right at the end is a scene depicting the king holding a council of war and another showing captured spies being beaten.

▲ *Painted carved reliefs on the papyrus columns of the Ramesseum's Hypostyle Hall depict Ramesses II offering to the gods.*

The whole of the South Tower is taken up with the great victory Ramesses claimed to have won against the Hittites at the Battle of Qadesh. Ramesses is seen larger than life, charging into battle in his chariot, while the Hittites, pierced by his arrows, fall into the River Orontes and are drowned, or else flee before him.

Temple courts and halls

Apart from fragments of the west wall, the First Court is totally ruined. Part of a colossal statue of Ramesses lies on the floor. From the measurements of the remains it has been estimated that the statue must have been 17.5m (57ft) high and weighed over 1,000 tons. The head of another colossal head of Ramesses from this temple is now in the British Museum, London. The Second Court has also largely been destroyed, although some of the Osiris pillars representing the

► *The statues of Ramesses II as Osiris in the Second Court of the Ramesseum are now largely in ruins.*

deceased Ramesses are still standing. The surviving part of the front wall is decorated with interesting scenes concerning the king's accession. On the left is the festival of Min, the fertility god, which was celebrated at this time. Ramesses is shown watching the procession, in which statues of his ancestors are carried by priests. In front of him are two poles decorated with the headdress of Min. Priests then send off carrier pigeons to the four corners of the earth, bearing the news of the king's accession.

On the right, Ramesses is seen cutting a ceremonial sheaf of corn in honour of Min as a harvest god. Several fragments of colossal statues are scattered in this court, including a piece from a throne inscribed with the name of Ramesses II. From here, three steps lead up into the portico where Ramesses is seen honouring the gods. Beyond this is the Hypostyle Hall, which is similar to that of the Karnak Temple. The roof was supported by a colonnade with three rows of lower columns at each side. The central columns have capitals of open papyrus flowers while the lower ones have buds, the whole representing the Mound of Creation. The columns are carved with images of Ramesses making offerings to the gods. As at Karnak, the temple was lit by clerestory windows set high up in the walls.

In the next hall, the First Small Hypostyle Hall, the reliefs show priests carrying the sacred boats of Amun, his wife Mut and their son Khonsu. At the end, Ramesses is seated under the sacred tree, while Thoth and Seshat inscribe his name on the leaves, thus acknowledging him as the worthy successor of his illustrious forebears. ◆

▲ *Ramesses II is blessed by the seated king of the gods, Amun, his wife Mut and son Khonsu.*

▲ *The fallen head of Ramesses II shows him wearing the double crown of the kings of Egypt.*

The granary

Around the temple itself lie an enormous number of vaulted mudbrick storage chambers which formed one of the state granaries. It has been estimated that, when full, this granary could have provided for the needs of 3,400 families for one year. The craftsmen of Deir el-Medina staged a strike outside the Ramesseum when their rations failed to turn up and were given food from these stores to tide them over until their 'pay' arrived.

Medinet Habu

The mortuary temple of Ramesses III (c.1184–c.1153 BC), the last great king of the New Kingdom Period (c.1550–c.1069 BC), was built at Medinet Habu and was closely modelled on the Ramesseum, both in layout and decoration. The temple takes its name from the associated village that grew up within its precincts. This was named after Amenhotep, son of Hapu, a very influential official of the reign of Amenhotep III (c.1390–c.1352 BC), who was so highly regarded that he was allowed to build himself a mortuary temple on the west bank among those of the kings (see *The Colossi of Memnon*).

Like the Ramesseum, the temple at Medinet Habu was dedicated to Amun. The king is depicted performing his cultic duties, and his military successes are prominently displayed. However, an unusual feature is the entrance to the temple. This was constructed in the form of a *migdol* or Syrian fortress. A massive mudbrick wall surrounded the whole complex and the temple became a place of security in unsettled times. The craftsmen of Deir el-Medina moved there at the end of the Twentieth Dynasty (c.1069 BC), when there was a constant threat of Libyan invasion.

▲ *The First Pylon of Ramesses III's mortuary temple at Medinet Habu is carved with scenes showing the king smiting his enemies and offering them to the gods.*

Temple reliefs

Ramesses III's victories are a constant theme. Inside the *migdol*, the heads of defeated enemies are used as a sill on which the king would tread when he appeared at the window. The outer walls of both the *migdol* and the Pylon at the entrance to the temple proper show the king in his traditional pose of smiting enemies and offering them, on the left to Amun and on the right to Re-Horakhty.

Between the grooves intended for flagstaffs is a long, bombastic account of Ramesses III's victory over the Libyans in the second year of his reign. This theme is repeated on the inner walls of the Entrance Pylon, where some rather grisly war trophies in the form of piles of hands and penises are also displayed, while on the face of the Second Pylon Ramesses' victories over the enigmatic Sea Peoples are recorded. This theme is expanded along the

◄ *Ramesses III ritually cuts a sheaf of corn and offers it to Hapy, the Nile god. A companion scene shows him ploughing the Field of Iaru.*

▲ *A lintel shows Ramesses III, accompanied by baboons, greeting the rising sun. This symbolized the king's resurrection.*

greater part of the northern exterior wall of the temple, where Ramesses is seen charging into battle against his Libyan enemies and their Sea People allies. Further scenes show a vast sea battle taking place.

Otherwise, the painted carved reliefs depict the king honouring the gods. Those of the Second Court, where an amazing amount of colour remains, are particularly beautiful. As in the Ramesseum, the festival of Min is being celebrated. On the rear wall of the North Colonnade, the king is seen carried in procession from the palace on a canopied litter. He is preceded by priests carrying censers, a lector-priest and soldiers, with a retinue of courtiers bringing up the rear. The procession is accompanied by trumpeters, drummers and castanet players. In the next scene, the king makes an offering to Min and a further section shows the god carried in a procession led by the king and queen. They are followed by priests carrying standards, ritual vessels and images of the king and his ancestors. The ritual is again connected with the king's coronation, and the event is announced by the release of pigeons who carry the message in all directions. The ritual closes with the ceremonial cutting of a sheaf of corn, which is offered to Min, and the burning of incense.

The Hypostyle Hall

The roof is missing, and only the lower parts of the columns that once supported it are extant, although the roof slabs of the colonnade of the Second Court have been restored and are most impressive from above. In the Hypostyle Hall beyond there are two pairs of statues, one of Amun and Maat, the goddess of truth and justice, and another of Thoth, the god of wisdom, and the king. These gods were very important in the ideology of kingship. Amun appointed the king and was regarded as his father, while the king had to reign in accordance with the concept of *maat* personified by the goddess. Thoth, the scribe of the gods, recorded the deeds of the king and so justified his reign. Some of the pillars in the preceding courts are in the form of Osiris, and associate the king with the god, with whom he hoped to become one in the Afterlife.

Ancillary buildings

The temple treasuries were built to the left of the Hypostyle Hall and are decorated with scenes showing the king offering to Amun costly ritual vessels, heaps of gold and bags of precious stones. Another chamber off this hall has an unusual scene showing the king ploughing and harvesting in the Field of Iaru (the 'Field of Reeds'), the name given to the domain of Osiris. This scene is more usually seen in the tombs of commoners of this period.

Adjoining the temple are the remains of a palace used by the king for occasional visits during his lifetime as well as being intended as a spiritual royal residence for use in the Afterlife. Although small, it was sumptuously decorated with glazed tiles and had bathrooms lined with slabs of limestone to protect the mudbrick. A church was built in the Second Court in the early Christian era. This has now been dismantled by the excavators. ◆

A plot against the king

In rooms at the top of the *migdol* are scenes showing the king enjoying himself among the ladies of his harem. It has been suggested that the plot to assassinate Ramesses III was possibly hatched here. This concerned one of the lesser queens, who wanted to install her son on the throne. The conspiracy involved several of the harem ladies, one of whom had a brother, a captain in the army, who was instructed to stir up revolt in Nubia in order to create a diversion. Some of the male officials procured wax images, which could be melted, with the intention of magically weakening the limbs of the guards. The plot was discovered and many of those implicated were put to death. Ramesses seems to have survived the conspiracy but the shock of its discovery may well have hastened the old king's end.

▲ *These ritual scenes from the Sacred Court show the king in his capacity as high priest taking part in the annual festival held in honour of the fertility god Min.*

The Temple of Seti I

Many of the mortuary temples on the west bank are barely recognizable today, but one that remains in relatively good condition is that of the Nineteenth Dynasty king Seti I (c.1294–c.1279 BC), the father of Ramesses II (c.1279–c.1213 BC). As well as being built for the *ka* of the deceased king, it was also dedicated to Seti's predecessor Ramesses I (c.1295–c.1294 BC), who reigned for only a few months so was not able to build a mortuary temple for himself, and to Ramesses II, who completed it after his father's death. Amun, the chief god, was also revered here.

Seti I was interred in one of the most spectacular tombs in the Valley of the Kings. However, he also had a cenotaph at Abydos, where Osiris himself was thought to be buried. Conversely, the Abydos temple, which was the main sanctuary of Osiris, also doubled as a secondary mortuary temple for the king. The Abydos temple was decorated in a similar way to the actual mortuary temple. In both cases, Seti is seen officiating in the cult and as a child being suckled by a mother goddess; at Abydos, Isis, the wife of Osiris, fulfilled this role.

▲ *The sacred boat of Amun with its ram-headed prow and stern is carried in procession during the annual 'Beautiful Feast of the Valley'.*

▼ *The mortuary temple of Seti I in western Thebes includes a chapel dedicated to Ramesses I, who reigned for too brief a time to build a mortuary temple of his own. The Theban triad were also worshipped here.*

The temple layout

Seti's mortuary temple was built of white sandstone on the usual plan of two courtyards, each with their own pylon, a six-columned hypostyle hall and a sanctuary where the sacred boat of Amun originally stood. Until the middle of the nineteenth century the temple was approached by an avenue of sphinxes. Only one now remains and even that has been damaged by recent floods. However, it is still possible to see that the base is inscribed with the motif of the 'Nine Bows', representing Seti's conquered enemies.

The central part of the temple is dedicated to Seti, while the southern part is dedicated to Ramesses I. The

► *Papyrus bundle columns support the portico of Seti's mortuary temple, plant forms being powerfully suggestive of creation and the re-creation of the king as he enters the Afterlife.*

cartouches of both Seti I and Ramesses II appear on the First Pylon. Most of the decoration of this temple refers to the cultic activities of Seti, but Ramesses II is also seen offering to the gods in the Hypostyle Hall and the side chapels. Seti makes offerings to the gods of the Ennead (the nine deities of the creation myth of Heliopolis). Ramesses, followed by Mut, the wife of Amun, and their son Khonsu, performs the rites of the *heb sed*, or royal jubilee festival, before Amun. In the main hall both kings are represented as children being suckled by goddesses, Seti by Hathor, the cow goddess, and Ramesses by Mut.

In the Sanctuary, which originally housed the sacred boat, there are scenes showing the boat of Amun with its ram-headed prow and stern, and Seti offering to the boat in procession. In the southern section there are dedication texts of Seti I and the figure of the deified Ramesses I.

Behind the temple is a pool, possibly the remains of a sacred lake, an essential element of any temple, representing as it did the primeval ocean from which creation arose. This would also have been appropriate in a mortuary temple as it was linked with the concept of re-creation and the king's passage to eternity. There are also the remnants of mudbrick houses, where the priests would once have lived, and storerooms where the ritual vessels and other treasures would have been kept.

The complex included mudbrick storerooms on its northern side and a royal palace, probably used for ritual purposes, on the south side. This feature was copied by later kings, such as Ramesses II at the Ramesseum and Ramesses III (c.1184–c.1153 BC) at Medinet Habu. A Coptic church was built in the Northern Courtyard with the coming of Christianity and the temple was used as a quarry to provide stone to build houses within the complex, as was the case in several of the temples on the west bank of the Nile at Thebes. ◆

◄ *A scene from the tomb of Seti I in the Valley of the Kings, which his mortuary temple served, shows Ptah, god of creation, offering him life, wellbeing and stability in the next world.*

The foundation of a dynasty

Seti I was the second king of the Nineteenth Dynasty. His father, Ramesses I, had been an officer in the army and was appointed as king by Horemheb (c.1323–c.1295 BC), who had himself served previous kings as a general. Ramesses I seems to have had no family connections with the previous dynasty, but he was elderly when he came to the throne and already a grandfather, so brought with him a ready-made dynasty. This may be why he was appointed – in order to prevent future disputes over the succession.

Although Ramesses I's own reign was brief, Seti I reigned very successfully for 17 years, during which he fought campaigns in the Levant and against the Libyans and Hittites, thus securing Egypt's prestige in North Africa and the Near East. Seti's success is reflected in the splendour of his tomb in the Valley of the Kings.

The Colossi of Memnon

Although the mortuary temple of the Eighteenth Dynasty king Amenhotep III (c.1390–c.1352 BC), one of the most illustrious of the New Kingdom rulers, was the largest on the west bank, very little of it remains today. It was used by later kings as a quarry when they built their own mortuary temples and had already been destroyed by the reign of the Nineteenth Dynasty king Merenptah (c.1213–c.1203 BC), who incorporated various architectural elements from Amenhotep's temple into his own. However, the site is currently under excavation and the pillar bases of the Hypostyle Hall and several pieces of colossal statues have now come to light.

The temple remains

The remaining features include a strange type of sphinx with the body of a crocodile lying near the road, a huge stela with a dedication text excavated in the nineteenth century, some recently unearthed statues of the lioness-headed goddess, Sekhmet, and the two colossal statues of the king, which once stood at the entrance. Many other statues that once adorned the temple have long since been removed and taken to museums around the world. Of these, some are conventional statues of the king and some are in a budding Amarna style.

▼ *Colossal statues, nearly 18m (59 ft) high, depicting King Amenhotep III, mark the entrance to his mortuary temple. Diminutive figures of his mother, Mutemwiya, and Queen Tiye, his wife, surround the legs of the southernmost statue.*

The statues of the king

The two huge seated figures known as the Colossi of Memnon both represent King Amenhotep III and once must have stood more than 20m (65ft) high. In each case, the king sits on a huge throne decorated on the sides with the symbol of the united land of Egypt: two images of Hapy, the god of the Nile inundation, tie the heraldic plants of Upper Egypt (the lotus) and Lower Egypt (the papyrus) to the hieroglyph meaning 'to unite'. The South Colossus is better preserved and has the figures of the

▲ *A black granite statue of the goddess Sekhmet found at the site. Hundreds more were discovered at Karnak in the temple of Mut, with whom Sekhmet is associated.*

king's mother, Mutemwiya, on the left, and of his wife, Queen Tiye, on the right. Both female figures are minuscule in comparison to the image of the king. There is another small figure between the king's knees but it is not clear who this represents.

▲ *This unusual sphinx with the body of a lion and tail of a crocodile may once have formed part of a processional way.*

The singing statue

The North Colossus was famous for its 'singing' in the Graeco-Roman Period (c.332 BC–AD 395). It was said that an earthquake in 27 BC had damaged the statue, which thereafter emitted a whistling sound early every morning. This was interpreted by visitors as the Homeric hero, Memnon, singing to his mother, Eos, the goddess of the dawn. The phenomenon is described by the first-century Greek geographer, Strabo, who wondered whether the whole thing was a trick, but later claimed to have been convinced that the noise was of divine origin. The life of the singing statue as a tourist attraction was short-lived, however, since the Roman emperor Severus (AD 193–211) repaired the damage, after which the statue no longer 'sang'. ◆

▼ *An aerial view shows the vast area originally covered by the mortuary temple of Amenhotep III.*

The royal architect

Amenhotep, son of Hapu, had an illustrious career during the reign of Amenhotep III. One of his titles was 'Director of all the King's Works' which roughly translates as 'Chief Royal Architect'. This means he would have been in charge of all the processes involved in the building of temples, from the quarrying of the building material and the construction and embellishment of the monuments with painted reliefs to the provision of statues. He may well have been responsible for the Colossi of Memnon.

Amenhotep's career is known from texts on the statues of himself that he was allowed to set up in the Temple of Amun at Karnak. That he was allowed both to do this and to build his own funerary temple among those of the kings indicates his importance. Several of his statues show him as a seated scribe, the epitome of the educated man.

Temples of Nubia

Nubia, Egypt's neighbour to the south, lay along the Nile between Aswan and Khartoum (in present-day Sudan). Ancient Egyptian interest in the area went back at least to the Predynastic Period (c.3500–c.3100 BC) and by the Early Dynastic Period (c.3100–c.2686 BC) the kings were mounting expeditions into Nubia, attracted by its rich resources. They returned bearing ivory, ebony, incense, animal skins and other exotic goods. From the Middle Kingdom (c.2055–c.1650 BC), the Egyptians began to exploit Nubian mineral deposits, especially gold.

The tomb autobiography of the late Old Kingdom official, Harkhuf, gives a wealth of information about Egyptian relations with the Nubian chiefs and the exotic goods he procured on behalf of the Sixth Dynasty king Pepi II (c.2278–c.2184 BC). Rock inscriptions of kings and officials on the island of Sehel provide further details, both about the expeditions and the royal attempts made to dig canals around the First Cataract, just to the south of Aswan. The kings of the Middle Kingdom also built fortresses at the Second Cataract to protect the trade routes. In the New Kingdom (c.1550–c.1069 BC) Egypt ruled Nubia directly, and several kings built temples to help maintain tight control over the territory.

◀ *The First Cataract is immediately to the south of the island of Elephantine and the town of Aswan. This was a major obstacle to trade in ancient Egypt.*

Aswan Dam Rescue Operations

Before the building of the dams at Aswan, the Nile flooded the cultivated areas in the Nile Valley every year between June and October. It then receded, leaving behind a rich deposit of alluvial silt, which replenished the fertility of the soil. In addition, by digging a system of dikes and ditches at the start of the inundation it was possible to bring additional land, some distance from the river and beyond the natural flood plain, under cultivation.

The inundation was so important to the ancient Egyptians that the time when the Nile began to rise – in conjunction with the dawn appearance of Sirius, the dog star, above the horizon after a long absence – was regarded as the start of the New Year. The population faced serious hardships and even death if the inundation was either too high or too low, which could result in disastrous floods or starvation.

Controlling the inundation

As the Egyptian population began to rise sharply at the end of the nineteenth century, the government began to make plans to control the waters of the Nile. The first dam at Aswan was designed by a British engineer, Sir William Wilcox, and was completed in 1902. The Nile Valley was flooded as far south as Wadi es-Sebua. However, this proved to be inadequate and the dam was raised twice, in 1912 and 1934 when the flooding extended to Wadi Halfa and the water level to between 87–121m (285–397ft). This caused many of the ancient temples above the dam to be submerged for much of the year.

▼ *Known as Elephantine in antiquity, this island on the Nile near Aswan was the point from which royal expeditions set out for Nubia to obtain ivory and gold. With the building of the High Dam, Aswan is again an important ecomomic centre.*

Nilometers

The kings of ancient Egypt had been interested in the height of the inundation from earliest times. The Palermo Stone, of which only fragments now remain, was once a record of the important events of every year of the reign of each king of the first five dynasties. It also gives the height of the Nile for each year. The king in his capacity as shepherd of his people needed to be warned of poor harvests: a concept that may be reflected in the biblical stories of Joseph interpreting Pharaoh's dreams. It is also seen in numerous Nilometers, such as the one at Aswan, constructed to gauge the river's rising level.

▲ *To the north of Aswan lie the tombs of the Old and Middle Kingdom Governors of the South, who led the expeditions to Nubia. Among them is the tomb of Harkhuf with its famous autobiography.*

The High Dam

The population continued to grow apace, and after the revolution of 1952 the new regime, under President Gamal Abdul Nasser, decided a new dam was needed. When completed in 1971, the new reservoir, now known as Lake Nasser, stretched 510km (317 miles) to the south. It has a capacity of 150 billion cubic m (5,300 billion cubic ft).

When the decision was made to build the High Dam it was realized that unless drastic measures were taken, many of the Nubian temples would be lost forever. Eventually, UNESCO responded to the appeals of Egypt and Sudan and mounted the Nubia Rescue Campaign. Fifty countries took part and between 1960–80 provided money and expertise in various fields. Wherever possible, the monuments were taken down or cut free from the rock into which they were built and reassembled in areas safe from the rising waters. It was not feasible to move the mudbrick fortresses, such as Buhen, but they were carefully excavated and recorded in detail. Surprisingly, these are at present still in remarkably good condition below the water. Unfortunately, the Nubian people did not fare so well. Their villages were drowned in the flood of water and the population moved elsewhere, some north to Kom Ombo and others to Khasm al-Girba, far to the south of Wadi Halfa. ◆

▶ *This memorial was set up to celebrate the completion of the High Dam in 1971. The dam provides most of Egypt's electricity and makes a major contribution to industrial development.*

Abu Simbel

The most famous of the Nubian temples that were moved to safety by UNESCO are those of Abu Simbel, some 250km (155 miles) south-east of Aswan. They were rock-cut in the reign of Ramesses II (c.1279–c.1213 BC), when Egyptian control of Nubia was possibly at its height. The larger one was dedicated to Re-Horakhty, Amun-Re, Ptah and the deified Ramesses II, and the smaller one to the goddess Hathor and Ramesses' favourite wife, Nefertari.

The two temples were rediscovered in 1813 by the explorer Jean-Louis Burckhardt, who found the heads of the statues of Ramesses protruding from the sand but was neither able to ascertain what they were nor to get inside. The temples were cleared four years later by Giovanni Belzoni, who was rather disappointed that there was little inside that he could take back with him to display in the museums of Europe. In the 1960s they were raised to a new position 65m (213ft) higher up the cliffs and 210m (690ft) to the north-west.

Moving the temples

Various schemes were proposed when the suggestion to move the temples was first put forward. The proposal from the USA was to float both temples on pontoons, which would carry them to the new site as the water rose, while the Polish suggestion was to enclose the site in a spherical shell: tourists would then have been able to visit the temples by going down in lifts within the sphere. Yet other proposals included encasing the site in a transparent tank, through which visitors could view the temples from glass cabins, and cutting the monuments free, setting them up on concrete bases and then using hydraulic jacks to raise the whole lot to safety. In the end it was decided to dismantle the temples by cutting them into carefully numbered blocks and to re-erect them on higher ground close to the original site.

▼ *The larger temple at Abu Simbel was dedicated to the sun gods Re-Horakhty and Amun-Re, the creator god Ptah and the deified Ramesses II.*

▲ *The head of one of the four statues from the façade of the main temple is 19.5m (31ft) high.*

▲ *Ramesses II destroys his enemies in this scene from the main Abu Simbel temple.*

Before the work began, a coffer dam had to be built to protect the temples from the rapidly rising water. Then the temples were sawn into blocks, taking care that the cuts were made where they would be least conspicuous when reassembled. The interior walls and ceilings were suspended from a supporting framework of reinforced concrete. When the temples were reassembled, the joins were made good by a mortar of cement and desert sand. This was done so discreetly that today it is impossible to see where the joins were made. Both temples now stand within an artificial mountain made of rubble and rock, supported by two vast domes of reinforced concrete.

The statues

The visitor is first confronted by the four colossal statues, each 20m (65ft) high, of the deified Ramesses II, which adorn the façade of his temple. Above and between the central statues, his throne name appears in the form of a rebus. In the centre is the figure of the sun god Re, flanked by the *user*-staff and the goddess of peace and justice, Maat. This spells out the king's throne name 'User-maat-re'.

Below the feet of the enthroned king are his traditional enemies: Nubians on the left and Libyans and Hittites on the right. Each throne is decorated with the heraldic plants, the lotus and papyrus, entwined around the hieroglyph for 'unite', to emphasize the fact that Ramesses is in firm control of both Upper and Lower Egypt. Statues of members of the royal family, diminutive in comparison with those of Ramesses but actually more than life-size, are arranged around the king's legs. A row of statues of the hawk-headed sun god Re-Horakhty stand on the platform in front of the statue of the king. ▶

The fallen statue

An earthquake in the 31st year of Ramesses' reign caused a great deal of damage to the temple. The pillars of the Hypostyle Hall cracked and one collapsed. The right arm of the colossus to the right of the doorway fell off, while the upper part of the statue on the left crashed to the ground. Paser, then viceroy of Kush, ordered the restoration of the temple and all but the upper part of the statue was restored. This was still lying where it had fallen when the temple was rediscovered. When it was moved to its new position, the engineers decided to leave the statue as it was found.

▲ *Nefertari is depicted in the temple dedicated to herself and Hathor presenting offerings to Anukis, the guardian goddess of the cataract at Aswan.*

▲ *Seth and Horus are shown crowning Ramesses as king of the Two Lands in this painted relief from the Nefertari temple.*

The temple of Ramesses II

Inside the temple, the ceiling is supported by square pillars embellished with half-engaged figures of the king holding the royal crook and flail. The ceiling itself is painted in the centre with flying vultures and at the sides with stars. The painted reliefs of the walls are very impressive and contain much of historical interest. The two usual themes are present: the king worshipping the gods and celebrating his military triumphs.

Ramesses' most famous victory was at the Battle of Qadesh in 1274 BC. The north wall of the Hypostyle Hall presents a lively account in both reliefs and text. Preparations for battle are being made in the Egyptian camp. Horses are harnessed or given their fodder while one soldier has his wounds dressed. The king's tent is also depicted while another scene shows a council of war between Ramesses and his officers. Two Hittite spies are captured and beaten until they reveal the true whereabouts of Muwatallis, the Hittite king. Finally, the two sides engage in battle, the Egyptians charging in neat formation while the Hittites are in confusion, chariots crashing, horses bolting and soldiers falling into the River Orontes. In the text, Ramesses takes on the whole of the Hittite army single-handed, apart from support rendered by Amun who defends him in battle and finally hands him the victory.

In the Sanctuary, the deified Ramesses sits with Amun-Re, Re-Horakhty and Ptah. Twice a year, on 21 February and 21 October, the rising sun shines directly into the Sanctuary and illuminates the figures of Ramesses and Amun-Re.

Temple of Hathor and Nefertari

The smaller of the two temples at Abu Simbel was dedicated to the local goddess Hathor of Abshek, goddess of love, beauty and motherhood, and to the deified Nefertari, the favourite wife of Ramesses II. The façade is hewn from the rock in imitation of a pylon and is embellished with colossal statues over 10m (32ft) high – four of Ramesses II and two of Nefertari. Here, the statues of Nefertari are the same size as those of her husband, but the royal children placed around their legs are much smaller, although the princesses are bigger than the royal sons.

The central doorway leads to the Hypostyle Hall, which is divided into three aisles by six pillars decorated on the inner side with Hathor-headed *sistra*, the goddess's sacred musical instrument. The other three sides show Ramesses and Nefertari making offerings to deities.

Although it is dedicated to Nefertari, Ramesses figures largely in the interior of the temple as well as outside. On the south wall is a painted carved relief of the gods Horus and Seth crowning the king. It was usually Horus and Thoth who performed this rite, Seth often being cast in the villain's role because of his murder of Osiris. However, in the Underworld, Seth was seen in a better light as he destroyed the great snake, Apophis, the archenemy of the sun god. Moreover, the family of Ramesses II came from the Delta, where Seth was an important deity, and Ramesses II's father was called Seti after him. On the east wall, Ramesses is shown smiting enemies while Nefertari looks on approvingly. He is also shown offering a tiny image of Maat, goddess of truth and justice, to Amun as a justification of his reign.

Nefertari comes into her own in the Vestibule. She appears on the right of the doorway as a slender figure wearing a close-fitting dress between the mother goddesses Hathor and Isis, who crown her. To balance this, on the left of the doorway, Ramesses, accompanied by Nefertari, offers flowers to Taweret, the goddess of pregnancy and childbirth. She is usually depicted as a pregnant hippopotamus, but here she takes the form of a woman. (Nefertari herself had seven or eight children, although none of her sons lived to become king.) At either end of the Vestibule is a painted relief showing Hathor as a cow emerging from a papyrus thicket. She is worshipped by Nefertari on the south wall and by Ramesses on the north wall.

Leading from the Vestibule is the Sanctuary, on the back wall of which Hathor is seen as a cow coming from the mountain. She is protecting the figure of Ramesses II, who stands under her chin. Otherwise the king and queen are shown making offerings to various deities. One of the most interesting scenes shows Ramesses II burning incense and pouring a libation in front of an image of himself and Nefertari, thus making the statement that they are also gods. Nefertari may not have been well enough to take part in the inauguration ceremony for the temple, and her place was possibly taken by the Princess Merytamun. In any case, she seems to have died shortly afterwards and to have been replaced by Queen Istnofret.

▲ *Nefertari, 'Beloved of Mut', styled here as 'Great Royal Wife and Mistress of the Two Lands', offers a lotus and a* sistrum *to Hathor.*

The Abu Simbel stelae

Several stelae were also rescued from the rising water and have been restored as near as possible to their original positions in relation to the two temples. One of the most interesting is on the left of the forecourt of the main temple. This records the marriage of Ramesses II to Naptera, daughter of a later Hittite king, Hattusilis III, which ratified the peace treaty drawn up 15 years after the Battle of Qadesh. Ramesses sits on a throne as the princess is led into his presence by her father. The text says that Ramesses asked Seth, the weather god, to withhold the winter storms until she had safely arrived in Egypt. When he saw her he was bowled over by her beauty and loved her more than anything.

Nearby is the stela of Heqanakht, viceroy of Kush at the time of the temple's dedication in the twenty-fourth year of Ramesses' reign. On the upper part of the stela, the king is shown with his daughter, Merytamun, making offerings to the gods, including the deified Ramesses. On the lower section, Heqanakht is depicted offering to Nefertari.

Further to the south is a double stela showing Ramesses smiting enemies before Amun and Horus, and Setau, another viceroy of Kush, who built the temples of Wadi es-Sebua and Gerf Hussein. The latter is now submerged, although a colossal statue of Ramesses from the site can now be seen in the Nubian Museum in Aswan.

Immediately to the north of the Temple of Hathor is the stela of Iuny, who was viceroy of Kush when the work on the temples was initiated. To the right of this stela is that of Asha-hebsed, who was in charge of the work force. The text tells of Ramesses' decision to build and to give Asha-hebsed the job of organizing the workmen. ◆

Beit el-Wali

The first of a series of temples built in Nubia by Ramesses II (c.1279–c.1213 BC), the Temple of Beit el-Wali lies near to the Ptolemaic Temple of Kalabsha. Both buildings were moved by the UNESCO project to their present location on the western side of Lake Nasser, near the High Dam at Aswan.

The name Beit el-Wali means 'House of the Holy Man' and may indicate its use by a Christian hermit at some point. Although it is relatively tiny, the temple is well worth a visit.

Political control

The Nubian temples of Ramesses II were part of a policy designed to maintain Egyptian control over the region. In the New Kingdom (c.1550–c.1069 BC) Nubia was not only administered by Egyptian officials, there was also a deliberate policy of acculturation, the intention of which was to break down Nubian identity. Many leading Nubians were educated in Egypt and adopted Egyptian dress, burial customs and religion. They spoke the Egyptian language and even changed their names to Egyptian ones. The decoration of the temples was to some extent royal propaganda intended to intimidate the population.

The temple Forecourt

There is a surprising amount of colour left in the inner part of this rock-cut temple, though unfortunately the colour has vanished from the interesting historical scenes in the Forecourt. In the early nineteenth century, the artist Joseph Bonomi removed much of it by taking casts of the painted reliefs. However, he also made careful notes about the colours used so that they could be reproduced later. His casts are now displayed in the British Museum in London. They are of great historical interest as they relate to the earlier part of Ramesses II's reign, when he ruled jointly with his father, Seti I (c.1294–c.1279 BC), and undertook campaigns against the Libyans, Syrians and Nubians.

▼ *A cast of a scene originally in the Forecourt of the Temple of Beit el-Wali shows Nubians presenting their annual tribute of exotic goods to Ramesses II.*

► *Ramesses II presides over the annual ceremony when Nubian chieftains and officials presented leopard skins, live animals, gold, precious woods and other exotic items to the king.*

Near the middle of the south wall, Ramesses charges into battle against the Nubians. The reins are tied loosely around his waist so that his hands are free to shoot with his bow and arrow. His young sons, Amenhirwenemhef and Khaemwese, who were then only six and four respectively, are also present. The Nubians flee before the Egyptian onslaught, taking a wounded comrade with them back to their camp among the palms, where all is confusion. The next section shows Ramesses enthroned, receiving the tribute of Nubia. The ceremony is recorded in two registers. In the upper register, Ramesses' eldest son and the viceroy Amenemope present the tribute procession. The viceroy is rewarded for his efforts with gold collars. Among the goods presented are logs of ebony, elephant tusks, ostrich eggs and ostrich-feather fans, rings of gold, elegant chairs and weapons. Below, animal skins, cattle and an exotic collection of monkeys, leopards, a giraffe and a gazelle are brought by the Nubians, some of whom are part of the tribute and would be destined to be taken to Egypt to work on the king's building projects, act as policemen or be recruited into the army for service in Syria.

The theme of Egyptian military success is hammered home on the opposite wall, where Ramesses II's campaigns in Libya and Syria are recorded. Here, Ramesses tramples enemies and holds others by their hair in his left hand while smiting them with his right. The king's personal heroism and military prowess is further displayed in the scene where, charging Bedouin in his chariot, he is shown with his left leg over the front, his foot on the shaft and the reins around his waist, allowing him to seize yet more enemies by the hair and brandish his scimitar at the same time.

The interior of the temple

The theme of the king's military might is carried inside the temple. On the walls of the Vestibule are further smiting scenes to the right and left of the doorway. Otherwise the theme of Ramesses as a pious ruler is taken up, and he is shown worshipping various deities. Beside the doorway leading to the Sanctuary are niches containing statues of the king with (on the left) Isis and Horus and (on the right) Khnum and Anuket, the gods of Elephantine and the First Cataract.

The Sanctuary is also decorated with fine painted reliefs of Ramesses offering to the gods. The most charming scenes are on either side of the doorway and show Ramesses as a child being suckled by the goddesses Isis and Anuket. The statue niche, however, has been destroyed, presumably in the Christian era when the temple was converted into a church. It probably contained a statue of the deified Ramesses sitting between two gods. ◆

◄ *Ramesses II built temples not only to honour the gods but to maintain his authority over a region vital to the Egyptian economy.*

Wadi es-Sebua

The temple at Wadi es-Sebua, which was rescued from the rising waters of Lake Nasser by the Egyptian Antiquities Department in the early 1960s, is perhaps the most attractive of all the Nubian temples. Like those at Abu Simbel, it was built by the Nineteenth Dynasty king Ramesses II (c.1279–c.1213 BC), and was dedicated to the gods Amun-Re, Re-Horakhty and the deified Ramesses II himself. An avenue of sphinxes leads to the temple and affords a most romantic view as it is approached across the desert. The scene from the temple down towards Lake Nasser is equally appealing.

▲ *The temple proper is entered by a stone pylon. On the left of the doorway is a statue of Ramesses II accompanied by one of his daughters.*

The temple precinct

The temple is partly free-standing and partly rock-cut. The gateway to the First Court is embellished with a large standing statue and sphinx of Ramesses II at either side, standing on bases carved with captured enemies. Inside the court there is a short avenue of sphinxes with portrait heads of the king. The avenue continues into the next court but here the four sphinxes represent various local forms of the god Horus. A small figure of Ramesses stands between the paws of each.

The main part of the temple is entered by a stone pylon with a central doorway, which originally had a statue of Ramesses on either side. Only the left-hand one remains in situ, while the other lies a short distance away, out in the desert. The remaining monument is a large standing statue of the king carrying the ram-headed staff of Amun. Ramesses' daughter, Bint-Anath, stands behind his left leg. The pylon itself is decorated in a conventional way, with the king smiting enemies and making offerings to the gods, including himself.

Next comes an open colonnaded court, with columns adorned by Osiris statues of the king. In mythology, before Osiris was murdered by his brother, Seth, he was a real king of Egypt who civilized his people, giving them laws and teaching them agriculture and to worship the gods. The Osiris statues are therefore an appropriate motif in this context, as well as in a mortuary temple, emphasizing Ramesses' role as both king and god, with the wellbeing of his people at heart.

▼ *Looking towards Lake Nasser, the First and Second Courts can be seen. An avenue of sphinxes leads to the main temple.*

Rock-cut halls

The rest of the temple is cut out of the rock and is possibly the most interesting part. It was later used as a Christian church and the original entrance was bricked up to form a double doorway with arches. (This has now been restored to its original state.) The Pillared Hall itself has 12 square pillars, of which

◀ *Ramesses II offers to Re-Horakhty, one of the gods to whom the temple was dedicated.*

the central six were once adorned with Osiris statues of the king: these were chiselled off by the Christians. However, the offering scenes on the walls survive, and some retain their colour. Better still are those of the Vestibule.

The subject of the scenes is traditional, Ramesses is again offering to the gods, but the representation of the goddess Hathor is very unusual. She is usually shown as a woman wearing a sun disc and cow's horns on her head; her face is human and only her ears identify her as a cow goddess. Here, however, she has the head of a cow.

The painted reliefs are in better condition where they were covered over with plaster during the Christian period and so preserved for posterity. The best examples of all are in the Sanctuary and its associated chapels, where there are colourful scenes showing Ramesses adoring the sacred boats of Amun-Re and Re-Horakhty. The central niche once held statues of these gods on either side of Ramesses II. These were hacked away by the Christians and replaced by an image of St Peter, complete with halo and large key. With the plaster removed from the offending carved reliefs the effect is somewhat bizarre, as Ramesses now appears to be offering flowers to St Peter, who has usurped him.

Viceroy Setau

The temple at Wadi es-Sebua was built on behalf of Ramesses II by Setau, who was viceroy of Nubia around 1236 BC. Eleven of his stelae were found in the courtyard of this temple and are now in the Cairo Museum. From these it is possible to trace his own career and to appreciate what the duties of a viceroy were:

I was one whom his Lord caused to be instructed...as a ward of the palace. I grew up in the royal abode when I was a youth...I was provided for, with bread and beer from all the royal meals. I came forth as a scribe from the school, I was appointed to be Chief Scribe of the Vizier; I assessed the whole land with a scroll, I being equal to the task.

Setau attracted the king's attention and was promoted to the posts of 'High Steward of Amun', 'Superintendent of the Treasury of Amun' and 'Festival Leader of Amun' and finally to 'Viceroy of Nubia':

My Lord again found my worth...So I was appointed Viceroy of Nubia... I directed serfs in their thousands and ten-thousands, and Nubians in hundred-thousands, without limit. I brought all the dues of the land of Kush in double measure. I caused the people to come in submission. Then I was commissioned to build the Temple of Ramesses II in the Domain of Amun [Wadi es-Sebua].

He goes on to say that the labour was provided by captives and funded by the booty captured by Ramesses on his campaigns. This statement is backed up by the inscription of an army officer, Ramose, who says:

Year 44: His Majesty commanded... the Viceroy of Nubia, Setau, together with the army personnel of the company of Ramesses II, Amun protects his son, that he should take captives from the land of the Libyans, in order to build the Temple of Ramesses II in the Domain of Amun... ◆

▼ *Ramesses II offers to Horus a figure of the goddess Maat, who represents the ideal world order, to demonstrate his fitness to rule.*

New Amada

The oldest of the temples rescued from Lake Nasser is that of the Eighteenth Dynasty king Tuthmosis III (c.1479–c.1425 BC) at Amada. Like many of the Nubian temples, it was dedicated to Amun and Re-Horakhty. The temple was moved by a team of French engineers, who dismantled the front section and then jacked up the rear on to flat-cars and painstakingly moved it backwards 2.6km (1.6 miles) to its present position.

Although the temple looks rather dull from the outside, it is well worth a visit. Inside, the painted carved reliefs are some of the most attractive in Nubia: they are finely cut and the colours are astonishingly bright and fresh. Like those of Wadi es-Sebua they have been protected by a layer of plaster placed over them by the Christians when the temple was used as a church.

▲ *Built by the Eighteenth Dynasty kings, this is the oldest of the temples dedicated to Re-Horakhty and Amun.*

The temple interior

The original plan of the temple had a pylon, forecourt and portico leading to a vestibule and sanctuary. However, Tuthmosis IV (c.1400–c.1390 BC) roofed over the forecourt and turned it into a pillared hall. The pillars and walls are decorated with offering scenes, with those involving Tuthmosis IV on the left and, on the right, Tuthmosis III and Amenhotep II (c.1427–c.1400 BC), his grandfather and father respectively. The strategic aspect of this Nubian temple can be seen in the title used here by Tuthmosis IV, 'Beloved of Senusret III'. This famous Middle Kingdom king was regarded as a god by the kings of the Eighteenth Dynasty because of his earlier conquest of Nubia.

The best painted reliefs are in the innermost part of the temple, where Tuthmosis III and Amenhotep II are shown being embraced by various deities or making offerings to them. On the left-hand side of the Vestibule, coronation rituals are illustrated: Amenhotep II is crowned by the gods Horus and Thoth and is shown running with oar and *hap* (a navigational instrument). The small cult room at the side of the Sanctuary contains some interesting scenes depicting the foundation ceremony and the consecration of the temple. They include the ritual of the 'stretching of the cord', the ceremonial making and laying of bricks, and the offering of the temple to its gods. Animal sacrifice and the consecration of ritual vessels and temple vestments are also shown.

Temple stelae

The temple contains several interesting inscriptions, which reveal something of the history of Egypt and Nubia, as well as of the temple itself, during the reigns of some of the New Kingdom rulers. From these it can be seen that the work was begun by Tuthmosis III and later completed by Amenhotep II and Tuthmosis IV, with restoration work and further decoration by kings of the Ramesside Period (c.1295–c.1069 BC).

▶ *Tuthmosis IV converted an open court to a roofed, pillared hall in the temple of Amada. His cartouche can be seen on the pillar.*

During the Amarna Period, the 'heretic' king Akhenaten (c.1352–c.1336 BC) obliterated the name of the god Amun throughout the temple, although this was later restored by Seti I (c.1294–c.1279 BC). The stelae of the viceroys Setau, Heqanakht and Messuy tell of their building activities on behalf of the Nineteenth Dynasty kings Ramesses II (c.1279–c.1213 BC) and Merenptah (c.1213–c.1203 BC), and of the chancellor Bay under Saptah (c.1194–c.1188 BC).

The two most important historical inscriptions deal with the military exploits of Amenhotep II and Merenptah. A large stela describes the success of Amenhotep's campaign against the rulers of Retenu, the city-states of Syria–Palestine, and show that he dealt with them ruthlessly:

...His Majesty returned with joy of heart to his father, Amun, when he slew with his own mace the seven princes who had been in the district of Tikhsi. They had been put upside-down at the prow of His Majesty's barge...He put six of those fallen ones on the wall of Thebes, and the hands as well. Then the other fallen one was taken up-river and hanged on the wall of Napata [a frontier city near the Fourth Cataract] to show His Majesty's victories forever and ever in all lands...to the ends of the earth, so that he may set his boundary wherever he wishes without opposition according to the command of his father, Amun-Re, Lord of the Thrones of the Two Lands...

The message is clear. Although the campaign had been conducted far away from Nubia, the hanging of the body of one of the princes of Retenu on the walls of Napata acted as a dreadful warning of the consequences of rebellion – and all in the name of Amun. Merenptah's inscription records the suppression of an insurrection in Nubia itself, which had Libyan backing. These inscriptions clearly show the way temples were used by the New Kingdom kings to maintain their hold on Nubia. ◆

▶ *Part of a coronation scene from the vestibule of the Sanctuary shows Thoth, god of wisdom, purifying Amenhotep II.*

The tomb of Penmut

Nearby is the tomb of Penmut, 'Deputy of Wawat' (Lower Nubia), 'Chief of the Quarry Service' and 'Steward of Horus, Lord of Miam', during the reign of Ramesses VI (c.1143–c.1136 BC). He was the chief administrator in Lower Nubia, second only in importance to the viceroy of Kush. So thoroughly did the Egyptians replace the native culture with their own that it is not possible to tell whether Penmut was Egyptian or Nubian. He was probably an Egyptianized Nubian, as members of his family also had tombs in the area, while there is a great deal of evidence to show that the Egyptians chose to be buried at home even when they died abroad. Penmut's tomb is rock-cut and has a small offering chapel decorated with scenes of his life: several concern his dedication of a statue of Ramesses VI and his reward of a gold collar.

▶ *Pillars in the Hypostyle Hall are decorated with cartouches of Tuthmosis IV and carved reliefs of the king.*

Expeditions to Nubia

From the beginning of ancient Egyptian history, the kings had been anxious to exploit Nubia in order to obtain the exotic luxuries it could supply. The expeditions they ordered for this purpose are described in the tomb inscriptions of Upper Egyptian officials and others who were responsible for organizing such missions.

Some tell of the hazards of their trips. Sabni, a governor of the South, writes that his father Mekhu was killed undertaking an expedition. Sabni set off in hot pursuit and managed to recover his father's body and bring it home for burial in Egypt. When the king heard about it he congratulated Sabni on his prompt action and provided the embalming materials for the burial of Mekhu.

Harkhuf's expeditions

Many of the expeditions used donkey caravans, as the autobiography of Harkhuf attests. It is inscribed on the façade of his tomb opposite modern Aswan. Harkhuf was a very important official during the reigns of the later Old Kingdom kings, Merenre (c.2287–c.2278 BC) and Pepi II (c.2278–c.2184 BC). His titles included 'Governor of Upper Egypt', 'Royal Seal Bearer' and 'Chief of Scouts', the two latter making clear that one of his main tasks as governor was to mount expeditions on behalf of the king.

Harkhuf's autobiography records three such missions, the first being undertaken with his father, another senior official, which was apparently very successful: 'I did it in seven months, I brought from it all kinds of beautiful and rare gifts and was praised for it very greatly.' A second expedition was equally successful, but Harkhuf experienced some difficulty on his third mission. The local chiefs put up some resistance until he won the support of the Chief of Yam. Then he was able to come home triumphant with 'three hundred donkey loads of incense, ebony, [precious] oils, panther skins, elephant tusks, throw sticks and all good products'.

However, the autobiography reveals that the thing that most delighted the child king Pepi II was a dancing pygmy (perhaps a dwarf) whom Harkhuf had obtained for him, and he anxiously insisted that great care was taken to look after him. The young king wrote a letter of thanks to Harkhuf, who proudly had a copy of it displayed on his tomb:

▲ *This typical fishing and fowling scene comes from the tomb of Mekhu and Sabni at Aswan. Sabni retrieved his father's body from Nubia after he was killed while on an expedition.*

Come north to the residence at once! Hurry and bring with you this pygmy whom you have brought from the land of the horizon-dwellers live, hale, and hearty, for the dances of the god, to gladden the heart, to delight the heart of King Neferkare [Pepi II] who lives forever! When he goes with you down into the ship, get worthy men to be around him on deck, lest he fall into the water! When he lies down at night, get worthy men to lie around him in his tent. Inspect ten times at night! My Majesty desires to see this pygmy more than the gifts of the mainland [Sinai] and of Punt.

Bypassing the cataract

The First Cataract, with its rocks and rapids, was a serious obstacle to river traffic south of Aswan. Attempts were made at an early stage to get around it by digging canals. The Autobiography of Weni, a governor of the south during the Sixth Dynasty (c.2345–c.2181 BC), mentions that he was instructed by the king to dig five canals in Upper Egypt. This may be a reference to such a venture.

The island of Sehel, which lies about 4km (2.5 miles) south of Aswan, is covered with over 200 rock inscriptions. They are dedications to the deities of the cataract, Khnum, Satet and Anuket, placed there to seek a blessing for the hazardous journey ahead into Nubia, or in thanksgiving for a safe and successful return home. Most date from the Eighteenth and Nineteenth Dynasties (c.1550–c.1186 BC) and several refer to the canals.

▲ *This inscription of Amenhotep II on the island of Sehel at the First Cataract commemorates an expedition to Nubia to procure luxury goods.*

▲ *Part of the letter from the child king, Pepi II, expressing his gratitude to Harkhuf for the dancing pygmy the official brought for him.*

Two of the inscriptions are of the Twelfth Dynasty king Senusret III (c.1874–c.1855 BC), and record his instructions for the digging of a canal as well as his conquest of Nubia. Later kings found the canal blocked and had to redo the work.

Two inscriptions from the reign of Tuthmosis I (c.1504–1492 BC), an early Eighteenth Dynasty king, have also come to light. One, in the name of Thure, the king's son, is incomplete but it has been possible to restore the text by comparison with an inscription of Tuthmosis III (c.1479–c.1425 BC), which repeats part of it:

Year 3, first month of the third season, day 22, under the majesty of the King of Upper and Lower Egypt, Aakheperkare [Tuthmosis I] who is given life. His Majesty commanded to dig this canal after he found it stopped up with stones [so that] no [ship sailed upon it]. He [sailed downstream] upon it, his heart [glad having slain his enemies].

Another inscription, also dedicated by Thure states:

'Year 3, first month of the third season, day 22, His Majesty sailed this canal in victory and in the power of his return from overthrowing the wretched Kush'.

In the inscription of Tuthmosis III, he adds:

The name of this canal is: Opener of the Way in the Beauty of Menkheperre [Tuthmosis III] Living Forever. The fishermen of Elephantine shall clear this canal every year. ◆

◀ *This agricultural scene is from one of the tombs of the high officials at Aswan.*

Nubian Temples of the Graeco-Roman Period

From the end of the Twentieth Dynasty (c.1069 BC), Egyptian power declined and Nubia became an independent state ruled from Napata. Three centuries later, the Nubians came into their own when the Kushite kings of Napata took over Egypt and ruled as the Twenty-fifth Dynasty. Unfortunately, in 701 BC one of their most illustrious kings, Taharqo (690–664 BC), antagonized the Assyrian king, Sennacherib, by going to the aid of his rebellious vassal, King Hezekiah of Jerusalem. This resulted in the Assyrian invasion of Egypt, culminating in the devastation of Thebes by Ashurbanipal in 664 BC, after which the Kushites were forced to retreat.

Not long afterwards the Nubians moved their capital further south to Meroe, between the Fifth and Sixth Cataracts. This Meroitic kingdom was contemporary with the Twenty-seventh to the Thirtieth Dynasties and the Ptolemaic and Roman Periods (525 BC–AD 395) in Egypt. During the Ptolemaic Period (332–30 BC), the two powers seem to have been on good terms and collaborated in the building of some of the temples in Nubia. All these have been rescued from the rising waters of Lake Nasser and removed to higher ground, except for Dabod, which was taken to Madrid, and Dendur, which is now in the Metropolitan Museum of Art, New York.

▲ *Originally located 50km (31 miles) south of the High Dam, the Temple of Kalabsha has been moved to higher ground much closer to Aswan. Built largely in the late Ptolemaic and Roman Periods, it was never completed, but is regarded as one of the best examples of Egyptian architecture in Nubia.*

Dakka

The Temple of Dakka was begun by the Kushite king, Arkamani, and was extended by his contemporary Ptolemy IV (221–205 BC). A pylon and sanctuary were added in the Roman Period (30 BC–AD 395).

The temple was dedicated to Thoth of Pnubs. The god's title is a reference to the sycamore-fig tree under which he waited for Tefnut, his wife, to return to Egypt. Tefnut was the goddess of moisture, born from the expectoration of her father, Atum, and in Ptolemaic temples her name was sometimes written with the hieroglyph of two lips spitting. In a demotic papyrus she appears as the eye of Re, who quarrelled with her father and rampaged through Nubia. Thoth, the god of wisdom, and Shu, the god of air, were sent to try to persuade her to come back. This story was used as the starting point for a series of further tales told by Thoth to entertain his wife on the return journey. A carved relief in the Sanctuary shows Thoth in his baboon form sitting under the sycamore-fig tree. In the Roman side chapel, Thoth, again in the form of a baboon, is depicted worshipping Tefnut in the form of a lioness. The son of Thoth and Tefnut was Arsenuphis, a Meroitic god. In this temple both Thoth and Arsenuphis wear short Nubian wigs and headdresses of four feathers. Throughout the temple the Ptolemies are shown as traditional Egyptian kings worshipping many of the Egyptian gods.

▲ *The Kiosk of Qertassi was possibly a way station on the processional route around Lower Nubia, which was regarded as the estate of Isis.*

Kalabsha

The extant Temple of Kalabsha appears to be Roman in date, although representations of Amenhotep II (c.1427–c.1400 BC) and one of the Ptolemies in the Hypostyle Hall suggest that it was built on the site of an earlier construction. The temple was dedicated to Mandulis, a Nubian form of Horus, and was also associated with Osiris and Isis. Mandulis was usually depicted wearing an elaborate headdress of ram's horns, cobras, and plumes surmounted by sun discs. Sometimes he is seen in the form of a hawk, but with a human head. His wife was Wadjet, the cobra goddess, and their child was a young form of Mandulis, so they appear in the temple decoration as counterparts of Osiris, Isis and Horus.

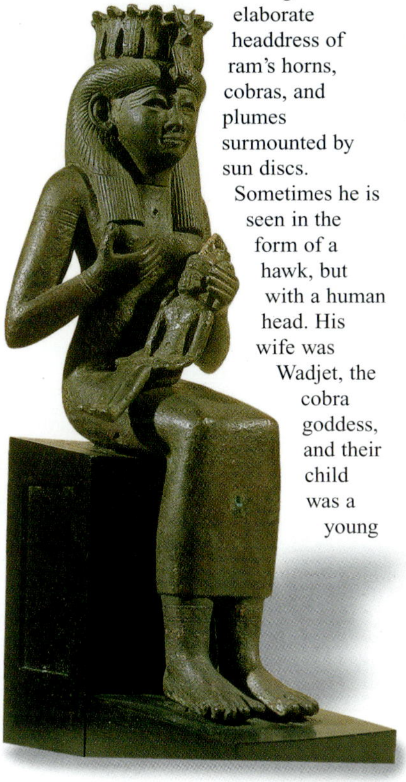

▲ *Hathor, identified by her diadem and erect* uraeus, *is often associated with Isis as the mother of Horus and, by analogy, of the king, to whom she offers her breast.*

Traditional scenes occur throughout, of Horus and Thoth purifying the king and the king or emperor making offerings to various deities. There are also some interesting inscriptions on the forecourt wall opposite the pylon. One, in Greek, is by a governor of Elephantine, ordering the pigs to be driven from the temple. Another is in the cursive Meroitic script and was written by one of the kings of the Blemmyes (c. AD 4), while the most interesting is an account by Silko, the Christian king of the Nubian kingdom of Nobatia, celebrating his victory over the Blemmyes.

Philae

The great cult centre of Isis, wife of Osiris and mother of Horus, was at Philae. The temple was built by the Ptolemies and Roman emperors between about 200 BC and AD 300. Isis was the epitome of motherhood and had a reputation for healing. Inscriptions show that Philae was an important centre of pilgrimage, dear to both Egyptians and Nubians, who remained faithful to Isis long after the introduction of Christianity. The temple was essential to the Ptolemies and Roman emperors who, although foreigners, continued to regard themselves, as the pharaohs had done, as reincarnations of Horus, and were depicted as such in the temple decoration.

The Kiosk of Qertassi

This charming little kiosk has been re-erected near to the Temple of Kalabsha, but once stood at the entrance to the sandstone quarries. The capitals are decorated with Hathor heads, in honour of the goddess who was patron of quarry-men and miners. As Hathor was often associated with Isis, as she is at Philae, it has been suggested that this kiosk and the small temples of Dabod and Dendur were way stations on the processional route taken by priests bearing the image of Isis around Lower Nubia, which was held to be her estate. ◆

Qasr Ibrim

Viewed from the deck of a Lake Nasser cruise ship, Qasr Ibrim appears to be an island. The site, however, once stood on the highest of three headlands on the east bank of the Nile, 70m (230ft) above the river. The waters of the lake have recently reached unexpected levels and each year encroach further on the site. Visitors are no longer allowed to wander around the ruins as they once did and can only view them from the ships, which moor close to the site while the guides point out the salient features. The Egypt Exploration Society continues its work at the site.

History of the site

The name means Fort of Ibrim and is ultimately derived from its ancient Meroitic name, Pedeme. In classical texts it was called Primis and in Coptic, Phrim, which was corrupted to Ibrim in Arabic. The fort may well have originated in the Middle Kingdom (c.2055–c.1650 BC) when the Twelfth Dynasty kings were establishing control of the trade route along the Nile, although the earliest archaeological evidence for fortification dates to c.1000 BC. The strategic importance of Qasr Ibrim was widely recognized, and fighting for the possession of the site took place for centuries until modern times. It was not finally abandoned until 1811.

The earliest inscriptional evidence at Qasr Ibrim is from the reign of Amenhotep I (c.1525–c.1504 BC) of the early New Kingdom. It is a stela dated to the eighth year of his reign and is now in the British Museum in London. The stela was not found in situ but in the cathedral, where it had been reused in one of the crypts.

That the site was of religious as well as strategic importance is clear from four New Kingdom shrines cut low down into the cliffs facing the ancient district capital of Miam (modern Aniba). These shrines were dedicated by high officials of the Eighteenth Dynasty (c.1550–c.1295 BC) and were dedicated to local forms of Horus as well as to the deities of the First Cataract and to Hathor, protectress of expeditions. Although the site in general was thought to be in no danger from the lake, these shrines, lying as they did close to the water's edge, were removed. The shrine of Usersatet, viceroy of Kush in the reign of Amenhotep II (c.1427–c.1400 BC) has been re-erected in the new Nubian Museum in Aswan, and there are plans to relocate the others at New Sabua. A stela of Seti I (c.1294–c.1279 BC) has already been moved to New Kalabsha where it has been re-erected just to the south of the main Ptolemaic temple.

After the defeat of Antony and Cleopatra at the Battle of Actium in 31 BC, Egypt became part of the Roman Empire and a Roman garrison was established at Aswan. This was

▼ *An important fortress in Pharaonic and Roman times, Qasr Ibrim is also the site of several temples, dating from the reign of Taharqo to the late Meroitic period.*

▲ *After Christianity had been introduced to Nubia, the Temple of Taharqo became a church. In the 7th century, a cathedral was built on the site and dedicated to the Virgin Mary.*

attacked by a Nubian queen, probably Amanirenas, and Aswan, Elephantine and Philae were briefly occupied by the Nubians. The bronze statue head of Emperor Augustus (27 BC–AD 14), now in the British Museum in London, was probably taken by the Nubians during this raid. It was found at Meroe, buried in front of the small temple there. The Nubians were driven south and the Romans occupied Qasr Ibrim where they hoped to fix their southern boundary. However, the Nubians again attacked, after which a peace treaty was drawn up and the Romans withdrew.

Temples and churches

The earliest religious building on the site was the mudbrick Temple of King Taharqo (690–664 BC). This was later converted into a Christian church. In the Roman Period (30 BC–AD 395), the traditional Egyptian gods continued to be worshipped here long after Christianity had taken root and become the official religion of the Empire. Christianity also had a long history at Qasr Ibrim and for several centuries held out against the growing influence of Islam.

Qasr Ibrim prospered in the years following the Nubian raids. Several new temples were built and the old Temple of Taharqo was repaired. These establishments gained reputations as healing centres and were much visited by those seeking cures. Although most of the temples dedicated to the old gods were formally closed by Theodosius I in AD 390, those of Qasr Ibrim continued to flourish.

At some point that has not yet been determined, Christianity was introduced at Qasr Ibrim. The Temple of Taharqo became a church and the Temple of Isis was destroyed. In the seventh century a cathedral church dedicated to the Virgin Mary was built on the headland, using some of the blocks from the old temples. Qasr Ibrim then became a great centre of pilgrimage and later, a bishopric. It was not until the sixteenth century that Christianity was replaced by Islam, when Egypt was conquered by the Ottoman Turks and a garrison of Bosnian mercenaries was installed. ◆

The grave of Bishop Timotheos

The intact grave of Bishop Timotheos was found in the north crypt of the cathedral. He had been buried in the late fourteenth century together with his letters of appointment from the Patriarch of Alexandria, which are dated 1372. At this time Christian burials were usually very simple, the body being wrapped in a shroud and laid in a pit covered with stones or a brick canopy. Grave goods were no longer provided in the burials of ordinary people. However, those of clerics were rather more splendid. Bishop Timotheos was buried in his bishop's robes with his benedictional iron cross and other belongings. These are now in the British Museum in London, which also has a page from the Book of Revelation written in the Old Nubian language using the Coptic alphabet. This, too, was found at Qasr Ibrim.

The Delta and Oases

The Delta is the triangular area to the north of modern Cairo, named by the Greeks after the fourth letter of their alphabet because it resembled its shape. In antiquity, the ancient capital of Memphis stood at the point where the River Nile, on leaving the Valley, divided into several branches as it wended its way to the sea. At least five channels existed in the Pharaonic Period, but most dried up between the tenth and twelfth centuries AD, leaving only two in evidence today. Low-lying and fringed by lagoons, wetlands and lakes, the Delta was a very fertile area famous for its rich pastures where goats, sheep and especially cattle were raised. Milk, honey and wine were also produced. Ancient cities grew up across the region, including Tanis, Bubastis and Alexandria.

In the Libyan Desert to the west of the Nile Valley, a string of oases lies virtually parallel to the Nile, the most important of which are Kharga, Dakhla, Farafra and Bahariya. They have been settled since the Stone Age and at Kharga there are traces of early agriculture. From the beginnings of Egyptian history, the inhabitants traded with Egypt, supplying aromatic woods, leather goods, agricultural produce, salt, natron and minerals.

◀ *The Siwa Oasis is a natural depression in the Libyan desert and the site of the famous oracle visited by Alexander the Great in 332 BC.*

Tanis

One of the most important Delta sites was Tanis. At the end of the Twentieth Dynasty (c.1069 BC), the rule of Egypt was divided: the kings ruled from new capital cities in the Delta while the high priests of Amun at Karnak governed the South from Thebes. Tanis was the capital city of King Smendes (c.1069–c.1043 BC), the first king of the Twenty-first Dynasty, and it retained its importance throughout the Late Period (c.747–332 BC). So many statues, carved reliefs and inscriptions of the Nineteenth Dynasty king Ramesses II (c.1279–c.1213 BC) were found there, however, that when the site was first excavated, it was assumed that Tanis was the site of Per-Ramesses, the brand new capital established by Ramesses and his father Seti I (c.1294–c.1279 BC). This caused great excitement because it was thought that the excavators had found the city where, according to the Bible, the Hebrews had worked as slaves. Modern excavation, however, has proved that it was not the city of Ramesses II, which lies a short distance away near the modern village of Qantir. Later kings used Per-Ramesses as a quarry when they were building the temples of Tanis, and this explains why there is so much Ramesses II material there.

The site of Tanis was first excavated by Auguste Mariette and Flinders Petrie towards the end of the nineteenth century. Since then, French archaeologists have been working at Tanis, in particular Pierre Montet, who made spectacular discoveries between 1921 and 1951.

▲ *A sphinx of Amenemhat III found at Tanis was originally from the Temple of Bastet at Bubastis. It was taken to Per-Ramesses in the eastern Delta and subsequently to Tanis by Psusennes I.*

The Temple of Amun

Excavation has revealed an enormous mudbrick enclosure wall surrounding the great Temple of Amun. The monumental gateway, or Propylon, was decorated in the reign of the Twenty-second Dynasty king Sheshonq III (c.825–c.773 BC), who is depicted on some of the blocks. Statues of Ramesses II, brought from Per-Ramesses, were also used to embellish the entrance to the temple precinct, including a fine quartzite colossus. On the right is a triad carved in high relief showing Ramesses II between the gods Re and Ptah-Tatenen. Another colossal figure, itself from an earlier period and usurped by Ramesses II, was also used to adorn the entrance.

Beyond the monumental gateway, fragments of yet more colossal statues and carved blocks, obelisks and columns can be seen. These had been used as fill

▶ *Strewn all over the site at Tanis are blocks bearing the names and image of Ramesses II, which led archaeologists to believe that Tanis was the Ramesside capital.*

for the Propylon. One block shows Ramesses II running his *heb sed* race before the god Horus. Sections of four columns with palm-leaf capitals, originally part of an Old Kingdom structure and also usurped by Ramesses II, had been reused in the building of a kiosk in the outer court of the temple. The entrance to the temple proper was once marked by two obelisks, as were the Second and Third Pylons. Beyond the wall is the smaller Sanctuary of Mut and Khonsu, the wife and son of Amun. Astarte, a goddess of Syrian origin regarded as the daughter of either Re or Ptah, was also worshipped here.

▶ *It is now known that statues and other architectural remains of Ramesses II were brought to Tanis from the Ramesside capital by the kings of the 21st Dynasty.*

Statues from the temple

From the Second Court of the temple came some of the statues now in the Cairo Museum. One of the most remarkable shows Ramesses II as a child, naked and with his index finger in his mouth, squatting in front of the Canaanite god, Horon. He wears a sun disc on his head and holds a plant in his hand. The whole thing is a rebus that spells out his name. The sun disc stands for Ra (Re), the child is *mes* and the plant *sw*. Ramesses is protected by the huge falcon representing Horon, who was worshipped mainly in the Giza area where workers from Canaan were installed during the New Kingdom Period (c.1550–c.1069 BC). They seem to have associated Horon with Horemakhet or 'Horus-in-the-Horizon', the Great Sphinx at Giza, which was regarded as the sun god at this time. According to the Egyptian tradition revealed in the Dream Stela of Tuthmosis IV (c.1400–c.1390 BC) erected between its paws, the Sphinx was the god who chose the next king. Thus, in the Tanis statue, Ramesses is shown as crown prince, chosen and protected by the sun god.

Another interesting statue from the Second Court takes the form of a sphinx. The unusual features of the king, and the fact that the statue was inscribed with the cartouches of one of the Hyksos kings of the Second Intermediate Period (c.1650–c.1550 BC), led the excavators to think that it was a Hyksos work. However, comparison with other statues has revealed that this was actually a portrait statue of the Twelfth Dynasty king Amenemhat III (c.1855–c.1808 BC), probably originating from the Temple of Bastet. It had been usurped first by the Hyksos king, Nehesy, then by Ramesses II who transferred it to his new capital at Per-Ramesses, and by his son Merenptah (c.1213–c.1203 BC). Finally, it was brought to Tanis by the Twenty-first Dynasty king Psusennes I (c.1039–c.991 BC), who added his own name to it and used it to embellish the Temple of Amun. ◆

The Royal Tombs of Tanis

The kings of the Twenty-first and Twenty-second Dynasties (c.1069–c715 BC) were buried at Tanis, rather than in the Valley of the Kings. The tombs were originally underground and were built of mudbrick and reused inscribed stone blocks. Those belonging to Psusennes I (c.1039–c.991 BC), Amenemope (c.993–c.984 BC), Osorkon II (c.874–c.850 BC), and Sheshonq III (c.825–c.773 BC) have been discovered. The tomb of Psusennes I, however, contained the silver hawk-headed coffin of Sheshonq II (c.890 BC) and the coffin and sarcophagus of Amenemope, while that of Takelot II (c.850–c.825 BC) turned up in the tomb of Osorkon II. Two other tombs have been found but the identities of their owners are not known.

▼ *The funerary mask of Psusennes I depicts the idealized features of the king. It is made of gold and lapis lazuli with inlays of black and white glass for the eyes and eyebrows.*

► *Found in the intact tomb of Psusennes I, this elegant vase was used to pour libations to the gods. It is decorated with the name of Amenemope, Psusennes' son and successor.*

The royal jewellery

During his excavations in Tanis, Pierre Montet found some wonderful jewellery in the tombs. It is considered to be even more splendid than the jewellery of Tutankhamun. Little attention was given to the discovery at the time, however, because Montet found it in 1939, just at the outbreak of World War II, when there were more urgent concerns. The royal jewellery is today on display in the Cairo Museum and is well worth a visit.

Ancient Egyptians of all walks of life loved jewellery. From the earliest days of Egyptian history there is evidence of gold-working and the use of semi-precious stones such as amethyst, carnelian and turquoise in jewellery-making. Much has been found in tombs, as the Egyptians took the jewellery they had worn during their earthly life with them to the Afterlife. They also had some jewellery made specially for the tomb.

The jewellery found at Tanis is full of religious imagery and significance. Worked into the designs are many amuletic devices to enable the king and his high officials to journey safely through the Underworld and become united to Osiris and the sun god in the Afterlife. The jewellery and other artefacts from the Tanis tombs are the most important evidence found so far concerning royal funerary equipment in the Third Intermediate Period.

▲ *This small vase with 24 gadroons is a type known since the Middle Kingdom. Found in the tomb of Psusennes I, it is decorated on the right with the king's cartouches and on the left with those of his mother, Queen Henuttawy. Part of the king's funerary equipment, it is a fine example of the craftsmen's work at Tanis.*

The pectoral of Psusennes I

An openwork gold cloisonné pectoral, or chest ornament, was found on the mummy of King Psusennes I. The decoration includes images of Isis on the right, and Nephthys on the left, on either side of a winged scarab. In mythology, Isis, the wife of Osiris, and Nephthys, his sister, searched for the body of Osiris after he had been murdered by Seth. When they had found it, they restored Osiris to life. The hope expressed here is that they will do the same for King Psusennes.

The winged scarab, of lapis lazuli, represents Khepri, the sun god of the morning. He is pushing the ball of the sun along in front of him, showing that he is responsible for its rising. The sun is placed over the cartouche of King Psusennes, and the imagery suggests that the king will enter his new life after his hazardous journey through the Underworld, just as the sun, having overcome his enemies during the hours of darkness, rises again as the new day dawns.

Below the main section is a row of alternating *djed*-pillars. These represent the backbone of Osiris, and in this context his resurrection, and the girdle of Isis, which she tied around her little son, Horus, to give him magical protection.

The pectoral of Sheshonq I

Some of the jewellery found at Tanis had been reused. Another pectoral, also made in gold-inlaid openwork, had been made for Sheshonq I (c.945–c.924 BC) but was found on the mummy of Sheshonq II. The inscribed lapis lazuli sun disc, sailing in the sun god's boat through the Underworld, is protected by images of Maat, goddess of justice and truth. The Eye of Horus between the wings of the goddess is a symbol of new life, as in mythology Horus restored Osiris to life by giving him his Eye. Lotus flowers are suspended below: they represent creation, as the sun god was born from a lotus. In this instance, however, they symbolize re-creation and the beginning of the Afterlife.

The bracelet of Sheshonq II

A particularly fine piece is the gold bracelet of Sheshonq II. It is made in imitation of a finger ring, with the bezel in the form of a lapis lazuli scarab beetle standing on a gold base decorated with braiding. The main part of the bracelet is beautiful in its simplicity, completely unadorned apart from the two stylized papyrus heads at either side of the bezel.

The bangles of Psusennes I

A pair of solid gold bangles was found on the mummy of Psusennes. Each is extremely heavy, weighing almost 1.8kg (4lb). The outside is plain, but the king's name is inscribed on the inside, together with a blessing to guarantee his safe arrival in the Afterlife. ◆

▼ *This gold and lapis lazuli bangle was found on the right arm of Psusennes I. Another lay in the sarcophagus beside him. Made of two unequal parts slotted into each other and fastened with a pin, the joins are hidden by the lapis lazuli set in the hollow ring of sheet gold.*

Bubastis

The ancient name of Bubastis was Per-Bastet, and the city was the cult centre of Bastet, the cat goddess. The town and the temple lie 80km (50 miles) north-east of Cairo.

Bubastis was an important town from the Old Kingdom (c.2686–c.2181 BC) to the Roman Period (30 BC–AD 395). The chief attraction was the Temple of Bastet, built of red granite and embellished with images of the goddess and the various kings who paid their respects to her here. Apart from the main temple, Bubastis is the site of the *ka*-temples of the Sixth Dynasty kings Teti (c.2345–c.2323 BC) and Pepi I (c.2321–c.2287 BC), and the jubilee chapels of the Twelfth Dynasty king Amenemhat III (c.1855–c.1808 BC) and the Eighteenth Dynasty king Amenhotep III (c.1390–c.1352 BC), as well as temples to Atum, the creator god, and Mihos, a lion god and son of Bastet.

The Temple of Bastet

Herodotus, the ancient Greek traveller and historian, visited the town in the fifth century BC and much of his description of the site tallies with what Edouard Naville found during his excavations at the end of the nineteenth century. Bubastis is in a rather ruinous condition today, having been used as a quarry at various times, although strenuous attempts are now being made to restore the temple to its former glory. The work was begun by the Fourth Dynasty kings Khufu (c.2589–c.2566 BC) and Khafre (c.2558–c.2532 BC), builders of the largest of the Giza pyramids, and continued by Amenemhat I (c.1985–c.1955 BC) and Ramesses II (c.1279–c.1213 BC).

Bubastis was also the home of the kings of the Twenty-second Dynasty (c.945–c.715 BC) and so grew in importance at this time, although the capital remained at Tanis. Osorkon II (c.874–c.850 BC) built a new hypostyle hall in the temple, and added a further

▼ *Bubastis, the cult centre of the cat goddess Bastet, is now in ruins. Little remains of the red granite Temple of Bastet.*

◀ *This bronze cat depicts Bastet. Her nose ring and earrings are ancient but may not have belonged to the statue originally.*

hall to celebrate his *heb sed*, or jubilee festival. He also decorated the walls and monumental gateway in relief. Many of these carved reliefs are now scattered in museums throughout the world. There is a fine example in the British Museum in London showing Osorkon and his wife, Karoma, making offerings to Bastet and recording his jubilee.

Further work was done by Nectanebo II (360–343 BC), the last king of the Thirtieth Dynasty. Present work on the site includes the restoration of the hypostyle hall of Osorkon II, with its closed papyriform columns. Numerous statues of Ramesses II and Bastet have also come to light.

Bastet, the goddess

Although Bastet was a local deity, she was of great importance to the kings of Egypt. Like Hathor and Sekhmet, the lioness goddess, with whom she could be associated, she was regarded as the daughter of the sun god. Cat-like, she had both gentle and fierce aspects to her nature. To the ancient Egyptians of the Late Period (c.747–332 BC) the cat epitomized the protective aspects of motherhood, so Bastet was honoured as one of the mothers of kings. She was mentioned on the façade of the valley temple of Khafre at Giza together with Hathor, another of the king's mothers, and in one of the spells in the Pyramid Texts she is specifically named as 'My mother Bastet [who] has nursed me'.

Although the earliest representations of Bastet, from the Second Dynasty (c.2890–c.2686 BC), depicted her with the head of a lioness, by the Late Period she was usually shown with the head of a domestic cat, often accompanied by her kittens. She was often shown carrying a *sistrum*, linking her with Hathor.

Bastet's festival

The fifth-century BC Greek writer Herodotus described the annual festival of Bastet at Bubastis, although he actually called the goddess Artemis. Artemis was the Greek goddess of hunting and so was appropriately equated with Bastet, the cat goddess:

The men and women come together in barges, each boat packed with large numbers of people. On the way the women shake their castanets and some of the men play flutes. Everyone else sings and claps their hands. Whenever they pass by a town on the river bank, they bring the barge close to the shore...Some of the women hurl abuse at the women of the town or start dancing and hitch up their skirts (in an unseemly manner). When they get to Bubastis they offer sacrifices and consume huge amounts of wine, more than that drunk during the whole of the rest of the year.

Cat cemeteries

Associated with the cult of Bastet were the cat cemeteries, which lay to the north of the city. These were underground vaulted galleries where mummified cats and hundreds of bronzes of Bastet were buried. The cemeteries were excavated by the Egyptian Antiquities Service in the early 1960s but most of the galleries had been robbed, the attractive figures of Bastet and her kittens being a favourite with antique collectors. In fact they were so popular that many fakes were produced and found their way on to the antiquities market. ◆

▶ *In the Late Period, Bastet was often shown as a mother cat with her kittens. The* sistrum *links her with Hathor, one of the traditional mothers of kings.*

Alexandria Lost and Found

According to the Greek historians, Plutarch (c. AD 46–c.126) and Arrian (c. AD 95–180), the city of Alexandria was not only named after, but also founded by Alexander the Great, who ruled Egypt from 332 to 323 BC. In his history of Alexander's campaigns, Arrian wrote, 'He designed the general layout of the new town, indicating the position of the market square, the number of temples to be built, and what gods they should serve…and the precise limits of its outer defences.'

Alexander, however, did not live to see the city take shape, and it fell to the early Ptolemies to carry out his plans. Strabo (c.63 BC–c.AD 21), the Greek geographer, described the city in such detail that it has been possible to draw a plan of it, including the island of Pharos with its famous lighthouse, the Heptastadium, which joined the island to the mainland, thus forming its two harbours, the royal palace, the Museum and Library, the Serapaeum and the necropolis.

▼ *Since 1994, major discoveries have been made during underwater excavations made by Jean-Yves Empereur and his team in Alexandria.*

▲ *A 13th-century mosaic in St Mark's, Venice, shows St Mark passing the famous lighthouse on his way to bring Christianity into Europe.*

The new city on the Mediterranean coast, designed by Deinocrates of Rhodes, was built on a strip of land between Lake Maroitis and the sea. It consisted of a network of streets lying at right angles to one another, embellished with the many impressive buildings mentioned by Strabo.

The Library

Alexandria's famous Library seems to have been initiated by Ptolemy I (305–285 BC) and developed by Ptolemy II (285–246 BC), who is credited with the idea of writing to the rulers of every other state asking them to contribute books. The Library eventually included most Greek literature, a complete collection of Egyptian literature and works on the religions of the ancient Near East. There was room for up to 70,000 papyrus rolls. Most of the items were bought, but other means were sometimes used. In order to procure coveted works, all ships entering the harbour were searched. Every book found was taken to the Library, where it was decided whether to give it back or confiscate it and replace it with a copy.

The Pharos

The lighthouse was one of the earliest buildings to be erected. The island of Pharos was chosen as the site and gave its name to the lighthouse itself. The construction began under Ptolemy I, and was completed by his successor.

The Pharos was an enormous building, said to be over 100m (330ft) high, built in three tiers, and was described in ancient and later Islamic sources. The lowest level was a square tower, 60m (200ft) in height. This was surmounted by a second tier, 30m (100ft) high and octagonal in shape. The top level was cylindrical, about 15m (50ft) high, and was crowned by a statue of Zeus the Saviour. (In the Islamic period this third tier was replaced by a mosque.) It seems, from the reports of travellers in the Middle Ages, to have been in ruins in the mid-fourteenth century, although it was apparently still in good condition around 1200, when it was depicted in a mosaic in the Chapel of St Zeno in St Mark's, Venice.

According to the descriptions of classical authors and the first-century Jewish historian, Josephus, a great fire was kept burning all night at the base of the lighthouse. This was reflected by mirrors from the top and could be seen from an enormous distance out at sea.

The Museum

In order to legitimize their rule, the Ptolemies had to project their city as the home of Greek culture and the main centre of scientific research. They invited all the great scholars of the age to come to work in Alexandria and offered them favourable conditions to do their work. It was a true intellectual centre, where all the disciplines were found.

Almost all of the great minds of the third century BC lived in Alexandria, at least for a while. Among them were Eratosthenes (c.276–c.194 BC), who calculated the circumference of the earth to within 80km (50 miles), and Aristarchus of Samos, who first put forward the idea that the earth turned on its own axis and at the same time moved around the sun. The mathematician Euclid also lived and taught at Alexandria around 300 BC, and Archimedes (c.287–212 BC) corresponded with the scholars and may have visited the city. It was also here that the Old Testament was translated from Hebrew into Greek, for the benefit of the Jews of Alexandria.

The Serapaeum

Under Ptolemy I the Egyptian cult of Osiris-Apis at Memphis was transferred to Alexandria, where the god was called Serapis. He was given the form of a Greek god but embodied both Greek and Egyptian deities: he was not only Osiris-Apis, but also Zeus, Dionysus, Hades and Asklepios. Serapis was thus a god of the Underworld, a healing god, a god of fertility and also the protector of sailors. He was depicted as a mature man with a beard and curly hair. On his head he carried a basket overflowing with good things. A temple, the Serapaeum, was built in his honour.

Rediscovery

Until recently, apart from the Serapaeum, very little of Ptolemaic Alexandria could be seen. However, since 1994, Professor Jean-Yves Empereur and his team have been uncovering the remains of the ancient city. A team of underwater archaeologists has been exploring the sea bed off Qaitbay Fort and has discovered thousands of columns, bases and capitals, many of red granite, removed from buildings of the Ramesside Period (c.1295–c.1069 BC) and reused by the Ptolemies. Parts of six colossal statues have been recovered, including a head of one of the Ptolemies. Other discoveries include obelisks, sphinxes and an enormous statue of a queen as the goddess Isis.

Work is also going ahead on land. One of the most exciting discoveries has been that of a Roman house with mosaic floors, one of which is decorated with a huge head of Medusa. Another is that of the Ptolemaic necropolis, already known from maps made during Napoleon's expedition of 1798. It was recently rediscovered during the construction of a bridge and new road to Cairo. The necropolis contained tiers of collective burials, with tombs that had been used and reused over several generations. They are dated to the Ptolemaic Period by their Greek inscriptions with Egyptian connotations, and decorative elements such as the classical handshake farewell. The deceased is often depicted as a cavalry man, or, if a woman, as a young mother with her new baby. ◆

▼ *A painted scene in the Tigrane tomb shows Isis and Nephthys guarding the mummy of Osiris.*

The Siwa Oasis

The Siwa Oasis lies in the Western Desert, not far from the border with Libya and about 300km (186 miles) inland from Mersa Matruh. It lies in a great depression, which is up to 60m (200ft) deep in parts. The oasis is enormous, about 80km (50 miles) long and 28km (17 miles) across at its widest point, with a population of about 10,000.

Water and salt are big problems in Siwa. Although there are more than 1,000 springs in use, the water is very saline and is of little use for agriculture. The crops produced are limited to dates, olives and a few vegetables. The lake is too salty for fish to survive.

The soil, which is used to make the traditional mudbrick houses of Siwa, is also full of salt. The salt appears in great chunks, which help to strengthen the walls. Unfortunately, on the rare occasions when it rains, the lumps of salt dissolve, causing the houses to collapse.

As the depression is well below sea level, drainage is another problem. In order to make any sort of agriculture possible the soil must be washed, but there is nowhere for the water to go. This also creates problems when there is a storm. There was major flooding in 1982, when it rained continuously for two days. The resulting floods devastated crops, killed livestock and destroyed houses throughout the oasis.

▲ *The ancient city was built of mudbrick. The buildings were devastated by heavy rains, which dissolved the salt in the building material.*

The history of Siwa

The ancient city was at Aghurmi, where the Temple of the Oracle and the Temple of Umm'Ubaydah still stand. It was probably founded during the Saite Dynasty (664–525 BC). Esarhaddon of Assyria had invaded Egypt in 671 BC, as did his son, Ashurbanipal, shortly afterwards. The Kushite king, Taharqo (690–664 BC), at first resisted but was forced to flee. Eventually, the Saite kings restored stability but in the intervening period unsettled conditions caused a diversion of trade from the Nile Valley to the oases and thence to the Mediterranean. Siwa thus lies at the hub of a network of desert routes.

Aghurmi was attacked by Bedouin in the Middle Ages and a new settlement, the Shali, was founded in 1203. The people were not allowed to build outside the walls so, as the population grew, the town extended upwards. Some of the salt-impregnated mudbrick houses reached seven or eight storeys high. After a rainstorm in 1928

◀ *The Temple of the Oracle at Siwa was famous throughout the ancient world. It was consulted by Croesus of Lydia before his disastrous attack on Cyrus of Persia in 546 BC.*

▶ *The tombs in the necropolis of Jabel al-Mawta (Hill of the Dead) were founded in the Saite Period during the 7th century BC and used by both Egyptians and Greeks.*

the ancient town had to be abandoned when the houses collapsed. No one lives there now but it is still possible to visit it. The modern town, with the mosque of Sidi Soliman, lies at its foot.

The Temple of the Oracle

During the reign of the Twenty-sixth Dynasty king Ahmose (570–526 BC), the Temple of the Oracle was built on the rock of Aghurmi, probably on the site of an earlier shrine to Amun and various local deities. In antiquity, the temple was famous all over the Mediterranean world.

Alexander the Great's visit to the oracle was recorded by the second-century AD Greek writer Arrian:

> *...[Alexander] suddenly found himself passionately eager to visit the shrine of Ammon [Amun] in Libya. One reason was his wish to consult the oracle there, as it had a reputation for infallibility and also because Perseus and Herakles were supposed to have consulted it...[and] Alexander longed to equal their fame [as] the blood of both flowed in his veins, and just as they traced their descent from Zeus so he, too, had a feeling he was descended from Ammon. His main concern was to have this confirmed.*

He seems to have had his wish granted; the priest meant to greet him in Greek with the words 'O, paidion' ('O, my son') but because he was Egyptian and speaking a foreign language he made a mistake and actually said 'O, pai Dios' ('O, son of god'). Alexander was delighted to have his divine origins confirmed.

The temple itself is relatively well preserved, although much remains to be excavated. The First Court has almost disappeared. Still standing are two halls and the Sanctuary, which Alexander the Great entered to hear the oracle. The Sanctuary is decorated with images of King Ahmose offering to Amun, Mut, Khonsu and other deities whose identity is not clear. To the right of the Sanctuary is a narrow corridor that leads around to the back. This could have been used to store ritual vessels or may have been involved in the delivery of the oracle's messages.

▶ *Alexander the Great was the ruler of Egypt from 332 to 323 BC, and visited the Temple of the Oracle so that it could confirm his divinity.*

The tombs at Jabal al-Mawta

Greek influence can be seen in the decoration of the tombs at Jabal al-Mawta, a short distance from the centre of Siwa. Of these, the tomb of Si-Amun is the most beautiful. The decoration is a mixture of Greek and Egyptian styles, explained by the number of Greeks encouraged to settle in Egypt during the Saite Period (664–525 BC). The owner, Si-Amun, is shown with a fair complexion but dark curly hair and beard, which suggest his Greek origins. Unusually, no titles appear in the tomb, which suggests he might not have had an administrative or religious post.

The tomb is decorated with Egyptian themes. Osiris is seated in his shrine beside a depiction of the ceremony known as the 'Weighing of the Heart'. The goddess of the sycamore tree pours cooling drinks in the time-honoured way. The sky goddess Nut appears on the ceiling near the entrance, with the morning sun emerging from her body. Further into the tomb Nekhbet the vulture goddess stretches her arms protectively. ◆

The Faiyum

About 60km (37 miles) south-west of Cairo, the Faiyum is another large depression in the Libyan Desert. It is a very fertile area surrounding a large lake, the Birket Qarun, called Lake Moeris by the classical writers. Originally, this was a vast salt-water lake but since the Palaeolithic period it has become smaller and the water has become fresh. Water is brought to the region by the Bahr Yusef, a branch of the Nile, which leaves the main river north of Asyut.

Farming is the main industry and yields are abundant. A wide variety of crops are grown and the orchards of the western Faiyum are among the best in Egypt and are famous for their oranges, lemons, apricots, guavas and mangoes. The Faiyum is also noted for its poultry farms, honey and flowers, which are exported to the perfume producers of Europe and America. Fishing on the lake and canals is important and fishermen can often be seen casting their nets and beating the water to attract the fish.

In Pharaonic times, the kings would visit the Faiyum to indulge in the sports of fishing and fowling. In the reign of Ramesses II (c.1279–c.1213 BC) some of the ladies of the harem were employed in the production of textiles in the Faiyum. One such was Maathorneferura, the daughter of the Hittite king, Hattusilis. She is known to have lived in a palace at Miwer (modern Medinet el-Ghurab), which seems to have been a textile production centre. Today, there is a cotton mill there, as well as a canning factory and hydro-electric station.

The history of the Faiyum

The area has been inhabited since the Stone Age, but really came into its own during the Middle Kingdom (c.2055–c.1650 BC), when a new capital city was established at Itjtawy. This has not yet been located but is thought to be near el-Lisht. Several of the Middle Kingdom kings built pyramids in the Faiyum and King Amenemhat III (c.1855–c.1808 BC) is known to have had a special interest in the area and was responsible for land reclamation work. He constructed a barrage to control the amount of water coming into the Birket Qarun and so was able to bring a large area of fertile land under cultivation.

Important work on the earliest settlers was done early in the twentieth century by Gertrude Caton-Thompson and Elinor Gardner in the northern Faiyum. In 1894, Flinders Petrie excavated the site of Kahun, the town that housed the workers on the pyramid of King Senusret II (c.1880–c.1874 BC) at nearby el-Lahun. From the wide variety of household objects and documents found, it was possible to build up a complete picture of life in the town.

▲ *Waterwheels are used in the Faiyum today to irrigate the exceptionally fertile land.*

Apart from the pyramids of the Middle Kingdom kings, most of the other archaeological remains belong to the Graeco-Roman Period (332 BC–AD 395), when the towns of Karanis, Tebtunis and Bacchias were flourishing. Many new settlers came into the Faiyum at this time, as the Ptolemies rewarded their veterans with plots of land. Thus it was necessary for the Ptolemies to continue the work of the Middle Kingdom kings by expanding the area of cultivable land. They too embarked on the work of draining the lake and building networks of canals.

Karanis was one of the largest of the Graeco-Roman cities. It was founded in the third century BC and inhabited by veteran settlers. Judging by the

The Labyrinth

Attached to the pyramid of Amenemhat III at Hawara was his mortuary temple, known to the classical authors as the Labyrinth. It was said to be bigger than all the other Egyptian temples put together. Herodotus paid it a visit during his travels in the mid-fifth century BC and described it as having 3,000 rooms connected by winding passages, hence its name. Pliny claimed that the Knossos labyrinth was actually copied from this building, and mentioned crocodile vaults in his description of the site.

When the area was explored by Flinders Petrie at the end of the nineteenth century he found only scanty remains. However, a bed of limestone chippings showed that it had been about 300m (1,000ft) long and 250m (820ft) wide. He also found crocodile burials, indicating that the temple had been dedicated to Sobek, the crocodile god.

numerous granaries and tax returns found here, Karanis was an important agricultural centre. The main crop was wheat, which was exported to Rome by way of Alexandria. Hundreds of houses, several temples and some splendid baths have been found. An important find was the discovery of a temple to the crocodile gods Pnephorus and Petesouchos, local variants of the Egyptian crocodile god, Sobek. Other temples to the crocodile god have been found at Narmouthis, where the Ptolemies extended a Middle Kingdom temple of Amenemhat III, and at Tebtunis where there was also a crocodile cemetery. One city, Crocodilopolis, was named in honour of the god. ◆

▲ *The ruins of the city of Karanis, which was a flourishing agricultural and administrative centre in the Graeco-Roman Period.*

▼ *This granite statue depicts Amenemhat III, who was famous for his land reclamation schemes and who built a mudbrick pyramid in the Faiyum.*

The Faiyum Portraits

In 1887, while searching for the entrance to the pyramid of Amenemhat III (c.1855–c.1808 BC), Petrie found a huge Roman cemetery. The mummified bodies were lying in brick tomb chambers, their faces covered with wooden panels on which portraits of the deceased had been painted: 'One was a beautifully drawn head of a girl, in soft grey tints, entirely classical in its style and mode. Another was of a young married woman of about 25; of a sweet but dignified expression, with beautiful features and a fine complexion. She wears pearl earrings and a gold necklace.'

From then on they came thick and fast and Petrie, somewhat overwhelmed by the great numbers that were coming to light, had to build a special store in which to house them. The mummies certainly seem to have kept him very busy. Giving an account of his activities he explained that he had to make containers for all the mummies himself, wash their garments and make accurate drawings of the sarcophagi. Always far ahead of his time, he realized the significance of his finds. When he found the burial of the young married woman, the mummy was in a fragile condition. However, aware of the importance to anthropologists of being able to match the portrait with a body, Petrie retained the skull.

▲ *For this portrait of a young woman, lead white was used as the background, haematite for the robe, a copper-based paint for the necklace and iron sulphate for the flesh tones.*

▲ *This portrait in encaustic on limewood was found by Petrie at Hawara in 1888. The clothes and jewellery indicate a 3rd–4th century date.*

The question of identity

The matching of the physical remains with portrait likenesses in modern times has had some interesting results, especially in answering the question of who these people were. This has proved quite tricky, and the answers are complicated by fashions in costume and burial customs. The portraits obviously belonged to members of the upper classes, as no one else would have been able to afford them. The question is, however, were the people of the Faiyum just like the upper-class inhabitants of the rest of Egypt at this time? As Petrie noted, the portraits have a distinctly Greek look. Does this mean that their owners were Greek? For instance, it is known that the Faiyum population was swollen in the Ptolemaic Period (332–30 BC) by numbers of Greek veteran soldiers who were settled here. However, they did not work their plots of land themselves but hired the

services of Egyptian agricultural workers, who must also have been immigrants to the area. Evidence for this is seen in Egyptian personal names and the names of gods and villages. Moreover, they seem to have come from all over Egypt, resulting in a very diverse population.

The Romans seem to have categorized people either as 'Greek' or 'Egyptian', but instead of simplifying things this makes the issue more complicated as the term 'Greek' really meant 'non-Egyptian' and could include people who were not Greek in the modern sense. The diversity of population is reflected in the adoption of Graeco-Roman hairstyles and Egyptian funerary practices, by people of whatever ethnic origin.

Historic survivals

The portraits are very important in the history of art, as all other examples of Greek painting elsewhere in the Mediterranean world have been lost. Only in Egypt has the climate been kind enough for them to have been preserved. Most of the Faiyum portraits were painted on wood, either in tempera (for which the pigments were mixed with a water-based binding agent, such as animal glue) or encaustic (using pigments mixed with beeswax). The actual 'recipes' used remain a mystery.

It is now thought that the paintings were made specifically for funerary purposes. As some of the portraits show signs of having been cut down to 'fit' the mummy, it has sometimes been suggested that they may have been painted during the lifetime of the deceased and hung for years on the walls of the family home; in support of this argument the point was made that many of the portraits were of young people. However, this is not now considered the case, and the youth of those portrayed is thought to show that many people died at a very early age.

Throughout their long history, life after death was a belief firmly held by the ancient Egyptians. They aspired to become an *akh* or transfigured spirit. In order to do this, the deceased had to overcome death by ensuring that his body did not decay and by providing for the needs of his *ka*, either by actual offerings of food and drink or by magical spells. These funerary beliefs and practices continued until the introduction of Christianity. The Faiyum portraits are more moving than the likenesses on earlier mummy cases as they are clearly pictures of real people. They are touching reminders of the eternal quest for immortality. ◆

▲ *The large size and high quality of this portrait suggest that the man came from an important family. It was excavated in 1911 by Petrie who dubbed it 'the Red Youth'.*

◀ *This painting in tempera of a young man holding a glass of red wine and a garland probably came from er-Rubayat, as it is similar in style to others known to be from that site. It has been dated by the hairstyle, with receding hairline, to the reign of Severus (AD 193–211).*

The Islands of the Blest

The oases of the Western Desert are depressions in the desert floor where life is sustainable thanks to the easily accessible water supplies. Much of the water comes from springs or, where the water is trapped underground, from wells. Wherever water is available, settlements have grown up within each oasis. How these depressions developed is still a matter of conjecture, but most geologists believe that they are the result of tectonics and water and wind erosion during the Pliocene period, while Europe was undergoing the ice age.

Herodotus called the oases 'the Islands of the Blest'. Their history reflects that of the Nile Valley, although most is known about the settlements from the Saite (664–525 BC) and Graeco-Roman (332 BC–AD 395) Periods. The people who live there now are largely farmers, and Bedouin who no longer roam the desert but have settled on the fringes of the agricultural land.

▲ *Qasr el-Ghueida, the Fortress of the Beautiful Garden, within which is a well-preserved sandstone temple, dedicated to Amun, Mut and Khonsu.*

Kharga

The Kharga oasis lies about 175km (109 miles) east of Luxor. Although there is evidence for agriculture here in the Neolithic period, there is little history of the area in Pharaonic times until the New Kingdom (c.1550–c.1069 BC), when records in Theban tombs state that the inhabitants of Kharga paid tax in the form of dates, grapes, wine and minerals such as ochre. Rebellions, and the expeditions mounted to quell them, are also mentioned. It seems, too, that the oasis was used as a place of exile then as it was for centuries later.

By the Twenty-second Dynasty (c.945–c.715 BC), when the kings were of Libyan stock, there was much more royal interest in the area. Sheshonq I (c.945–c.924 BC) ordered the improvement of the desert tracks and also had to deal with a rebellion. During the Persian occupation, Darius I (522–486 BC) built temples to Amun-Re at Hibis and Qasr el-Ghueida.

The time of greatest prosperity was in the Roman Period (30 BC–AD 395), when the caravan routes were protected by a chain of fortresses, and new roads and wells were constructed. The period is marked by the building of temples, many as part of fortress complexes. By AD 390 Kharga was Christianized and many of the old fortresses and temples were converted to use as churches and monasteries. At Gebel el-Teir, in the mountains, several churches and hermitages came into being, and these are among the earliest Christian buildings in Egypt. Two famous exiles to the oasis were Athanasius (c.AD 296–373), Patriarch of Alexandria and Primate of the Church in Egypt, and Nestorius, Patriarch of Constantinople (AD 428–431), who were both banished here when their beliefs conflicted with the prevailing dogma.

◀ *The el-Qasr mosque in Dakhla was built during the reign of Saladin (AD 1171–93). Its 21m (69ft) high minaret is typical of this brilliant period of Islamic architecture.*

Dakhla

Several settlement sites and cemeteries have been found dating from the Old Kingdom (c.2686–c.2181 BC) in this

◀ *The view over the Dakhla Oasis, with its high fields and overlands and the distant escarpment. Dakhla is regarded as the bread basket of the area.*

region, the most important being the town and associated mastaba tombs of Sixth Dynasty officials near the modern village of Balat. As Dakhla lies about 300km (186 miles) west of Luxor, these clearly demonstrate the extent of Egyptian control at this very early period.

Near modern Arnhada there is a cemetery belonging to the First Intermediate Period (c.2181–c.2055 BC) and a late Ramesside temple (c.1130 BC) to the goddess Mut near Ezbet Bashindi. Otherwise, the most important remains again belong to the Graeco-Roman Period. These include a temple of Thoth at el-Qasr and a further temple dedicated to Amun, Mut and Khonsu at Deir el-Hagar. There are decorated tombs of the Roman Period at Qaret el-Muzawwaqa, while the most exciting finds so far come from Arnhada, where a Canadian team have excavated a two-storey building of 15 rooms, each decorated with scenes from Greek and Roman mythology.

Bahariya

The Bahariya Oasis lies in the Western Desert, about 200km (125 miles) west of the Nile. The earliest archaeological remains date to the New Kingdom (c.1550–c.1069 BC), represented by the tomb of the Nineteenth Dynasty provincial governor, Amenhotep Huy, near Bawit. The necropolis contains the tombs of several officials from the Saite Period. Nearby is a sacred bird cemetery associated with the worship of Horus and Thoth. This is partly of Saite and partly of Roman date. There are also two temples at Bawit, one built by the Twenty-sixth Dynasty king Apries (589–570 BC) and the other by Alexander the Great (332–323 BC). From the Roman Period there is a triumphal arch, also at Bawit, and a garrison, basilica and small settlement at el-Hayz.

Farafra

The Farafra oasis is about 300km (186 miles) west of Assiut. Texts mention occupation of the area from the Old Kingdom but as yet there is no archaeological evidence for settlement before the Roman Period. There are the remains of a town of the early Christian Period (c.AD 450) at Ain Dallaf. ◆

New discoveries

By far the most exciting find in the region in the last few years has been the discovery of hundreds of the most beautiful and well-preserved mummies ever found in Egypt. The cemetery lies near the Temple of Alexander the Great at Bawit and is vast. Eventually, thousands of mummies may be recovered.

There are four different styles of mummy in the necropolis. The first has a gilded mask placed over the face of the mummy, while the second is covered with cartonnage (plaster-stiffened linen) painted with the funerary gods, Anubis, the four sons of Horus, Osiris, Isis and Thoth. The third style is a burial of an undecorated mummy within a pottery coffin, while a fourth group was simply wrapped in plain linen and not placed in any kind of coffin.

The Antiquities Service is preparing to open the Temple of Alexander to tourists, but the mummies will not be on view.

▶ *Wind-eroded chalk sculptures create the surrealist landscape of the White Desert in the Farafra Oasis. The powdered chalk makes much of the spring water undrinkable.*

Monasteries, Mosques and Synagogues

The temples of the old gods are not the only sacred sites in Egypt. From the time of the Hebrew Exile there had been a Jewish settlement on the island of Elephantine, and in the Graeco-Roman Period (332 BC–AD 395) a substantial Jewish population existed in Alexandria.

According to tradition, Egypt was one of the earliest places to accept Christianity, which was said to have been introduced in the middle of the first century AD by St Mark. It was first adopted by the Greek-speaking upper classes of Alexandria, and spread only gradually to ordinary Egyptians during the third century AD. Egyptian Christians, known as Copts, denounced the ancient religion, although some elements of the old beliefs survived. Egypt was also the home of monasticism; the desire for a life of seclusion was perhaps stimulated by the Roman persecutions of the third century.

The conversion of the country to Islam effectively began with the capture of Alexandria by the Arab general, 'Amr Ibn el-'Asi in AD 641. The Fatimid caliphs who ruled Egypt in the tenth century were great builders. They founded the new capital, Cairo, with the intention of making it as splendid as Baghdad, and some of the mosques they constructed can still be seen today, together with the medieval mausoleums of the Mamelukes.

◀ *The skyline of Cairo reveals the domes of the many Muslim mosques that have been erected in the city since the 10th century AD.*

Early Christianity in Alexandria

The Egyptian Church claims to be the oldest in Christendom, but its origins are actually obscure. In his *Ecclesiastical History* written in the fourth century, Eusebius of Caesarea (c.AD 264–340) stated that Christianity was brought to Egypt by the gospel writer St Mark and that he established the first churches in Alexandria itself. This was early in the reign of Claudius, about AD 41–3, and only a few years after the death of Christ. Eusebius further wrote that Mark stayed in the Jewish quarter of Alexandria and that his first convert was a shoemaker. However, there is no reliable contemporary literary evidence for this. Neither has the early Church left any trace in the archaeological record.

Whatever the truth concerning its beginnings, the Church in Egypt was certainly established by the reign of Commodus (AD 180–92), as it is known that one of his concubines was a Christian. By this time, too, the Egyptian Church was presided over by a Patriarch.

Eusebius also credited Mark with the foundation of the See of Alexandria. He claimed that Mark was the first Patriarch and gave a list of those who followed. The list is, however, considered to be suspect, as the reigns of the first 11 are all of 12 years, which seems rather too much of a coincidence. There is evidence, though, for the twelfth, Demetrius, who held office from AD 190–223. In spite of all the doubts, the head of the Coptic Church in Egypt is still called the Patriarch of the See of St Mark and Pope of Alexandria.

The scholars of Alexandria

The Church in Alexandria was very well organized and converts were given training in the Christian faith in the Catechetical School. The catechetes, or teachers, could be either clergy or lay people. They taught the converts and prepared them for baptism. Two of the most famous scholars to be head of the Catechetical School in the late second and early third centuries were Clement (c.AD 150–215) and his pupil Origen (c.AD 185–254).

Clement may have been born in Athens. He was very interested in philosophy and seems to have spent much of his life visiting the great centres of learning in the Mediterranean world. He converted to Christianity in Alexandria and went on to become a presbyter and then head

▼ *St Sebastian is depicted before the Emperor Diocletian, under whom the Egyptian Church suffered its most severe persecution when church buildings and the scriptures were burnt.*

▲ *A mosaic in St Mark's, Venice, shows St Mark passing the Alexandria lighthouse as he brings the gospel to Egypt.*

of the Catechetical School. In his teachings, he emphasized the intellectual approach to Christianity. He appealed to the Greek population through discussions on the philosophers and tried to demonstrate the superiority of Christianity by attacking paganism.

Origen was born in Alexandria. When he was about 17 years old, the Roman emperor Severus (AD 193–211) visited Egypt and issued an edict forbidding conversion to Judaism or Christianity. Origen's father was arrested and imprisoned and Origen encouraged him to suffer martyrdom rather than give up his faith. In fact, Origen was eager to seek martyrdom himself but it is said that his mother hid his clothes so that he was unable to go out. When he became a catechete he castrated himself in order to avoid a scandal concerning himself and a female student, although he is said to have regretted this later.

Origen became head of the Catechetical School after Clement's death. By this time he was very famous and was invited all over the Near East to discuss knotty theological problems, much to the annoyance of the Patriarch Demetrius, who exiled him from Alexandria. Altogether, Origen wrote about 6,000 learned works, including the *Exhortation to Martyrdom*. His most important work was the *Hexapla*, in which the Old Testament is presented in six different versions, in Hebrew and Greek, arranged in columns for comparison. Origen died at Tyre as a result of the torture he had suffered during the persecution ordered by Diocletian (AD 284–305).

The spread of Christianity

Christianity encountered opposition from Gnosticism and the cult of Serapis and it spread only slowly to other parts of Egypt, and then only to the Greek-speaking areas. By the third century, churches were established in Oxyrhyncus, Antinoopolis and Panopolis. As Christianity spread, the need arose to provide the converts with scriptures. This led to the emergence of Coptic, the ancient Egyptian language written using Greek letters, as a standardized literary form in the third century. The earliest surviving books in Coptic, which are versions of the Old and New Testaments, date from the early fourth century.

With the acceptance of Christianity, Coptic styles of architecture and sculpture were also introduced. These were based on Greek classical style rather than Christian motifs, and were imitated in the images used to decorate textiles. Biblical themes did not appear until the eighth century. However, in mural painting, Old Testament themes such as Adam and Eve, Noah's Ark, Daniel and the three Hebrews in the fiery furnace, and local saints, such as Damien and Cosmos, were popular. New Testament scenes commonly used were the Massacre of the Innocents, the Flight into Egypt, the Wedding at Cana, the Baptism of Christ and the Last Supper, though otherwise there were few scenes relating directly to the life of Christ. After the fifth century, when Egypt became mainly monophysite (believing that Christ is divine only), the Nativity and the Crucifixion disappeared entirely from the repertoire. Burial customs also changed: bodies were wrapped in a shroud and buried without grave goods, a complete break with the long tradition of ancient Egypt. ◆

▶ *The Serapaeum, the cult centre of Serapis, is marked by 'Pompey's Pillar', in reality set up in AD 297 in honour of Diocletian.*

The Monasteries of Wadi Natrun

The Wadi Natrun is a depression in the Western Desert, 32km (20 miles) long, which lies midway between Cairo and Alexandria. A series of salt lakes, joined to the Nile by subterranean channels, lies along the valley floor. These evaporate in the summer, leaving behind deposits of salt and the natron that gave the valley its name. Natron was extremely important to the ancient Egyptians for mummification. Today it is used for bleaching cloth and in the manufacture of soap and glass.

Persecution

Wadi Natrun is also famous for its monasteries and hermitages, founded following the persecutions of early Christian communities by the Romans. The worst was under Diocletian (AD 284–305), when churches were razed, scriptures burnt and clergy and laymen imprisoned and tortured. Those who persisted in declaring their faith were often put to death. In an attempt to stamp out Christianity, an earlier emperor, Decius (AD 249–251), had issued an edict requiring all inhabitants of the empire to take a loyalty test, which involved making an offering to the emperor as a god. Those who did so were given a certificate to say they had. About 50 of these certificates are extant. Some Christians, fearing for their lives, performed the sacrifice and received certificates. This was the cause of much bitterness later when Christianity became acceptable and those who had thus denied their faith sought readmission to the Church.

The desert fathers

The traditional founder of monasticism in Egypt was St Anthony (AD 251–356), who lived at a time when the empire-wide persecutions were at their height. Coming from an affluent family, Anthony was moved by the gospel story of the rich young man who came to Jesus seeking the Kingdom of God and was advised to sell everything he had and give to the poor. He went off to the Eastern Desert and lived as a hermit. Others followed his example, including Abu Maqar, the founder of monasticism in the Wadi Natrun. Formerly a camel driver, Abu Maqar felt called by a vision to seek a solitary life and thereafter lived in the Wadi Natrun as a hermit. He seems to have attracted others and a small community grew up. Each monk had his own cell, well removed from

▲ *Five churches lie inside the walls of the monastery of St Bishoi. The monastery is named after a disciple of Abu Maqar.*

▲ *Deir el-Baramus, also founded by Abu Maqar, is the oldest of the four monasteries remaining in the Wadi, dating from AD 340.*

those of his neighbours, although they met weekly to celebrate the Eucharist.

This remains the basis of the monastic system in the Wadi Natrun today. Some of the monks still seek the solitude of their predecessors, but they first have to spend ten years in a monastery before they are allowed to apply for permission to become hermits. If this is granted, the monk has to go into the desert to look for a suitable cave. A truck from the monastery delivers food once a week, and once a month the hermit has to go back to the monastery to take part in the liturgy with the other monks.

There are four monasteries in Wadi Natrun today. Each is surrounded by a high protective wall (which originally had no entrance) and a keep where the monks of the Middle Ages could hide when the monasteries were attacked by Bedouin. Several have churches built according to the traditional eastern plan of open altar, choir and nave.

▼ *Deir Abu Maqar was founded by Abu Maqar, the first of the thousands of monks and hermits to seek the solitary life in Wadi Natrun.*

Deir el-Baramus

Called the Monastery of the Romans, Deir el-Baramus is the oldest of the surviving monasteries. It was founded in AD 340, and is said to have been named after two sons of the emperor Valentinian (AD 364–75), St Maximus and St Domidus, who came to stay in the area, having been ordained as monks in Syria. They lived in a cave 3km (2 miles) away from the monastery. After they died, three days apart, they were buried under the middle altar of the Church of the Virgin Mary, to whom the monastery was originally dedicated, and it was then renamed in their honour.

The monastery church contains the relics of another fourth-century saint, Moses the Black, who before his conversion had been a thief and a murderer. Afterwards he became the founder of a now ruined monastery near Deir el-Baramus. The church also contains the pillar of St Arsenius (AD 354–450), who was tutor to the sons of Theodosius I (AD 379–95) before he came to Wadi Natrun. The most important antiquities in the church are the frescoes. They were discovered recently behind four layers of plaster and are thought by the French team engaged on restoration work to date from the fourth century. They include scenes from the life of Christ, images of Jesus, six of the Apostles, the Virgin Mary and the monastic fathers.

The Monastery of the Syrians

Founded in the sixth century, the Monastery of the Syrians was given its present name in the ninth century, when it was bought by a merchant from Syria for Syrian monks. The monastery once housed a vast library but the manuscripts have now been dispersed. The Church of the Holy Virgin within the walls is the most interesting in Wadi Natrun and is decorated with tenth-century frescoes.

The Monastery of St Bishoi

Opposite the Monastery of the Syrians is the Monastery of St Bishoi, named after one of the first hermits who lived in Wadi Natrun. His relics are housed in the Church of St Bishoi within the walls, and are often visited by pilgrims.

The Monastery of Abu Maqar

This monastery was named after Abu Maqar, also known as Father Macarius, the first of the hermits and monks to live in Wadi Natrun. Although he founded this monastery as well as the Monastery of the Romans, he remained a hermit to the end of his life. In the eleventh century, this monastery became the seat of the Coptic Church. ◆

Abu Mena

According to Coptic tradition, St Mena was an Egyptian who was martyred in Phrygia during the persecution of the Christians under Diocletian (AD 284–305). Originally a soldier, he had left the army when the persecution began. He went out into the desert where he had a vision in which he was told that he would be martyred and his martyrdom would be of great importance. A sanctuary would be built in Egypt in his honour and would draw pilgrims to it from all over the world. It was also foretold that miraculous cures would be effected there.

Mena himself subsequently entered the arena at Kotyaion during a festival and declared himself a Christian, whereupon he was arrested and tortured before being beheaded. Before he died, he begged that his body should be taken to Egypt for burial. The body was retrieved by fellow Christians and given to an officer in the Phrygian army, Athanasius, who had been ordered to Egypt. He was reluctant to bury the corpse because, apparently, he thought it brought him good luck. Eventually, however, he had no option, as the camel carrying the body refused to go any further. At the spot where St Mena was buried, between Alexandria and the Wadi Natrun, springs of healing water gushed from the desert floor, and pilgrims began to flock to be cured.

St Mena, whose image is often seen standing between two camels on the famous pilgrim flasks associated with the site, may once have been a camel driver himself. Whether this is the case or not, his association with the animals led to his becoming the patron saint of merchants and camel drivers. Between the fifth and seventh centuries a great

► *The remains of the city of Abu Mena have been excavated since 1905 by German and Egyptian archaeologists. Attacked by Bedouin and Arabs in the early Middle Ages, it was deserted by AD 1000.*

◀ *The monastery of St Mena is now in ruins but it was an important focus for pilgrims from the 4th to the 10th centuries. A new monastery was built near the original site in the 1980s.*

▶ *St Mena is here depicted between two camels, which were said to have knelt beside his body after its miraculous transportation from Asia Minor.*

city, Abu Mena, arose near the springs. Within the city, the Byzantine emperor Arcadius (AD 395–408) built a splendid basilica over the saint's burial place, while the emperor Zeno (AD 474–91) built a palace near the basilica and garrisoned the city to protect the pilgrims.

The pilgrim flasks

When pilgrims came to the site to honour the saint and be cured of their ailments they took home with them little pottery flasks of the healing waters. These were made locally and are often decorated in high relief with the characteristic scene of St Mena standing between two camels. These flasks have been found all around the Mediterranean and in other parts of the Christian world, indicating how far pilgrims would come to visit the site. So many flasks were found at the site by the German archaeologist Kaufmann in 1905 that he was able to identify it as Abu Mena, even though the city itself was completely ruined.

The end of Abu Mena

The city flourished after its foundation, but in the seventh century it was attacked by Bedouin tribes and again later by the forces of Islam during the Abbasid era. Its buildings were dismantled and architectural elements were taken to Cairo and Alexandria and incorporated into new buildings there.

The city of Abu Mena was seen and described by an Arab traveller around AD 1000. He mentions the palaces, marble sculptures and holy icons that he saw, as well as the famous vineyards and gardens with their almond and carob trees. But by that time the city was already a ghost town, solely inhabited by marauders and thieves.

The rediscovery of the city

The site seems then to have been largely avoided by travellers until the nineteenth century, when J. R. Pacho went there in 1825. So little was left by this time, he assumed it was a Roman ruin. It remained unrecognized as the great pilgrim centre it had once been until the arrival of the German cleric and archaeologist, Kaufmann, in 1905. Since then it has been extensively excavated by a team from the Coptic Museum in Cairo and by German archaeologists. They have discovered the ruins of several churches, a monastery, a pilgrim hostel, baths where the pilgrims could immerse themselves in the healing waters, potters' workshops and kilns where the pilgrim flasks were produced, cisterns, private houses, shops and two cemeteries. Many of the finds from the site can now be seen in the Coptic Museum in Cairo. ◆

The Monasteries of the Eastern Desert

The life of St Anthony (AD 251–356), traditionally the founder of Egyptian monasticism, was recorded in a mixture of fact and legend by the fourth-century theologian and Patriarch of Alexandria, St Athanasius (c.AD 296–373). According to his account, Anthony was born into a wealthy Christian family at Coma, near Beni Suef. He seems to have been a serious youth, and after his parents died he decided to leave home and lead an ascetic life. At first he lived just outside his village supporting himself by his handiwork and giving part of what he earned to the poor. Then, under the influence of an old man who had practised asceticism since his youth, Anthony travelled about meeting like-minded men from whom he learned much about this way of life. He went without food for several days at a time and when he did eat he only ever had bread, salt and water. He also deprived himself of sleep.

Eventually he went to live in an ancient tomb and blocked up the entrance. While he was there he was attacked one night by the Devil. He was discovered by a friend coming to bring him food, who carried his apparently lifeless body back to the village and laid him in the church, where the people came to pay their respects to the dead man. In the middle of the night, Anthony came round and asked to be taken back to his cave. Once more, the Devil attacked him, aided this time by an army of demons and monsters. However, Anthony was able to withstand the onslaught and his ordeal was eventually brought to an end by a beam of light shining down from the roof. Anthony heard a voice telling him that because he had stood firm he would always receive divine help and would become famous everywhere.

▲ *The Monastery of St Anthony today. Although the foundations date to the third century AD, most of the building dates to 1560.*

Anthony's troubles were not yet over, however, as the Devil put several temptations in his way. He always resisted, and at last took refuge in an abandoned fortress at Pispir, on the east bank of the Nile. Anthony lived here for the next 20 years, never going out and seeing no one. He became famous for his asceticism. One day a crowd came to Pispir and broke down the door of his cell, expecting to find him pale and emaciated. To their amazement he was fit and well and of a sound mind. Many of their number were sick and Anthony cured them. He also managed to persuade many to take up the hermit's life, and so began the monastic movement.

▶ *This is an icon of St Paul, said by Jerome to be the first of the hermits.*

At first there was no organized community. The hermits lived alone in caves near to the fortress of Pispir. Gradually two different types of community developed: one where the hermits lived entirely alone, and the other where they lived alone but met at times for prayer.

The Monastery of St Anthony

After a time Anthony withdrew from Pispir to seek solitude in the Eastern Desert. Even here his fame attracted visitors, so leaving behind a second community of anchorites he moved into a cave in the mountains. Anthony is said to have died at the ripe old age of 105, having sworn two trusted monks to secrecy concerning the whereabouts of

▶ *Frescoes from the church of St Paul in his monastery in the Eastern Desert.*

his body. He did not want his tomb to be venerated. Some say he was buried under the floor of the cave. Another tradition maintains that the body was moved in AD 561 to the Church of St John the Baptist in Alexandria and thence to St Sophia in Constantinople. Otherwise, the body is said to rest in various locations in France. Whatever the truth, a monastery was eventually set up in the fourth century in the Wadi Araba in the Eastern Desert, near the cave where Anthony lived for the last years of his life.

St Anthony's Monastery is the oldest and largest Coptic monastery in Egypt. There is little to see of the original monastery today, as it was rebuilt in later centuries. It remained a great centre of scholarship where Coptic works were translated into Arabic until 1483, when it was attacked by the Bedouin and the monks killed or expelled. It has now been reoccupied, and a self-supporting community carries on its tradition.

▼ *The monastery of St Paul is the second oldest Coptic monastery in Egypt. It is situated in the Wadi el-Deir.*

The Monastery of St Paul

St Paul's Monastery in the Wadi el-Deir is the second oldest Coptic monastery in Egypt. The life of St Paul the Hermit (AD 228–341) was recorded by St Jerome (c.AD 342–420) but it contains much that is tradition and legend. Born to a wealthy family in Thebes, he fled into the desert during the persecution instigated by Decius (AD 249–251) to become a hermit. He is said to have lived on dates and the bread brought to him by a raven that visited him daily. As he lay dying, he was visited by St Anthony, who buried him with the help of two lions.

By AD 460, a church had been built over his grave and by the sixth century this had become a place of pilgrimage. The monastery was built in the Middle Ages. It is surrounded by defensive walls, from the top of which there are magnificent views of Mount Sinai. There is a Chapel of the Virgin in the watch tower and next door is the Church of St Michael, which contains an icon said to have been painted by St Luke. ◆

Pachomius

St Pachomius also lived in the fourth century and developed a different sort of monasticism. He started a community of ascetics near the Nile at Tabennisi around AD 323. Here, the monks lived an organized, communal life that involved strenuous manual labour and strict discipline. Prayer was an important part of life in the monastery. The monks were divided into houses according to their trade or nationality. Each house had a head and the whole monastery was presided over by the superior-general and his deputy. Pachomius died of plague in AD 346, by which time he had established 11 such communities, including two for women.

St Catherine's Monastery

At the foot of Mount Sinai, according to tradition, lies the place where Moses tended the flocks of Jethro, his father-in-law, and where he saw the Burning Bush. From the end of the third century the area was settled by small communities of monks escaping persecution by the Romans and seeking the spiritual life in the isolation of the mountains. Some time after AD 313, when Constantine (AD 312–337) had granted freedom of worship throughout the Roman Empire, the monks of Sinai petitioned his mother, Helena, for patronage. Helena answered this request in AD 330 by erecting a small church dedicated to the Virgin Mary, and also a tower on the traditional site of the Burning Bush to provide refuge for the monks.

In about AD 530 Emperor Justinian (AD 527– 65) ordered the building of the great walled monastery, with its magnificent church, which remains to this day. The church incorporated Helena's earlier building and was also dedicated to the Virgin Mary, since the church fathers saw the Burning Bush as a symbol of the Annunciation. The monastery was originally called the Monastery of the Transfiguration but since the eleventh century it has also been known as St Catherine's.

▲ *To protect the monks who settled around the site of the Burning Bush from marauding Bedouin, the Byzantine emperor Justinian ordered the building of a fortified monastery.*

The life of St Catherine

St Catherine was born into an aristocratic family of Alexandria in AD 294. She was clever, highly educated and, according to tradition, beautiful. However, she was converted to Christianity by the teaching of a Syrian monk and rejected all her many suitors. During the last years of the persecutions she publicly confessed her faith. The story goes that 50 wise men from all over the Roman world were brought to reason with her, but to no avail: instead, she converted them to Christianity by her persuasive arguments. When she was later tortured, she even managed to convert members of the imperial family and the Roman aristocracy.

Catherine was executed. Her body vanished and tradition has it that it was carried by angels to the peak of Mount Sinai. Some three centuries later, the monks brought it down and buried it in the church.

The sanctity of the monastery

A tradition claims that in AD 625 the monks of St Catherine's sent a delegation to Medina to ask for Muhammad's patronage and protection. The request appears to have been granted, as in the Icon Gallery there is a copy of a document stating that the Muslims would defend the monks and that they were exempted from taxation. According to another legend, Muhammad actually visited the monastery while he was a merchant.

When the Arabs invaded Egypt in AD 641 the monastery itself was not harmed. However, the number of monks began to decline until, by the early ninth century, only 50 were left. Many of the Christians of Sinai converted to Islam, and in the eleventh century a mosque was built within the complex. During the Crusades, pilgrims from Europe came to St Catherine's in ever-increasing numbers and a special order of Crusaders was formed to protect them. The story of St Catherine's martyrdom was brought to Europe by the Crusaders, and she became a major saint.

Conditions were more difficult under the rule of the Mamelukes but the monastery's fortunes revived in the early sixteenth century under the rule of the Ottoman sultan Selim I (1512–20), when the rights of the monks were respected and the archbishop was granted special status.

By the seventeenth century the monastery owned property in several other countries, as branches had been established in other parts of Egypt, Palestine, Turkey, Romania, Russia, India and Greece. Especially important was the school at Heraklion in Crete, where the greatest Greek scholars of the time were educated. At the end of the eighteenth century the monastery came under the protection of Napoleon, who also paid for the reconstruction of the north wing. During the later nineteenth and earlier twentieth centuries, however, the monastery lost much of its property abroad. In spite of this it continues to function and in 1951 a new wing was added to house the library, Icon Gallery, a new refectory and the archbishop's apartments. The monastery celebrated its 1,400th anniversary in 1966.

The Icon Gallery

The monastery owns a large collection of 2,000 icons, of which 150 are on display. They are of great artistic and historical importance. Twelve of the oldest and rarest icons date from the sixth century and were painted using the encaustic method (mixing pigment with beeswax). Part of the collection is Byzantine, dating from the sixth to the tenth centuries, while most of the icons date from the eleventh to the fifteenth centuries.

The library

The monastery's library is second only to that of the Vatican in importance and contains about 3,000 manuscripts. Most are in Greek while others are in Arabic, Syriac, Georgian, Armenian, Slavonic, Coptic and Ethiopian. Most of them are Christian works but there are also historical documents in the collection granting rights and privileges to the monastery and authorized by the seals of emperors, patriarchs, bishops and even Turkish sultans. At present the oldest document is the Codex Syriacus, dating to the fifth century, which is the oldest translation of the gospels. Until the mid-nineteenth century the Library also owned the even more important fourth-century Codex Sinaiticus, which is now in the British Library in London. ◆

Codex Sinaiticus

The Codex Sinaiticus was found in 1844 in the library of St Catherine's by the German scholar Konstantin von Tischendorf (1815–74). His interest was aroused when he saw some manuscripts in a basket waiting to be burned. Concealing his excitement, he asked for the pages, which he recognized as part of a very early Bible, and presented them to Frederick Augustus of Saxony. He managed to obtain the remaining pages on a later visit in 1859, as the result of a rather dubious deal, which the monks still resent. This document was presented to Tsar Alexander II of Russia as head of the Orthodox Church, and was purchased from the Russians in 1933 by the British Library.

Until the nineteenth century the Codex was complete. It once contained both Old and New Testaments, as well as several books of the Apocrypha. Unfortunately, about 300 pages are now missing. It is still the oldest complete New Testament in the world and has proved invaluable to Biblical scholars. Notes in the margins of the Codex show that it had been checked in antiquity against the *Hexapla* of Origen, the second-century scholar, and corrected by Antoninus and Pamphilius in the fourth century.

▼ *The interior of the church of St Catherine, from a painting by David Roberts. The decoration and iconostasis date from the 17th and 18th centuries.*

The Islamic City of Cairo

The city of Cairo is the largest in Africa and in the Islamic world. It came into being after the Arab conquest of Egypt in AD 641. The main part of the city lies on the east bank of the Nile, where there had been a settlement from the beginning of ancient Egyptian history. The settlement was called Kher-aha, meaning 'Place of Combat', because it was said to be the spot where Horus and Seth had fought over the succession to the throne of Egypt after Osiris had gone to be the ruler of the Underworld.

Cairo is an exciting place to visit. As well as the mosques and mausoleums there are the medieval bazaars of the Khan el-Khalili, the Museum of Islamic Art and the Wakal of Kait Bey, a caravanserai built in 1480.There is also the seventeenth-century House of Sheik es-Sihaimi, the Bab el-Futah ('Gate of Conquests'), which marks the northern limits of the Fatimid city, and the Nilometer on the southern end of Roda Island, constructed by the Omayyads in AD 716.

▲ *The Mosque of Muhammad Ali, also called the Alabaster Mosque, is in the medieval city of Cairo. It was built between 1830 and 1848.*

Babylon and Fustat

The Ptolemies called the area Babylon, perhaps a corruption of Per-Hapi en Yun, the Egyptian name of the island of Roda nearby. Later the Romans built a fortress here, the remains of which can still be seen today. This stronghold was besieged and conquered by the armies of Caliph Omar in AD 641, after which a new city, Fustat, was founded just to the north of Babylon. The first mosque was built here but this was destroyed in 1158, along with the rest of Fustat, to prevent it falling into the hands of the Crusaders. Until AD 868 Egypt was ruled by governors representing Arab dynasties based in Damascus (the Omayyads) and Baghdad (Abbasids). Then, for a brief spell of about 40 years, Egypt became independent under Ahmed ibn-Tulin, who built the mosque named after him that still stands today.

El-Kahira

Egypt was finally conquered in AD 969 by Gawhar of the Fatimid dynasty, who traced their descent back to Fatima, the

◀ *The mosque of ibn-Tulin, built in AD 876–9, is the second oldest in Cairo. The fountain in the central courtyard was added in the 13th century.*

▲ *Originally built by Saladin in 1176, the Citadel was the stronghold of the city until the time of Muhammad Ali, and home to Egypt's rulers for nearly 700 years.*

daughter of Muhammad. Gawhar then founded a new capital city called el-Kahira, meaning 'the Victorious One'. It was named after the planet Mars (el-Kahir in Arabic), which was apparently passing over the city at the time when the foundations of the ramparts were being laid. The Fatimids were followed by the Ayyubids, a new dynasty founded by Saladin, and the Ayyubid period is the most brilliant in the medieval history of Cairo. One of Saladin's claims to fame is that he began the building of the citadel and the city walls, although he himself spent only eight years in the city. For the rest of his reign he was on campaign in Syria, Palestine and Mesopotamia.

The Mamelukes

The Ayyubids were followed by the Mamelukes, originally slaves bought by the sultans and trained to become both their bodyguards and an élite force of troops. During the thirteenth and fourteenth centuries they further embellished the city with mosques, the most important being the Mosque of Sultan Hasan. They also began the practice of building elaborate mausoleums. Those of the later (Circassian) Mamelukes are in the eastern part of the city, that of Kait Bey, one of the last independent Mameluke rulers, being particularly noteworthy. It was built in 1474 and restored at the end of the nineteenth century. With its intricately carved arabesques and interlaced patterns it is considered to be one of the jewels of Islamic art.

Egypt was conquered by the Turks in 1517 and remained under their rule for the next 300 years. The power of the Turkish sultans and their governors, the pashas, soon declined however, the pashas being required to obtain the consent of the Mameluke beys (the district governors) before bringing in any new measures. The beys collected the taxes and commanded the army but paid tribute to the pasha.

European influence

In 1798, Napoleon's fleet appeared off Alexandria. Although the French were defeated by Nelson at the Battle of Abukir Bay, Napoleon went on to conquer Middle and Upper Egypt the following year. However, his triumph was short-lived as in 1801 he surrendered to the British in Cairo and Alexandria and was forced to leave Egypt.

The French withdrawal saw the rise to prominence of Muhammad Ali, who threw out the Turkish governor, proclaimed himself pasha and took possession of the Citadel in Cairo. He and his successors enjoyed some military successes and introduced railways, bridges, canals, a postal and telegraph service and factories, as Egypt came under increasing European influence. The Suez Canal was one of the major enterprises undertaken during this time, though these public works resulted in a huge rise in the national debt. ◆

▼ *Khan el-Khalili, the main Cairo bazaar, where brassware, perfume, jewellery and leather goods are on offer. Having always drawn in foreign merchants, it is now a major tourist attraction.*

The Coptic Churches of Old Cairo

The oldest Coptic churches in Cairo are within the Roman fortress of Babylon. Their plan seems to have been based on the Roman basilica used for administrative purposes, which was oblong in shape with a double colonnade and a semicircular apse at one end. The churches are aligned east–west, with the main entrance at the west end and the sanctuary at the east. In some cases there are three sanctuaries, said to represent the Trinity. There is a dome over the main sanctuary and if there are more sanctuaries these will have a dome too, each topped by a cross. The windows are high up on the wall to cut down on the amount of light, heat and sand entering the building.

In order to protect the congregation from Muslim attacks, the outside of the church was made to look little different from an ordinary house. The main door was often blocked up and the church entered through an unobtrusive side entrance. Bells were forbidden under Muslim law, so there are no bell towers in Coptic churches.

Inside, the churches are divided into narthex, nave, chancel and sanctuaries. In the narthex or entrance hall of the oldest churches a large basin, about 3m (10ft) long and 2m (6ft 6in) wide, is set into the floor. This was used for the blessing of the water on the night of Epiphany, when the congregation bathed in it, and for baptism. The nave is usually divided into three aisles by two rows of superimposed columns. A gallery often runs around the top, which was originally used by the women in the congregation. Another basin is usually found at the west end of the nave, for use during the ceremony of Washing the Feet on Maundy Thursday.

The chancel, which goes across the whole width of the building, is a very important part of the Coptic church as it is the place from which the choir leads the worship. Apart from occasional use of triangles or cymbals, Coptic church music is purely vocal. At the back of the chancel an iconostasis, or screen, separates the sanctuary from the rest of the church. This is made of intricately carved wood, inlaid with ivory. The upper part is decorated with icons and lamps, and ostrich eggs are suspended in front.

A central door with a window to either side leads into the sanctuary. Nearly all Coptic churches have three sanctuaries, each with its own altar. The central altar is covered by a wooden dome, the underside of which is painted with images of Christ in glory surrounded by cherubim and seraphim. Behind the altar is the bishop's throne, with a perpetually burning lamp in front of it. Every church also has a baptistry, with a font deep enough to allow the priest to immerse the baby completely.

▲ *Dedicated to the Virgin Mary, this church is known as the 'Hanging Church' as it rests on the bastion of the old Roman fortress of Babylon.*

▶ *The Coptic cross on the gate of the Hanging Church in Babylon. Crosses are not used in the altars of Coptic churches.*

The Church of St Sergius

Built in the fourth or fifth century, St Sergius is one of the oldest churches in Cairo and traditionally stands on the place where the Holy Family rested during the Flight into Egypt. A round stone font in the south aisle of the crypt chapel marks the exact spot, and the event is commemorated annually on 1 June. The church is dedicated to Sergius and Bacchus, two soldiers in the Roman army said to have been put to death in the third century for refusing to take part in sacrifices to Jupiter. The wood and ivory iconostasis is also decorated with panels of ebony inlaid with ivory crosses, above which is a row of icons depicting the 12 Apostles and the Virgin Mary. The Nativity and the Last Supper, together with three warrior saints, are portrayed either side of the sanctuary door.

The Church of St Barbara

There are two churches on this site. The first was built by a rich scribe, Athanasius, in AD 684 and was dedicated to St Cyrus and St John. The second was built later when the body of St Barbara, a young woman put to death by her father when she converted to Christianity, was brought here. It is one of the largest and most beautiful old churches in Egypt. The icon of the Virgin and Child, in a frame of carved wood inlaid with ivory, is particularly fine.

The Church of St George

This church is also said to have been built by the wealthy scribe Athanasius, in AD 684. Unfortunately, it was burnt down in the nineteenth century and only the fourteenth-century Wedding Hall remains.

The Church of the Virgin

The Church of the Virgin was built in the ninth century and is also known as the Church of the Pot of Basil, which may be a reference to the use of basil in the Greek Orthodox ceremonies of Blessing the Water, which take place every month and on the feasts of the Holy Cross. It is thought that the church may have acquired this name when it was taken over temporarily by the Greek Orthodox Church during the caliphate of el-Hakim, whose mother belonged to that faith. The original church was destroyed and then rebuilt in the eighteenth century.

The Hanging Church

One of the most beautiful in Old Cairo, the Hanging Church was built in the late seventh century. Its name is derived from the fact that it rests on the remains of the bastions of the Roman fortress of Babylon. The original church was replaced by a larger one as it increased in importance. It became the seat of the Coptic Patriarchs in the eleventh century, when the Patriarchate was moved from Alexandria to Cairo, and remained so until the fourteenth century. ◆

◀ *An icon of the Virgin and Child from the church of St Sergius, associated with the Flight into Egypt.*

▶ *The interior of the church of St Barbara with its beautiful 13th-century screen of wood inlaid with carved ivory.*

Jewish Synagogues and Temples

Jews probably settled in Egypt at the time of the Exile at the beginning of the sixth century BC, when they were not only taken to Babylon by King Nebuchadnezzar, but were dispersed throughout the known world.

The Synagogue of Ben Ezra

One of the most interesting sacred sites of Old Cairo is the Synagogue of Ben Ezra, which stands in a pleasant, shady garden near the churches of St Sergius and St Barbara (see *Coptic Churches of Old Cairo*). According to tradition, there has been a Jewish community in Old Cairo since the time of Moses. The earliest written records, however, are those of medieval travellers, such as Benjamin of Tudela (died 1173), who visited the synagogue and claimed to have seen the Torah of Ezra the Scribe.

The first synagogue was destroyed when the Romans took Egypt. Later, at the time of the Arab conquest in AD 641, the site was given to the Copts by the Muslim general, Amr. The Copts built a church there and dedicated it to St Michael. This church, in turn, was destroyed by Caliph el-Hakim and in the twelfth century the site was given back to the Jews and a new synagogue built by Abraham Ben Ezra, the great Rabbi of Jerusalem.

At the end of the nineteenth century, a hoard of ancient manuscripts was found here, including the ancient Torah. Sadly, this was split up and portions are now owned by various institutions in Europe and America. However, some interesting documents remain, including a copy of the Torah dating to the fifth century BC written on gazelle skin, a drawing of a seven-branched candlestick on deer skin, and the manuscript known as the Atlas of Moses.

Elephantine

A small community of Jews also existed at Elephantine: they and their temple are known from Aramaic papyri of the fifth

▼ *The Roman city on the island of Elephantine is now in ruins. In the sixth century BC, the island was inhabited by a small community of Jews.*

▲ *Rams sacred to Khnum were buried next to his temple at Elephantine. Antagonism between the Jews and the priest of Khnum can be seen in the Aramaic papyri.*

century BC. The Temple of Yahweh was in existence before the invasion of Egypt in 525 BC by the Persian king, Cambyses, but its precise location is not known. The papyri reveal that in 410 BC the priest of the nearby Temple of Khnum persuaded the local governor, in the absence of the Persian satrap (the provincial governor), to attack and destroy the Temple of Yahweh.

The Jews wrote to Bagoas, Governor of Judea, and Yohanan, High Priest in Jerusalem, in protest. At first their communication was ignored, but two years later they wrote again to Bagoas and to the two sons of Sanballat, an earlier governor of Samaria. This time they had the answer they were hoping for. A messenger was sent to request the permission of the Persian satrap to rebuild the temple. The temple was restored and in 401 BC is mentioned in a document, but shortly after the end of Persian rule in Egypt in 332 BC, the Jewish colony was dispersed and its temple disappeared.

Leontopolis

A later Temple of Yahweh, at Leontopolis in the Delta, is known from the work of the first-century Jewish historian, Josephus. He wrote that, after the murder of the High Priest Onias III, his son Onias fled to Egypt where he became commander of the Jewish military colony at Leontopolis (Tell el-Yahudiyeh). While in this post he obtained permission from Ptolemy VI (180–145 BC) to build a temple to Yahweh. According to Josephus, this was built on the site of an old Egyptian temple and was modelled on the Temple in Jerusalem, although it was smaller and not so splendid. The temple was founded in 160 BC but was destroyed by the Romans in AD 74 after the Jewish Revolt. ◆

The 70 scholars

Under the Ptolemies, there was also a large Jewish community in Alexandria. They were mostly Greek-speaking and the Old Testament was translated from Hebrew into Greek mainly for their benefit. The tradition of the 70 scholars who gave their name to the translation comes from a fictional work, The Letter of Aristeas to his friend Philocrates. This says that Ptolemy II (285–246 BC), at the suggestion of Demetrios of Phaleron, decided to make a collection of all the books in the world. When it was realized that the Library of Alexandria did not contain a copy of the Jewish Law, Ptolemy sent a letter to Eliezer, High Priest of Jerusalem, asking him to send to Egypt six elders from each of the 12 tribes, all of whom must be experts in Hebrew and Greek, in order that a translation might be made. On arrival in Alexandria, they were taken to the island of Pharos and set to work.

According to Philo of Alexandria (c.20 BC–c.AD 40), the scholars were inspired as if by an invisible authority, while an anonymous third-century source claims that the scholars were isolated from one another in separate rooms while they translated. St Epiphanius (c.AD 315–403) claimed they were given 36 little houses in which they were installed two by two and locked in from dawn to dusk. Whatever the story, the result was the same: when the translations were compared they all turned out to be identical.

The Mosques and Mausoleums of Cairo

There were no mosques at the time of Muhammad. He and his followers prayed in his home, which consisted of a collection of huts around an open courtyard, surrounded by a high wall. This court was later roofed over and became a place of prayer. After Muhammad's death, when the new faith was spread by military conquest, the Arab armies came into contact with Byzantine and Sassanian culture and this eventually had a great influence on Islamic architecture. In the later seventh and eighth centuries, the semicircular Islamic prayer niche, the pulpit and the screened-off area where the caliph sat were all inspired by the art and architecture previously encountered abroad.

In Syria, the first mosques had originally been churches. The old entrances on the west side were blocked and new ones opened up in the north side. A niche would be made in the south side to indicate the direction of Mecca. A different type of mosque developed in Mesopotamia when the seat of government of the Arab world moved eastwards. The first large mosque to be built in Baghdad occupied an area 120m (1,292ft) square. It consisted of a central court surrounded by a large prayer hall on the south side and on the three other sides by roofed and columned halls or liwans.

▲ *The Sultan Hasan Mosque is possibly the finest example of Islamic architecture in the world.*

The Mosque of Ahmed ibn-Tulin

For about 50 years in the mid-ninth century, the Caliphate was at Samarra, about 100km (60 miles) north of Baghdad, where excavation of the palace has revealed pointed arches and carved stucco. When Ahmed ibn-Tulin, a native of Samarra, became ruler of Egypt, he brought with him the architectural ideas from his own part of the world.

The mosque of Ahmed ibn-Tulin has a ground plan similar to that of the mosque in Baghdad and the decoration is like that found in the caliph's palace at Samarra. All the main types of ornamentation in carved wood and stucco are repeated here. Pointed arches are integrated into the structure. The lower parts of the arches on the south-west side of the court are decorated with the earliest-known examples of geometric patterns in Islamic art.

The el-Azhar Mosque

Of all the Fatimid examples, the el-Azhar Mosque is considered to be the finest. It was finished in AD 972 by Gawhar. In AD 988, it was given university status by Caliph el-Aziz. It was rebuilt after an earthquake in 1303 and since then several rulers and governors have made it their religious duty to restore and maintain the buildings. It remains the leading university of Islam.

The principal lecture hall is the vast liwan on the south-east side of the central court, while the smaller ones on the

▲ *The Sultan Hasan Mosque was built between 1356 and 1363 and was once used as a fortress.*

south-west and north-east are used as student workrooms and sleeping quarters. Around the central court there is an arcade with Persian-type arches, decorated with niches and medallions and crowned by crenellations. The mosque owns a magnificent fourteenth-century library, which houses 60,000 volumes.

The Sultan Hasan Mosque

The Sultan Hasan Mosque was built in 1356–63 and is often said to be the finest example of Islamic architecture in Egypt. It is also one of the largest and it has been suggested that it may have been designed by a Syrian architect.

The ground plan is in the shape of an irregular polygon with the liwans arranged around the central court in the form of a cross. The outer walls are plain except for blind niches and twin round-arched windows. The impressive main doorway is 26m (85ft) high, while the minaret, which is well over 81m (265ft), is the tallest in Cairo. The central courtyard contains an elegant fountain and the decoration of the inner walls is in coloured marble cut into attractive geometric shapes. All the liwans are used as prayer halls while the medrese, or teaching rooms, occupy the areas between them.

The main liwan has a carved stucco frieze of kufic lettering. A doorway on the left of the pulpit leads to the Mausoleum of Sultan Hasan, containing a very simple sarcophagus under a dome decorated with carved stalactites.

◀ *The minaret of the el-Azhar Mosque was added to the building in the 15th century. The original mosque dates from the founding of the new city of Cairo in* AD *970–971.*

▲ *An interior view of the richly decorated dome of the Muhammad Ali Mosque, also known as the Alabaster Mosque, which stands on the site of a former Mameluke palace.*

The Citadel

The Cairo skyline is dominated by the Citadel. It was begun in 1176 by Saladin, who is said to have used the Pyramids at Giza as quarries to provide the stone. Very little remains today of the original structure, except for the walls on the eastern side and some of the internal towers. The two Ayyubid palaces that stood on the site at the time of Saladin's conquest have vanished completely.

One of the most striking sights on entering the Citadel is the Mosque of Muhammad Ali, otherwise known as the Alabaster Mosque. Begun by Muhammad Ali in 1824, it was finished some 30 years later by his successor. The architect was a Greek from Istanbul, whose design was ultimately derived from the Byzantine Church of St Sophia. As in other mosques, there is a fountain for ablutions in the central courtyard, which is surrounded by various halls. The huge main prayer hall has Byzantine-style domes resting on square piers and is impressively lit. The mosque also houses the Mausoleum of Muhammad Ali. ◆

Index

Acknowledgements

Picture Credits

AKG Photographic: pages 4, 8 (inset), 12/13, 14, 15 t, 18 (Musee des Beaux Arts, Liege), 19 tr, 19 b, 20, 23 t b, 25 b, 26 br (private collection), 39 t, 40, 41 b, 51 b (Louvre, Paris), 61 b (Egyptian Museum, Cairo), 90 (Rijksmuseum van Oudheden, Leiden), 105 b (National Museum, Cairo), 112, 117 b, 126, 127 t b, 129 b, 130 t, 151 b, 152, 153 b, 154, 163 t, 179 (Egyptian Museum, Cairo), 180 (Egyptian Museum, Cairo), 182 b (Egyptian Museum, Cairo), 183 t, 189 b, 197 l, 207 b, 209 b, 218, 220 t, 226 l r (British Museum, London), 227 r (Petrie Museum of Egyptian Archaeology).
Alan Fildes: pages 43 t, 91 br.
Ancient Art and Architecture Collection: pages 51 tl, 83 b, 85 b, 91 t bl, 113, 178 t.
Ancient Egypt Picture Library: pages 3, 6, 8, 26 bl, 34 b, 39 b, 44 t, 48 b, 49 all, 55 b, 56 t, 58 t, 59 t, 60, 64 t, 66, 82 b, 84 b, 86, 87 t b, 88 b, 89 b, 102 b, 104 t, 109 l r, 110 b, 111, 118 t, 120 t, 121 all, 128 t b, 129 t, 130 b, 131 b, 140, 142, 143 t b, 148 b, 149 t, 166, 170, 171 t b, 181 t, 191 tr, 197 r, 199, 200, 201 b, 206, 210, 215 t b, 251, 254.
The Art Archive: pages 5 l, 22, 24 (Louvre, Paris/Dagli Orti), 27 (Egyptian Museum, Cairo), 37 b, 38, 120 b (Egyptian Museum, Cairo), 173 t (Dagli Orti), 216 l (Archaeological Museum, Cairo) r.
Axiom: pages 52/53, 63 (Luke White); 54, 55 t, 80 t b, 81 b, 136/7, 138, 144 b, 147 t b, 148 t, 149 b, 15 1 t, 176 l, 177 t b, 188 t b, 189 t, 198 l r 202 t, 212/213, 222 b, 224, 228 t b, 229 t b, 230/231, 239 t b, 242 b, 252 (James Morris); 158 t, 255 (Chris Caldicott).
The Bridgeman Art Library: pages 15 b (National Archaeological Museum, Naples), 28 b, 56 b (private collection), 57 b (private collection), 59 b (Egyptian Museum, Cairo), 107 t, 132 t, 150, 161 tr, 184, 185 c, 187 t, 219 t (Ashmolean Museum, London), 233 b (private collection), 241 (Stapleton Collection), 256.
The British Museum: pages 34 t, 51 tr, 92 b.
J L Charmet: pages 16 (Biblioteque de Mazarine, Paris), 21 t, 26 t.
Christine Osborne Pictures: pages 234, 235 t b, 238 t b, 243 t, 244, 245 all.
Corbis: 46 t (Gianni Dagli Orti), 65 (Roger Wood), 73 (Roger Wood), 81 t (Roger Wood), 83 t (Roger Wood), 93 t b (Roger Wood), 100 (Gianni Dagli Orti), 101 (Gianni Dagli Orti), 114/115 (Roger Wood), 117 t (Roger Wood).
A M Dodson: pages 67 t, 221.
Dyan Hilton: page 167 bl.
Egyptian Museum, Cairo: page 108.
Eye Ubiquitous: page 222 t.
The Hulton Archive: pages 25 t, 28 t, 29, 30 t b.
Jacke Phillips: pages 50.
Dr Joann Fletcher: page 69 t, 158 b.
Jurgen Liepe: pages 32/33, 57 t, 134/135, 139 t, 162 t, 164 t b.
Liason International/© Kurgan-Lisnet: pages 10/11.
The London Library: page 17.
Lorna Oakes: pages 36 b, 37 tr, 44 b, 47 b, 61 t, 76 l, 85 t, 92 t, 110 t, 124, 125 t b, 141 all, 146, 153 t, 155 all, 165 all, 167 br, 168, 169 tl tr, 182 t, 183 b, 186 b, 187 b, 191 tl b, 194, 195 t b, 202 b, 204 t b, 207 tl tr, 225 t b, 236 t b, 237, 246, 247, 249 tl.
Mary Evans Picture Library: pages 19 tl.
Michael Holford: pages 21 b (British Museum, London), 31 r (British Museum, London), 219 b (British Museum, London).
Nowitz Photography: page 243 b.
Panos Pictures: page 249 tr.
Paul Hardy: page 242 t.
Peter Clayton: pages 67 b, 167 t, 181 b, 201 t, 203 t b, 205 t b, 211.
Peter Sanders: page 249 bl.
Rick Strange: page 196.
Robert Harding Picture Library: pages 1, 7, 74/75, 76 r, 94/95, 96 b, 104 b (F L Kenett),105 t, 106 b (R Ashworth), 107 b (R Ashworth), 116 (Tetrel), 131 t, 132 b, 139 b, 144 t, 145, 156/157 (Julia Bayne), 160, 174/175 (Gavin Hellier), 176 r, 185 t (Etan Simanor) b (Gavin Hellier), 186 t (Philip Craven), 208 (Philip Craven), 209 t (Philip Craven), 248 (Nigel Francis), 253.
Scala: pages 41 t (Egyptian Museum, Cairo), 62 (National Archaeological Museum, Naples), 98, 99 t b, 106 t, 159 (Louvre, Paris), 162 b, 172 (Egyptian Museum, Cairo), 223 b (Acropolis Museum, Athens), 232, 233 t.
A Siliotti: pages 46 b, 47 t, 68, 69 b, 70 t, 71 t b.
Silvia Cordaiy Photo Library: pages 192/193.
Sonia Halliday Photographs: pages 37 tl, 78, 79 b, 133 t, 190, 240.
Spectrum Colour Library: pages 161 tl, 163 b.
Sygma/Stephane Compoint: page 220 b.
Theban Mapping Project: pages 122, 123 t b.
Travel Ink/Stephen Psallidas: page 96 t.
Trip: page 118 b.
Veneta Bullen: page 36 t.
Werner Forman Archive: pages 2, 5 c r (Egyptian Museum, Cairo), 31 l (Egyptian Museum, Cairo), 35 (Louvre, Paris), 42, 43 b, 45 t b, 48 t (Metropolitan Museum of Art, New York), 50 t, 58 b, 64 b (Egyptian Museum, Cairo), 70 b, 72, 79 t (Egyptian Museum, Cairo), 82 t, 88 t, 89 t, 102 t, 119 (Dr E Strouhal), 133 b (Dr E Strouhal), 173 b (Egyptian Museum, Cairo), 214 (Egyptian Museum, Cairo), 217 t b (Egyptian Museum, Cairo), 227 l (J Paul Getty Museum, Malibu), 250.

Acknowledgements

The author would like to thank Hany Zarif for his information on the temples of Nubia and Elephantine.

Sources of Quotes

The author and publishers would like to thank publishers for permission to quote from the following titles. Every effort has been made to identify sources and we apologize for any omissions:

Page 14: Austin, M M, *The Hellenistic World from Alexander to the Roman Conquest*, Cambridge, 1981
Page 19: Denon, V, *Travels in Upper and Lower Egypt*, London, 1802
Pages 26, 93: Vercoutter, J, *Search for Ancient Egypt*, London, 1992
Pages 28–29: Edwards, A, *A Thousand Miles Up the Nile*, London, 1877
Page 30: Petrie, W M F, *Seventy Years in Archaeology*, London, 1939
Pages 42–43, 84–85, 142, 165, 170, 206–207: Lichtheim, M, *Ancient Egyptian Literature*, Vols 1–111, Berkeley, 1973, 1976, 1980
Pages 62–3, 92, 219: Herodotus, *The Histories*, (trans. Aubrey de Selincourt), London, 1954
Page 81: Lauer, J-P, *The Pyramids of Sakkara*, Paris, 1991
Page 90–91: Martin, G T, *Hidden Tombs of Memphis*, London, 1991
Page 100: Romer, J, *Valley of the Kings*, London, 1881
Pages 104–105: Carter, H, *The Tomb of Tukankhamun*, London, 1923
Pages 112–113: Spencer, A J, *Death in Ancient Egypt*, London, 1982
Page 123: Weeks, K, *The Lost Tomb*, London, 1998
Pages 153, 168–169: Gardiner, A H, Peet, T E, and Czerny, J, *Inscriptions in Sinai*, London 1952–55
Page 167: Bierbrier, M L, *Tomb Builders of the Pharaohs*, London, 1982
Page 183: Naville, E, *The Temple at Deir el-Bahri*, London, 1894-1908
Page 203: Kitchen, K A, *Pharaoh Triumphant*, Warminster, 1982
Page 205: Breasted, J, *Records of Ancient Egypt*, London, 1906
Page 207: de Morgan, J, *Sehel Inscriptions*, Paris
Page 223: Arrian, *Life of Alexander*, (trans. Aubrey de Selincourt), London, 1958

Notes

Notes

NOTES

Notes

Notes

Notes

Notes

Notes